embers

Ark House Press
PO Box 1722, Port Orchard, WA 98366 USA
PO Box 1321, Mona Vale NSW 1660 Australia
PO Box 318 334, West Harbour, Auckland 0661 New Zealand
arkhousepress.com

Cataloguing in Publication Data:
Title: embers
ISBNs: 978-0-6485077-3-4 (pbk.) 978-0-6485077-4-1 (ebk)
Subjects: Autobiography; Christian Living; Divorce;
Other Authors/Contributors: Chilver, H A
Design by initiateagency.com

Author's Note

I've never written a book before so I don't know what is normal. I just had this feeling inside that something needed to come out. I've always enjoyed writing in my journal and sending newsy letters home when travelling. But about now I am waking each day and thinking, 'What am I doing? Whatever possessed me to think I could write a book? *Write* at all?' Then I come to my desk and am amazed: chapters unfolding. How did they get there?

For as long as I can remember I've yearned to be creative; not that I could have described what that may look like. In my mind it certainly didn't look like hours and days of solitude with a laptop computer and enjoying it. Nor feeling this sense of completeness that jostles in stark contrast with hollow suspense. The suspense of wondering whether anything legible will appear on the page today. As for anyone else ever wanting to actually *read* what I've written 'flying pigs delivering milk' springs to mind as a more likely occurrence.

I began by writing down whatever thoughts came into my mind for forty minutes a day as a discipline to see how it might feel. It felt positive and satisfying. I loved coming to the clean empty space of a new page each morning. If you are wondering if you have a gift or dream of doing a particular thing, have a go. Start the journey without looking too far ahead. I couldn't imagine this writing ever really becoming a book but as I worked something grew, changed and developed in me. Perhaps this is what it looks like when God cultivates a gift in our lives? I can't think how I got started and, as my writing became a book, I didn't know how I would end it. There isn't an ending. I have had these thoughts regularly for some months and strongly suspect they are an integral part of the creative process.

Deep breath then… I will keep turning up at the keyboard and be grateful. I love words and am free to express myself. I leave any outcome in the Creator's hands.

Contents

Author's Note iii

Introduction vii

1. Halcyon Hostage 1

2. Sinking Sand 17
3. Truth Hurts 25
4. Faith Leaps 33
5. Guiding Hand 49
6. Painful Obedience 63
7. Slippery Slopes 77
8. Go…Where? 93
9. Over The Border 101
10. By Still Waters 117
11. Deeper 135
12. Then We Were Five 147
13. Hope Deferred 157
14. Clouds Gather 175
15. Rock Bottom 189
16. Freedom Promise 197
17. Silent Protest 213
18. Undignified Sacrifice 229
19. The Cloud Moves 248
20. New Beginnings 262
21. Not The End Of The Story 279

Bibliography 293

Introduction

When life began to unravel I was experiencing a hunger for intimacy, intimacy with God. I wanted to go deeper, know more, sense him and have his tangible presence in my life, church and family. It seemed to me he offered a safe enough invitation to walk down the beach, leave the sand and wade out further into him. I prayed he would take me deeper even using the words, 'out of my depth in your love'. I had flown through my Bronze, Silver and Gold Life Saving Awards so treading water held no fear for me. My skill with a pair of inflated pyjama bottoms was unrivalled. I had no concept then of violent undercurrents, rips. I never dreamed of the need for total abandonment to the tide of his influence. I couldn't conceive of overwhelming loss birthing priceless gain. I was in fact clueless as to the process of divine love and therefore unprepared for the tsunami that would bring the answer to my prayers.

The banned substance in my school was testosterone. The name of the establishment even had 'for young ladies' in it, reflecting the heartfelt optimism of those in power that the male of the species would not feature. This never deterred my beau who somehow managed to win over even the sternest housemistress with his charming ways. He wrote copious amounts of beautiful love poetry and my plump post was the envy of the common room. Everyone was intrigued and enthralled as I mysteriously found bunches of red roses or even champagne on my bed in the dorm. He drove a blue and white Ford Anglia, which added greatly to his appeal as most of us were feverishly ticking off the days till the magic birthday that meant we could start driving lessons. Motorbikes were his passion and by the time we met he already had plenty of hair-raising stories to tell. The night our lives collided I had gone to a village some twelve miles away for a youth service. It turned out it was a baptism service and Nick was a conspicuous candidate, not just because his audible comment about the water temperature raised a laugh. He was the only one on crutches. Months previously he had broken his hip in a motorbike accident and was not long out of hospital. He had thick, dark, shoulder-length hair and I was mesmerised from the start. Eventually, parents permitting, groups of us would venture out of school with him on weekends. It was all very exciting as romance visited an otherwise passionless environment. In the staff room, where the revered role of spinster was worn like a medal on countless ample bosoms, the collective pulse quickened.

An exciting five-year courtship ensued. We were 'sensible' and had times apart. Nick went to gain work experience in his brother's business in Denmark for a year and I spent an interesting time in a small chateau village in the hills overlooking Lake Geneva. Working as an au pair in a family with no English was challenging but my French improved rapidly and time apart only fanned the flame of love as we missed each other terribly. A twelve-month engagement culminated in a large frothy wedding with all the traditional trimmings. Having admired stunning sunsets together I had the romantic notion that wearing a pink underskirt beneath my white crinolined gown would bless the groom, as I travelled up the aisle, with a beautiful apparition reminiscent of said sunset moments. The effect would have been breathtaking but when it came to it Nick was acutely conscious of the nervous perspiration streaming down the back of his knees; said perspiration washed all received instructions (about turning around) from his mind and he stood squarely facing front until I joined him at the altar, by which time the moment was well and truly passed.

After twenty-one years I'm still not sure I can write this book. I first heard the whisper to write, to share my story, our journey, a decade ago now. Perhaps I thought God would somehow pen it while I slept and leave it on my desk. Maybe I fear I am not as whole or recovered as I like to think. Certainly the battle to begin, to actually get something on the page, has raged for some time and the urge to recount has remained strong. The hope that some small gleaning may ease the pain for another and the overwhelming longing, that something clean and strong and honourable in the spirit realm should be seen to remain, does not dissipate as years pass. And yet, I don't know the end of the story. For some years I felt I must await a rapturous conclusion before putting pen to paper but here tonight, in the sticky mist of a heat wave on the far side of the world in Canberra, Australia, it seems the moment can be deferred no longer.

When my marriage – I should perhaps say here that at the time it was very much 'our' marriage but since this book is not a joint venture and is my personal story, I use the personal pronoun. When my marriage broke…Broke. Such a neat, clean, matter of fact word.

A child's toy or a fingernail breaks. 'Broken' nowhere near describes the ravaging devastation I'm writing about. A sense of pillaging assault and wrenching loss invading relentless days and nights. Fragments of the person I was and the partnership we had become lying mutilated and deformed. The puzzle of me not designed to fit these ugly, misshapen pieces; trying to make them was agony for which there is no analgesia. The marriage relationship ending was profoundly shocking. I had heard of people in the village, couples that 'had parted', and I'd felt a vague sense of sadness. I suppose I wondered if they had suddenly realised they had married the wrong person. I hoped the children wouldn't suffer too much. Perhaps I even knew a smug frisson as I relished the fact that our relationship was special. God had definitely joined us for a purpose. Our life together was fun, passionate and we shared the dream that God could use us to be part of the answer for hurting people. I know the social landscape looks very different today; but back then not one of my friends was divorced.

The eldest of four in a Christian family I had praying grand and even great-grandparents. My aunt and uncle were taking Jesus to black Africa and I had been active in church and youth work all my life. Divorce was not on the agenda. Cast adrift on the vast ocean of marital breakdown with two small dependants I had no map, signposts were scarce and I had zero sailing experience. I had no ability to read the stars, no knowledge of the tides and certainly no emergency plan up my sleeve.

1

Halcyon Hostage

Married a year, and in a fairly traditional church, we found ourselves carrying responsibility for the leadership of a youth group of struggling teenagers. We had approached the elders expressing our need of a father figure. We asked if one of them would be willing to provide us support just by meeting to pray with us regularly. We were only a few years older than the young people in our care and the majority of them were offspring of the elders. Their response jarred. 'No, we think this will be a good learning experience for you, it will teach you to lean on God for yourselves.'

We felt let down and very disappointed by the lack of support from those much older in the faith but attempted to plough on. We both worked shifts at the time. I had to stay away overnight each week for work and life was full. Drained by the challenge of giving ourselves to the group we seriously questioned the purpose of our Christian walk. We couldn't see at the time how in that season of desperation God specifically lured us to be more dependent on him for what we needed. We didn't dream that he intended the experience to connect us with a couple called Andrew and Sue, which in turn would result in us having a role in his purpose for West Sussex. We just recognised we were inadequate and unequal to the task assigned to us.

We had been married for eighteen months and youth leaders for eleven. Trying to prepare for the next youth evening we came across the scripture in John 10:10 where Jesus says, 'I have come that they may have life and have it abundantly' (ESV).

Time to face facts. The only evidence of 'abundance' in our lives was the overflow from the linen bin as we struggled to keep up. Nick was a police constable in Sussex and I was completing my nursing training in a London hospital, which meant I regularly needed to stay in the nurses' accommodation for my run of shifts. Even in these early years God wanted to show us that he alone was to be our resource. We knelt together right then on the lounge floor and politely but resolutely spelled out to the Almighty that our take on 'living abundantly' at that stage meant we would receive some encouragement from someone. Anyone. Perhaps not so politely but with complete sincerity we agreed that if no encouragement were forthcoming we would have to review our commitment to God, the youth group and the church. Within a month the offer of encouragement came: through a complete stranger.

Nick was a member of the Christian Police Association and small teams would be invited to contribute in church services all over the county. These were often struggling little chapels with waning rural congregations. On the Sunday in question it was Nick's turn to preach and the venue a pleasantly warm, rather lively Baptist church. There were a good number of people there and he gave a convincing talk entitled 'Victorious Christian Living' whilst I sat in the pew glowing with wifely adoration. At the end of the evening a man from the congregation approached Nick, shook him by the hand and said, 'I'd really like to encourage you. Would you like to meet up?'

We were in awe as we drove home. Actually, that's not completely true. Nick was elated, excited and sure God had a purpose in the invitation he had accepted. I was irritable. With my spiritual antennae shoved to the bottom of my handbag, arranging to travel halfway across the county to have a meal with a couple we didn't know seemed an extra commitment we didn't need. Unfamiliar with God reaching into our lives in such a specific way I was most uncomfortable with the idea of accepting such an invitation from a total stranger. I was apprehensive; what might unfold?

As a teenager Nick had experienced God in the person of the Holy Spirit tangibly intervening in lives with supernatural healings and strange languages. He and a group of mates had been invited each week to the home of an elderly man in their church. He had taught them about listening for God's promptings and then stepping out in faith. They would practise asking God for pictures or words to encourage each other and enjoyed the risk of sharing those things. The old gentleman challenged the lads to push the boundaries in their spiritual journeys, which meant they would offer to pray for people who were ill and sometimes saw God heal. He taught them from scripture making events and teachings from Jesus' life vital and alive. The teaching and fellowship together stimulated the group to explore spiritual truth from the Bible and expect to see increasing evidence of God changing the environment around them for good. They were passionate, expectant and excited. I, on the other hand, had my feet firmly on the ground, thank you.

Growing up I had been present during countless family discussions about the relevance of the Holy Spirit. Usually on a Sunday night around the kitchen table, often provoked by yet another cold, seemingly to us teenagers, completely 'Holy Spirit Free' Evensong. Debates, particularly about anything of the 'supernatural' variety, were often heated and had left me in no doubt. Those who were less fortunate than myself, particularly if their misfortune bred emotional instability, were far more likely to be attracted to the idea of 'gifts' and external displays of power; maybe, they even needed them. However, for stable, well-educated Anglicans like ourselves, who, fortified by their Bible-based Brethren roots, were busy working their evangelical butts off, it was different. The Holy Spirit was living in us from conversion but had the decency to remain in permanent hibernation. Suffice it to say that gabbled languages and supernatural expectations were viewed as at best suspect and at worst a dangerous distraction promoted by those with a psychiatric history. These incomprehensible indications of a possible power source beyond our imminently respectable 'Church of England Darling' experience, were more than likely to be American in origin. Naturally, if they had been at any stage demonstrated on television, the common view was that the humans concerned were quite possibly 'possessed' and thus beyond all hope. We definitely came from different perspectives.

About six weeks later the dinner date with our 'encourager' arrived. In my mind this rather outspoken and scary man from

Worthing warranted a cautious approach but Nick sensed familiar stirrings from those teenage gatherings and was hooked. The evening we spent with the encouraging gentleman and his wife proved to be life changing. Andrew and Sue had moved from their church in Worthing to build a new church family in a village on the other side of the South Downs. The story of God providing support and finance for their adventure was exciting. But trusting God for things like house deposits? It all sounded a bit on the radical side of sensible to me. Nick told them our story of desperation and didn't hold back as he enthused about Andrew approaching him that evening after he had preached. I felt slightly uncomfortable and didn't think he needed to be quite so honest. We had, after all, only just met these people. All my apprehensions burst into the room as Andrew leaned in and offered to pray for Nick. I had a sinking feeling that there was no going back as Nick knelt on their lounge floor. Nick embraced new hope, the atmosphere seemed to fill with liquid warmth and he began emitting strange articulations that formed into a foreign sounding language. Andrew explained this was 'tongues' which did little to reassure me. Nick came away full of excitement and peace with an expectation of God showing himself to be in our lives in increasingly tangible ways.

Over time the evidence of this experience was that Nick remained hopeful, stronger and consistently excited about his faith. His passion for knowing as much of God as possible was contagious. He urgently encouraged me to ask God for more of his love and power whilst telling me not to worry because the Holy Spirit definitely had my number! I found his enthusiastic confidence slightly daunting but I began spending time alone in our bedroom, tentatively praying. I told God I was willing to have my opinions influenced and that I wanted to desire whatever he wanted to do in my life. A few months later I knelt down by the bed. Feeling I could be risking my family rushing me for psychiatric attention I hesitatingly asked the Holy Spirit to please come and be in complete control of my life so that I could more fully represent heaven on earth. While I was praying God put a picture in my mind that helped me.

I was swimming in a big river. The river was fast flowing and deep. I felt apprehensive so was splashing along in the shallows clutching reeds and overhanging branches to slow myself down and control my journey downstream. I realised this was a picture of my Christian life. I loved God and wanted to co-operate with his intentions for my life but the concept of yielding completely, the idea of abandoning myself to some unseen spiritual force was unnerving. In the picture God was calling me to the middle of the river where the current was strong and fast flowing. I would be completely out of my depth. If I left the safety of the shallows I would have no control over my direction or speed but then I would no longer be straining to reach every stick or branch that appeared to offer stability. I would stop grazing my knees and jarring my joints on the boulders that lurked in the shallows. It felt scary as I grappled with the option to fling myself into the deep and 'go with the flow'. Something about the smooth, fast-flowing water seemed magnetic. I had always loved swimming: floating on my back in a pool I can feel the stresses and tensions of any day drift away. But the current was so fast and powerful. What if I changed my mind?

As I knelt holding my breath, I suddenly felt as if I wanted to cough but when I opened my mouth a combination of sounds came out and I experienced a rush of peace. I made myself try the sounds again and then again. It was real: I had a new language and as I trusted I was not just making the sounds up, more came. Experimenting I found I was in control. I could stop and start at will. I was excited and it seemed as if love enveloped me. I wasn't scared although I didn't feel wholly safe either. I saw myself in the picture pushing away from the riverbank and as I did so I was saying, 'Yes, yes, yes, Lord.'

I had been a Christian since I was six years old but this was a turning point for me when I relinquished any right to pursue my own ideas and invited God to infuse and overwhelm me with his Holy Spirit. I understood I had been making every effort to live the Christian life but all along God intended I move over and allow him to live through me. What a relief. I knelt still and calm for some time and then prayed, 'Lord, whatever you ask, my answer is, "Yes" every time.'

The Bible says the gift of tongues is to build us up or 'edify' us so I reasoned that was why it was a battle; it had the potential to make me stronger. I practised my new language often and was delighted to discover God's presence no longer ebbed and flowed but became the constant in my life. Nick and I talked often about how God was working in us. Our new understanding led to us hungrily seeking out a church that was demonstrating New Testament Christianity. Over a couple of years we travelled across the county to have regular meals with Andrew and Sue until Nick was transferred by the police force into their area. Later we were able to move right into the village and then join the growing church led by this dynamic couple. As they patiently taught and encouraged us we steadily grew spiritually.

Our new church family shared life together between Sundays. They ate in each other's homes and often looked after one another's children. Cars and lawn mowers were freely shared and not just between those who attended church. Neighbours and friends were included in the blessings. If anyone in the street were ill someone from the church would arrange meals to be delivered. A rota to offer support for laundry, cleaning and provision of meals was organised for new mums. This was demonstrating a loving openness we had never experienced. We were very attracted by the power of love impacting the community. These people seemed genuinely to be constantly putting other people's needs before their own. And without any grumbling. A church family atmosphere with the absence of gossip, back-biting or criticism was undeniably compelling. We were inspired by this graphic exhibition of what we had only read about in stories of the early New Testament church. We were magnetically attracted to this Jesus lifestyle. These people were sharing their days with a level of honesty and humility we had hitherto only dreamed about.

Their faith together was affecting the area where they lived and worshipped. Lives were enhanced by selfless love and sharing. One doctor in the local health centre attended the church and was able to link those with loneliness and depression with church families offering friendship. She prayed with some patients who recovered. Members of the church worked in the local school supporting students who struggled. Opportunities for developing parenting and relationship-building skills plus workshops on time management and nutrition were all hosted by church members keen to contribute to community life.

The leaders of the church met regularly with other leaders in the region. As they had prayed and fasted over years God had inspired them to host meetings, youth camps and numerous events calling Christians together, to believe God for revival. Prophetic words and pictures were recorded and shared. They were united in their conviction. God intended his church in West Sussex to be a catalyst where the powerful things he was doing, in healing physical illness, freeing people from addiction, restoring broken marriages and letting people experience his love for them in a way that influenced their circumstances, would result in a significant number of the population becoming followers of Jesus. This passionate vision influenced how we lived every day. The weeks were full and enriching. Nick became more and more involved until it seemed there was hardly time for him to go to work.

After managing to secure a midwife who was game to attend home deliveries, we had welcomed our first son Sam into the world. Sam was about ten months old when Nick went off to work one Sunday. He was working a late shift in a patrol car with his partner Lee. Not long into their shift a radio message announced the shooting of one of their colleagues. This policeman had waved a car down in order to do a routine search and the driver had produced the weapon and opened fire. A countywide alert was put out and Nick and Lee decided to sit for a while on a major junction thinking the villain may head for London. It wasn't long before the car they were looking for came past and they set off in pursuit.

Meanwhile I was getting ready to go to a service. Being a small community church we didn't have our own premises but, like many similar groups, hired the local school each week. We borrowed a separate church building when we needed to use a baptismal pool. This was one of those occasions and I was driving with friends to Worthing for the mid-afternoon service. As we made our way down the A24 there seemed to be an unusually high number of police cars about and a siren could be heard every few minutes. Completely ignorant of the shooting drama that had unfolded only twenty minutes' drive away I commented, 'Seems to be a lot of police activity this afternoon. I wonder if something has happened? Maybe they're doing a big exercise.'

We arrived at the church and continued to hear sirens faintly wailing in the background as the service progressed.

It was as we were moving through to the church hall for tea and cake that I felt a hand on my elbow. The minister of the church we were visiting gently said he needed to talk to me and nudged me towards his office. As we entered Andrew rose to meet us. I was offered a seat and, noting their rather sombre demeanour, I lowered myself into it feeling bemused. The minister's tone was grave.

'I need to talk to you and it is rather serious. It's about Nick.'

I was puzzled thinking, 'Nick? He's at work.' Another siren screeched in the distance as he continued.

'There is a rather dramatic situation unfolding. A policeman has been shot . . .'

He paused for a deep breath.

'. . . and Nick has been taken hostage.'

I felt sorry for this man across the desk. He seemed to be weighed down with the need to impart bad news to someone. We had been celebrating resurrection life less than five minutes ago but he didn't appear to be having a great afternoon. I was unable to absorb what he was saying, only that it was something relatively serious. It was very quiet. A picture of Sam tottering delightedly on rubbery legs deep in Nick's black uniform boots, flashed onto the screen in my mind. The boots he had left for work in today.

The statement pounded in my head, 'A policeman has been shot. A policeman has been shot.' I felt calm but suddenly wanted to go home, to be in familiar surroundings and out of this alien context. Andrew gazed at me his face full of concern.

'Can we pray for you and for Nick and then perhaps you'd like a lift home?'

I nodded. My mouth felt too full of sawdust to speak. I remember being ushered to a vehicle. I recall weaving through plates of cakes and sandwiches suspended in the hall as people became aware that something unexpected was unfolding. I don't recollect anything of the journey home or what I did with my own car. I imagine a friend delivered it to the house later.

By now we had been friends for several years and Sue came over. Together we gave Sam his tea and then bathed him. We put the news on and gaped as familiar lanes and road junctions, littered with emergency vehicles, flashed across the screen. We watched in silence as the story unfolded. The news ended and with Sam tucked up in his cot I decided to tackle the ironing whilst the next programme unfolded. It seemed the obvious thing to do; carry on as normal. I wasn't afraid. I felt 'held' and enveloped in peace. I knew Nick would be praying and felt a quiet confidence in his ability to cope with disaster. He is brilliant in any emergency. Suddenly, a voice said the programme was being interrupted for an 'update on the dramatic circumstances unfolding in Sussex'. By now several hours had passed and the clipped voice was hardly able to disguise the relish he felt about reporting these unprecedented events.

'Still nothing is known about the whereabouts of the two policemen hi-jacked and taken hostage, we believe at gunpoint, in their patrol car earlier today. Helicopters are now being brought in to search the area. The patrol car was last seen . . .'

Within a few moments the telephone rang.

'Hello, Darling, I'm watching a programme and they interrupted it, something about a policeman in Sussex and I thought I'd give you a call but of course I realise it couldn't be Nick. It isn't…is it?'

I had been so focused on remaining calm and carrying on as normal it hadn't occurred to me to contact Nick's mother.

'Oh, Mum,' I said quietly, 'I'm sorry, I'm afraid it is.'

In the quiet I sensed her trying to decipher what she thought she'd heard.

'I probably should keep the line open, Mum, but I'll let you know the minute I hear anything. Try not to worry; I'm sure he'll be fine.'

Next the doorbell rang and there stood a clutch of people in uniforms. The most senior stepped forward and introduced first himself (I think he was the Assistant Chief Constable but I can't honestly remember) and then his colleagues. As we stood in the kitchen he explained that all that could be done was being done but it was important I realise that the situation was serious. One policeman had been shot and we should be prepared for the worst. I felt sorry for him. He clearly thought that bodies would be found. I did not. I felt peaceful and confident. Nick would think of something. We had deliberately moved to the village to become part of the church there and life was full of hope and promise. We were excited and blessed as God provided a home and we sensed he had a specific purpose for us in the area. Nick being shot dead would hardly enhance the plan. I did realise that injury was a possibility though. I prayed under my breath and tried to accept graciously the presence of the WPC (woman police constable) who was left to 'keep me company'.

As it happened we only had a few hours together before word came through that Nick and his partner had been found and were unharmed. The news was a huge relief and the longest part of the whole ordeal for me was the waiting to see Nick and hold him, once we knew he was safe but had not yet come home. There was a fairly lengthy de-briefing and he finally arrived bone weary but in one piece. I did ask him if at any point he'd thought he was going to die but he said he hadn't and told me the story.

They had spotted the villain's car heading north on the main road, where they sat just out of sight. With Lee driving they set off in pursuit. They followed the villains who turned down a more minor road and before long pulled onto the forecourt of a garage. As Nick approached the car a man got out and, pointing a gun, ordered him to get into the back seat of his own patrol car. The second man got into the front passenger seat snarling at Lee to do as he was told.

Knowing Nick had a gun sticking in his ribs behind him Lee obeyed the instruction to ignore the radio and drive off. As they approached a roadblock littered with police, nobody was suspicious because they believed the villains to be travelling in their own vehicle. Nobody was looking for a police car although later it was registered that there appeared to be extra people on board. Waved on through they drove at high speed for a few miles before the car suddenly swung off the road and into the driveway of a large country house.

The unsuspecting family were at home enjoying afternoon tea. The gentleman of the house responded to the knock on the front door and beat a hasty retreat as he registered the situation and sensed the urgency felt by the agitated villains. There was a teenage boy in the household who had brought a pal home for a school exeat. A quiet weekend in the country! Their game of chess was rudely interrupted but I guess the story they had to tell on returning to school was some compensation.

Nick and Lee were unceremoniously ushered upstairs to the old nursery and ordered to sit on the floor back to back. They were tied up with their hands wedged together between their backs. This position made drinking the tea that was placed on the floor in front of them a bit of a challenge but by rocking in turn they managed to catch the straw between their lips and grab sips. They heard the police helicopter pass overhead but had also heard the villains hiding the car in one of the family garages so knew there was no hope of their patrol car being spotted. (This incident precipitated all patrol cars having roof markings for clear identification. It was recognised that once the villain's car had been found and Nick and Lee no longer responded to radio calls, the police car they were hostages in, had it been roof marked, could have been spotted and tracked from the air thus pre-empting events at the house.)

Ultimately Nick worked the knots free or they may've shuffled across the room and found something to work against the rope (I can't remember the detail) but they got free and rushed downstairs to find the family, and their by now animated house guest, locked in a large cupboard. They were shaken but unharmed. A family saloon car was missing. Within a short time of the details of the car and the address it was stolen from being circulated the villains were apprehended as they attempted to leave the county. Talking things over later Nick never thought he was going to die. He did admit that the drive in the patrol car with a gun in his ribs was pretty hair-raising. He always claimed he was unaffected by the experience which was 'all in a day's work'.

Towards the end of the year our second son was on the way. The leadership team at church approached Nick to see if he might be interested in becoming assistant to the pastor, Andrew. We mulled and prayed together and it was decided Nick would hand in his notice to leave the police force the following spring. May arrived and Nathan was born. The plan was for Nick to do part-time work to supplement what the church could afford to pay him. They were halcyon days brimming with hope and healthy relationships when we believed that together we could be influential in the county turning to God.

2

Sinking Sand

There were no man-eating wild animals prowling around our little corner of rural England, no terrorist alerts or violent storm warnings on the radio. Or, looking back, had we let our spiritual guard down, becoming complacent, perhaps taking for granted our comfortable middle-class existence? We believed completely in spiritual warfare; prayed, fasted and donned our spiritual armour routinely. Is it possible we had inadvertently fallen into a subtle trap that Father John Woolley highlights? In his book *I Am With You* he writes down what God says to him in his prayer times, 'Consciousness of status in My service is far more deadly than in a worldly context. Do not strive after status…or even covet it.'

We disciplined our children, made love often and hospitality was a lifestyle. But the ambush when it came brutalised and stunned us.

Sally was a friend from church and she came for coffee one day. We were on the leadership team together and savouring the journey as we built community. We sat in the garden (where I would sit some years later and watch a small hedgehog snuffle past). She told me that God had highlighted a particular verse as she had been reading in the book of Jeremiah, prompting her to share it with me. What she read out to me was Jeremiah 17:7–8:

> *But blessed is the one who trusts in the LORD, whose confidence is in him. They will be like a tree planted by the water that sends out its roots by the stream. It does not fear when heat comes; its leaves are always green. It has no worries in a year of drought and never fails to bear fruit.*

These words took root in my life and the prophetic power of them infused my inner self as I read and reread them over the years. I'm sure they are part of how I managed never to totally lose hope. Reading and meditating on these verses empowered me to love and continue giving to others even through some of the darkest days.

I had not long ceased breastfeeding when something began to come undone in that hidden place. Nathan was fifteen months old when I was having lunch with my mother one day. He toddled over to me and began undoing my blouse thus demonstrating that in his opinion it was time for a drink. Fortunately it wasn't a time when she was entertaining, so Mum was spared the embarrassment of explaining to anyone that at the time *Breast is Best* was my mantra and I really was not unique in my mothering style. She did however offer her opinion, suggesting that a child who could undo buttons so deftly probably had the dexterity required for using a cup. I duly helped Nathan understand that reducing 'feeds' to just a bedtime drink from Mummy really would suffice. He was quickly weaned. I felt lumpy, wholly unattractive and unworthy of my popular, handsome husband. At this time people were being saved, healed and set free through his ministry so I knew the problem must be with me. Nick would set off for another John Wimber conference. Before the car had left our street, I would be comfort munching on another packet of biscuits whilst giving myself a firm talking to in which I would vow to do better tomorrow. I decided aerobics was the way forward and duly reacquainted myself with Lycra.

I became friends with the girl who ran the class (I'll call her Millie) and eventually introduced her to my husband. She suffered with a back problem and when I explained people were being healed as Nick prayed for them she declared herself as 'up for it'. Millie was attractive, lithe and magnetically free of any church inhibition. This was most obvious by the lack of a certain undergarment, presumably burned. She often wore a tight white t-shirt and regular visits to Lanzarote gave her skin an exotic glow. Millie was a free spirit and her sense of humour, as free from inhibition as her body, immediately appealed to Nick. My background was far more structured than Nick's and I had been immersed in church life from the very beginning. Perhaps I had an overdeveloped idea of what was appropriate but I often had to squash the slight sense of unease I felt. Like the time a mutual acquaintance, whose job was selling fabrics, curtain material, and other soft furnishings, had died and one of them said, 'It's curtains for Clifford then.' Their delighted chortling made me squirm with discomfort but I couldn't express it. I just felt gradually more and more left out. Nick's obvious ease in the company of those whose lives were going in such a different direction, compounded my misery as I chided myself on not being able to relax and blend in. We were supposed to be looking for ways of blessing and including people who weren't experiencing God's love and yet him fitting in so comfortably made me feel totally awkward inside. I just couldn't find any rest in the inner turmoil.

Attempts to explain my apprehension were unproductive. Nick would groan, 'Oh, lighten up, Hazel.'

I did try to fit in; I wanted to be fun to be with but it just seemed that in some subtle way the atmosphere had changed and something vital was slipping away. Disguised as light relief from focused commitment, as 'fun' that had the potential for spreading God's love, the enemy had begun his revolting work. No roaring announced his intention but an insidious, stealthy prowl began around the quietly bleeding body of our marriage. Weakened and dispirited I had no inkling and in fact nothing actually happened for some while. We know the battle is first won or lost in our minds. The seed of temptation lands in the soil of thought life. If not destroyed immediately the imagination fertilises it causing a subtle shift in heart temperature. Slowly the fantasy of sin influences the climate of a life until a monumental paradigm shift occurs and the heart releases the body to translate the daydream into action. Conscience is seared. That all takes a while to unfold.

Millie enjoyed our home and we included her and her little girl in family days out. Her husband worked long hours and they were both excited when the home they had renovated together sold. Sharing with her about God knowing our needs and answering prayer it seemed amazing a house in our street came up for rent. They moved into the property next door and we found ourselves playing card games, eating meals and chatting together. Millie confided in me that she was dissatisfied in her marriage and quizzed me about how deeply I loved Nick and how much we appeared to enjoy one another. I sensed she was subtly fishing for inappropriate confidences. Even as I talked about our love for and relationship with God being key to our marriage, a squirming in the pit of my stomach warned against exposure of my tender inner self. I hoped she would soon want to come to church so that she could know and enjoy God's love for herself. The enemy had another agenda.

I became increasingly unhappy over time. There was a tremor somewhere in the core of our marriage, a disturbance in my spirit. More and more frequently this expressed itself in silent weeping; embarrassingly I seemed to have no control over the tears that gushed silently down my face, most particularly when a meeting was held in our home or Nick was leading worship on a Sunday morning. I was disquieted by the sense of a growing independence in him.

We both loved people and had worked in jobs where communication was vital long before helping people grow and enjoy healthy relationships under the church banner became our life. We had always been open, enjoying chatting for hours about our hopes, dreams and longing for God. We knew healthy interaction was a crucial ingredient for the survival of a relationship. But where once we used to discuss things, seeking and respecting each other's perspective, a prickly silence grew; a subtle pressure to perform had developed in Nick. Something was very wrong.

I noticed that time when Nick would have lingered, enjoying God's word and cultivating his presence, seemed now to be devoured by the determination to produce a great sermon. He used to love singing and worshipping. Where he used to go out in the car with his Bible and return with insight and inspirations to share, he now poured over reference books making sermon notes. He had become reluctant to delegate and asking for support increasingly became a last resort. One Sunday over breakfast Nick was so focused on getting to church the morning took on an uncomfortable sense of haste. I wondered if something had happened and had the disconcerting feeling I wasn't being told the whole story. I knew he was preaching so causing turbulence wouldn't be helpful, but my toast just wouldn't go down. I quietly asked Nick why he needed to be at the venue three hours prior to the service beginning. In an agitated tone he explained he was going to put out the chairs and set things up ready for the morning. I suggested calling some others to give him assistance but he vehemently stated he wasn't going to ask anyone to do anything until he could do it well himself. I was flummoxed by his response and the belt of anxiety I now seemed to wear constantly, tightened a notch. The church was built on a foundation of team; Nick lived and breathed team. I couldn't think where this perspective of needing to do everything himself had come from. It didn't seem the right time to open a discussion around the adage, 'delegation is the art of leadership'. It seemed it was less and less the right time for me to broach any subject beyond the domestic routine. I sat for ages at the table smarting from his heated response. I was churning inside.

My private, personal struggle felt endless; if I had been desperately treading water to stay afloat the water now morphed into a quagmire. Weak from striving to keep my head above the water line, I now experienced life as if stillness was all that could keep glutinous mud from filling my lungs. Every muscle ached with the effort of not struggling against the impossible pressure. It seemed I had no choice but to live with the strain of waiting. Waiting for…I hardly knew what.

The stark reality that I could not initiate change was numbing. Would Nick realise the direction he seemed to be drifting in? Would the light flick on one day? Did he care I was unhappy? I was in trouble for being tearful in meetings. Nick was frustrated because I could not explain why I was unable to control the sadness. I craved the intimacy I knew with God in worship as it drew me to a familiar place of safety; but then we had revelled in that place as a couple and I couldn't draw near to God without experiencing the loss of a closeness now withheld. The salt of great loss poured into the gaping wound in my chest. The pain made me weep. I was deeply distressed about our growing lack of togetherness as church plans unfolded. I worried about my impression that expectancy to perform had lured Nick away from a place of intimacy with me and with God. I felt benefit from the physical stimulation of aerobics but I was still a pear-shaped size 14, wondering if I could ever be enough; enough woman for this vibrant man of God who was clearly going places in the kingdom.

During this season Nick was keen to go to the cinema. The movie content would definitely have caused more than the odd palpitation in the staff room and holiness was not the hot topic. I'm not proud of the fact that against my conscience I acquiesced. Having my eyes closed most of the time hardly compensates. I was there and uncomfortable about it. I prayed someone would see us and confront us but that was trickier when the mixed sauna began to feature; then my worst fear became bumping into someone who knew me, in a context where no swimsuits were allowed. One visit was more than enough. I found it so stressful it was a relief when Nick decided to go alone even though I was mortified. Mortified as my sensibilities were thrown in the bin and it seemed he was happy to be around other women naked. The evil presence of diminishment that had been lurking now gleefully set up camp in my life and hammered in the guy ropes. I was exposed. I wasn't even valued enough to be shielded from the indignity of other men watching me. If only I had been strong enough to resist persuasion, if only nudity had featured in my conservative upbringing, if I hadn't been so fearful of being written off as a killjoy, if I hadn't weakly hidden behind Nick as 'my head', who knows?

The deep, constricting fear that I was simply not enough for my man, pervaded every day blurring any ability to see the slimy serpent lust, as it wrapped its deadly coils deliberately around our love.

3

Truth Hurts

As months passed, discerning members of the leadership team, who had been our friends over years, began to express kindly concern. When Andrew, by this time the senior elder and leader, asked me directly if something was wrong it jolted me to admit that I was unhappy but 'something wrong'? By this time the fog was so thick I didn't know. Everything was not all right because I obviously needed help. A weepy blob of a wife would not do for the helpmeet of God's man of faith and power. Survival was my focus.

I think of myself as being a good communicator but actually verbalising my own emotions was beyond me. Probably I wasn't clear myself what I was feeling. I berated myself on a regular basis, convinced I should be able to pull myself together. Nick and I seemed to be on opposite sides of an ever-widening gulf. We had less and less time together as the business of community life, and the delight of meeting other people's needs, expanded. Leadership was about team and Nick was a vibrant member. He was a fervent advocate of accountability. Committed to honest, open relationships he enthusiastically promoted this perspective from the pulpit. For my part, although it was not verbalised until some years later, I was no longer cherished. Deprived of this essential to healthy marriage something vital quietly died in me. The pain of trying to make it through the following months uncovered and vulnerable, with the essence of me once so highly treasured, now totally exposed like a crab with no shell, almost broke me. Emotionally emaciated I had less and less to offer.

We shared life with the other leaders; our friendships were at the core of all we did. Together we were passionate about having a healthy, vibrant church touching the lives of all around us with God's transforming love. Then one day in an eldership meeting the men expressed the concerns they were feeling to Nick. I wasn't there but I understand they gently confronted him about what they saw as a need for him to take stock of how life was unfolding. They expressed concern for me and encouraged him to take a few weeks leave to spend time with God. They urged him to recharge his batteries and, having observed I was not quite my normal self, suggested some quality family time.

Nick came home furious. The brief glimmer of hope I had known, once the meeting was mentioned, was snuffed out. Life got worse. Much worse. Overnight the people I loved, lived with and looked to for spiritual guidance, those I worshipped and ate with, were divided. As surely as if the prowling beast none of us had observed had mauled and gored it, the tapestry of our lives was viciously shredded. Ripped. Desperately the frayed ends of trust and truth reached for each other in a futile attempt at repair.

My husband was deeply offended, aghast; he felt accused and unfairly judged of some illusive crime. I was greatly troubled by the strength of his reaction and dared to think that now at last perhaps the huge pressure could be relieved. I yearned for the thing that seemed to have invaded our relationship, and hidden itself there, to be exposed but it didn't have a name. Nick desperately needed to hear me say he was right and they were wrong. I could not. I wept often and filled the kitchen with endless worship songs longing for lines such as 'and now let the weak say I am strong' to be my reality. Nick felt completely ravaged and abused. At the hand of those he had trusted most he felt utterly mistreated. Unable to find any resolve he walked the streets at night wailing for comfort but finding none. God seemed to have moved very far away and Nick's deep wounding provided a ripe bed for offence to be planted. Over time the seed put down a root of bitterness. There seemed no way back.

Over the ensuing months everyone in our lives expressed an opinion as to what had happened and how. Among the suggestions were mental illness or the fact that Nick had lost his father in his early teens and was therefore unfamiliar with boundaries of discipline. Some of his previous colleagues wondered if he could be suffering from post-traumatic stress disorder related to his hostage experience. That had all happened three years previously and Nick always claimed he was unaffected.

None of the comments or suggestions did anything to relieve the pain or soften the shock of living with someone who, for whatever reason, was unable to practise what he had preached for years. He rejected outright the counsel of the team of men he loved, respected and to whom he was committed. I was stunned, confused and distressed. When pressed by an angry husband I couldn't truthfully say I felt there was nothing wrong or that the other leaders were barking up the wrong tree. I wondered if this was God reaching into our circumstances but I couldn't define the problem or name a specific stress factor either and this infuriated Nick. I silently yearned for rescue and thrashed around internally for truth because surely, the truth is what sets us free?

Desperate to salvage the marriage and longing to understand how I had let my husband down, I began seeing a counsellor. As Nick's absences from home and changes in behaviour increased communication had become more and more strained. To my horror the Christian counsellor started intimating that this pattern was familiar and that I should prepare myself for the reality of 'another woman'. He stated that if this should indeed prove to be the case I would surely have to consider a separation. I was appalled that an older, wiser Christian should even entertain such a thought much less verbalise it to me, a committed Christian wife determined to preserve her marriage. I knew my husband was under extreme pressure, was angry, was slipping into our bed in the early hours having left his clothes on the landing in the hope that I would not smell the clinging odour of cigarettes; but I was certain he would definitely draw the line at being unfaithful. How little I knew.

I was disquieted enough by the counsellor's suggestion to pray specifically about it. One day in the bathroom I heard that still, small voice audibly for the first time. I was praying, 'Father, there must be another way; separation can't be your answer. Please show me some other way, anything else I can do.'

He responded in an audible whisper, 'There is no other way.'

I held still; frozen. As I began to tell myself it was the wind rustling outside I heard it again, clearly.

'There is no other way.'

Awed but chilled it literally felt as if the axis of my life tilted to a new angle as I tried unsuccessfully to absorb the statement. I eventually emerged into the hallway feeling stunned that it looked just the same as it always did. I recorded this in my journal and locked it in the recesses of my mind where it remained for nearly two years.

Though decades have passed the scene remains vivid on the screen of my memory. Two less than happy years, triggered by Nick's independence and fuelled by the ongoing tensions in the leadership team at church, culminated in my husband grudgingly admitting his adultery. With no previous experience I have no idea how this errant behaviour is normally confessed. I had been fasting and praying the previous week whilst staying at my parents' home. (Don't be too impressed, for me this meant eating just an evening meal and using the time freed up by not needing to plan, shop, prepare, eat and clear up after food each day, for prayer.) I was desperate for some kind of release or change. I sensed there was something lurking in the black cloud of tension that filled our home and begged God to expose it. I simply believed that exposing something that was hidden to the light, would shatter the web that secrecy weaves thus rendering it powerless to continue spoiling things. I had been reading in John's gospel where Jesus tells his disciples various things about the future.

He explains that it was so they would be prepared. I had felt strangely calm about coming home after the week away with the boys. As Nick and I sat that evening, on opposite sides of the lounge, I felt prompted to remain quiet. Far, far out to sea, plates shifted, a low rumbling could be heard, currents changed, water swirled and the wave slowly swelled. Gaining ruthless momentum as it hit land the relentless wall of water continued its unstoppable progress. Reaching the bottom of our street it was already many times the size and height of our home, our life…

Finally into the silence my husband grunted, 'Well, I've needed cuddles, you know.'

Haltingly he enlarged upon the statement explaining that he had been so unhappy that he had sought solace in the arms of another. Unleashing a torrent of septic waste into the sanctuary of our home he continued, 'I had to.'

He explained that he believed his actions had saved him from certain mental illness and therefore he had had no choice. One bank holiday when the boys and I were visiting old friends, Millie had taken my husband to her bed for the first time. It was many months before confession reluctantly exposed truth and unspeakable damage occurred in the meantime.

The conflict at church being unresolved, Nick had been suffering and seemed unable to see anything but his pain. As repeated excuses floated across the room I felt in danger of suffocating under the pressure of the torrent of unwanted truth. A deafening siren wailed in my head warning of the total obliteration of trust and destruction on a mammoth scale. My heart cut wide open, the fear of infection from what felt like a tidal wave of toxic waste filling the room, propelled me out into the garden. Reeling, I gulped in the fresh air, grateful for the canopy of darkness; in a far-off life we had loved, played and laughed where I sat but that night shock robbed me of emotion. Giddy with horror I sat screaming silently under the stars to the one who flung them there. I was wearing my pink velour dressing gown. I loved it but I could never bear to put it on after that night. Eventually I gave it to a friend. I needed help as never before as I thought of my precious sons. I needed wisdom as trauma threatened to swallow me. I watched as a hedgehog obliviously snuffled past and I felt strangely reassured by his small prickly innocence.

It was many months previous to that dark night when I had returned home with a weight in my heart. Words from the counsellor heavy as lead. But God had whispered. Now in the garden as I cried despairingly to the heavens, 'God, I don't know what to do,' the still small voice came again, gentle, strong.

'Yes you do, I have told you. Separation. A month.'

Infused with courage and overcome by a strange calm I returned indoors and heard myself gently yet firmly announce to my husband that I would like him to live somewhere else for a month. The month became twelve.

I suppose this could be the beginning of a book. But I can't shake off the feeling that I am surely kidding myself. What could my story really offer anyone? Who would *ever* want to read something I write? If this was a God idea wouldn't it feel more 'anointed'? How does it feel when God is doing a creative work that has a spiritual purpose but requires a human tool? I don't always read the introduction of a book but I did recently. In *Walking with God* by John Eldredge, he writes,

> *There is something more than a little disconcerting about writing your autobiography. When people have occasionally asked me what I am working on, I have found it impossible to tell them without an inward blush. As if anybody cares or should care...But I do it anyway. I do it because it seems to me that no matter who you are, and no matter how eloquent or otherwise. If you tell your own story with sufficient candour and concreteness, it will be an interesting story and in some sense a universal story . . .*

So, I will trust that the timing of my reading this is an encouragement from God to press on regardless of how unlikely it feels to me. I am way out of my comfort zone in unfamiliar territory but the scent of adventure lures me.

4

Faith Leaps

That first year of separation it seemed we were living at op[ends of a long, dark corridor and the boys, wearing trainers with little roller balls in the soles, hurtled blindly fron end to the other and back. Bleak weeks were punctuated by bleaker weekends when cries of, 'Why can't Mummy come wit[split the air and tore my heart.

The ongoing stress of Nick's late arrivals, changing plans and minute cancellations rendered me numb. I constantly found half of cold coffee around the house but had no recollection of maki[drinking any of them. My brother Andrew arrived from Londo[was just 'with me' in the house. We were living quite different li[different cities and hadn't seen much of each other for a few yea[his reassuring presence comforted me. He didn't comment, cri or utter platitudes; he just offered a shoulder and played with the Without any need for explanation he demonstrated a level of wo[empathy that was profoundly comforting. He seemed instinctiv[

know my deep pain. Much later I wondered if perhaps he, too, had been betrayed. We didn't know the details of one another's lives and he soon returned to the big smoke but I have never forgotten how safe his kindness made me feel in the raw exposure of Nick's infidelity.

Supportive friends came and sat each evening. I suppose we had conversation. I climbed and re-climbed the stairs to settle a sobbing four-year-old. Comforting his frightened older brother, then six, was more of a challenge. Sam wept with anxiety because Daddy had always been vehement about smoking causing cancer and now he had acquired the habit himself: was he going to die?

About this time I read in an old book (*Streams in the Desert* by Mrs Cowman) that in years gone by when ships hit enormous storms, seamen would lash themselves to the mast and abandon their fate to the seaworthiness of their trusted vessel. Having set the ship's instruments on a course they tied themselves up and waited for the storm to pass.

As the months and years unfolded people would ask me how, in the midst of so much pain and loss, I managed to continue trusting and believing that God loved me and had a purpose in it all. They questioned my dogged belief in him being able to bring something good from the debris of my life. As the storm raged and tumultuous waves churned, I found God to be the mast that did not crack or splinter. The tree of my life was battered and stripped bare. As I clung with blind, clenching grip to the one remaining branch it continued to support my weight. God was all I had left that was certain. Letting go was simply not an option. 'Holding on' seemed to burn calories though. 'Slim' came and went as my body began to feel more coat

hanger than woman. When I was with my mother the word 'gaunt' hung in the atmosphere. I felt fine as I watched this other lean woman cleaning for hours and organising social activities for my children. Their father expressed appreciation of her new physique when collecting his sons.

The church had a healthy reputation. We were known in the local area for being a caring community of people committed to sharing our lives honestly. Part of our mission statement declared our desire to 'speak the truth in love'. Honesty and openness were hallmarks of the relationships we shared. The exposure of one of the leaders, living a life of deceit and immorality, inevitably brought the integrity of the church into question. Rumours were rife. I felt ugly, worthless, somehow disfigured, misshapen so that familiar places and relationships felt alien. I didn't fit; could no longer belong. If I saw an attractive woman my tummy would turn over. Sometimes I couldn't stop trembling. Subsequent admission of one-night stands caused me to feel completely vulnerable: skinless. After his admissions I felt I could be connected to any female I met because she could have been intimate with Nick; as if I was somehow contaminated by a physical act to which I had never consented. With betrayal my constant companion the normal routine of life took on the proportions of an Everest climb. Just breathing…a discipline. Undeserving of the heartache thrust upon them family and friends shared the dark days. Needy children filled every space. The tunnel stretched ahead further than I could see but I grew up knowing there is always a light at the end. In this season I let others believe it was there. Only a spluttering wick of hope remained in my heart and the darkness was thick. I could only get out of bed, dress and support the children. We inhabited a strange new world where Daddy was not living with us anymore.

During this year following Nick's initial admission of adultery I hit what I presumed to be an all time low. I had only ever been intimate with my husband but it became apparent that his choices had exposed me to many others. When pressed, Nick admitted to unprotected sex with various women. I battled to keep my attitude right, knowing my life depended on not giving space in my spirit to the sense of injustice I felt. It was unjust; because of someone else's actions I was facing anxiety and humiliation. What if he was now carrying a disease? If I had caught something I had to know.

I felt sick. People would surely presume it was my own promiscuity that put me in the queue at the Clinic for Sexually Transmitted Diseases. I could hardly sit in the grubby, dingy waiting room, walls adorned with, well, you can imagine the scintillating NHS (National Health Service) posters in such an establishment, wearing a badge stating, 'It wasn't me that done it!' What if someone from the school gate spotted me coming out? But as the open arms of resentment and shame tried to goad me into darkness, I turned and lurched into the hopeful light of openly confessing my anguish to Sue. The habit of speaking out negative feelings is equivalent to putting the light on in a darkened room. I have found this denies the devil the opportunity of trying to convince me that a thing is best kept hidden, like a secret, where it can grow out of all proportion. Darkness is banished in the light of spoken truth so find a trustworthy friend and let confession set you free. With his devious intention of taking another prisoner thwarted, the enemy retreated, pushed back by the love of a faithful friend. Once exposed, his tactics shrivelled to powerless dust. I think this chapter was more painful for Sue as she offered me support. I felt wretchedly numb. The boys would need me; they would need a healthy mother. I had to know I was all right. I felt tossed about by indecision: faith or wise action? Maybe some would receive prayer and trust it would all be okay. Perhaps it was the nurse in me. I felt I needed to be sure that nothing was left festering in my body. It was a hideous feeling. Sue, loyal friend that she is, accompanied me. It helped. The 'all clear' took a few weeks to arrive but was reason to thank God for his protection over me even before I was aware I needed it.

As reality began to sink in my options appeared starkly before me. As a Christian of course I wanted to forgive, knew I had to forgive in order to remain in the blessing of God's forgiveness in my own stumbling life. I am forever thankful for the wise advice that scripture does not instruct us to forget; only choose to forgive. The forgetting is God's prerogative when we are sorry for our own failings and confess them. I got busy. Dumping our now thoroughly defiled 'marriage bed' I slept in a new single and re-arranged the bedroom. Nick moved into a room in his mother's house and collected the clothes and personal things he needed to live and work from there. Replacing bed linen and curtains I indulged in a riot of pink and lilac. The neighbours watched with mild interest as a rather undignified assortment of unwanted items appeared outside the back door and found their way to new homes, but I could not help myself. I felt desperate to create space. It felt important to me that I was not surrounded by things that had significance for us as a couple.

We had frequent conversations, usually on the telephone, and my husband was making it clear that he wanted to make a go of the marriage. His perspective was that his unfaithfulness had been necessary to protect his sanity. In a time when nobody understood him or his needs the deceit and betrayal were unfortunate consequences. In his mind all this was about him and had little to do with our actual marriage. He constantly reiterated his belief that we were meant to be sharing our lives. He remained adamant that God intended us to be together. I was thoroughly confused. (And dot.com hadn't even been thought of!) I just couldn't grasp how he could have acted in the way he had if he really believed what he was now declaring.

Just because someone hurts you and lets you down it doesn't mean the immediate death of love. If you have had children with a man, given yourself in total abandon and adored him with every cell in your body, you are joined. The leaving and cleaving that Jesus spoke about happens; a done deed. Convinced that God's heart is for restoration, healing and promises fulfilled I set my sail to make things better. We began having discussions with the leaders who felt certain steps should be taken for the process of restitution to be complete. For his part Nick went through the ordeal of public confession in a meeting where church members gathered (pretty humbling for me too, actually). And so began the long journey back. His mother's house was near to the church of his youth and he began attending there. Old friends encouraged Nick to see a spiritual counsellor and he went for a number of sessions. We were encouraged to take time to forgive and gently rebuild our relationship. Nick was encouraged to consider courting me again and began making appropriate gestures with flowers and notes.

My inner anguish over all that was lost was immense. The decision to work at rebuilding was not. Two small boys needed a father, their father. It must surely follow that as their mother I had a responsibility to do all within my power to reunite the family. My heart had been towards Nick since I was seventeen years old so turning away from him to strike out on my own, rather than press into a restoration journey with God, looked like a much tougher option. I can see now how devotion and desire actually paved the slippery slope into idolatry. In my naivety something ostensibly wholly good, such as a husband who was passionate about living with God, could never usurp God's place in my life. It was a huge lesson as I began to recognise that anything at all that draws passionate commitment from me has potential to subtly tilt the balance and become an unholy priority. Soon choices are influenced and life becomes coloured by the posture of worship at a wholly unhealthy altar. I truly believed that being married meant we somehow lived before God as a conglomerate. I saw our life together as a misshapen lump of clay, full of potential. God was working on the clay and Nick (as my head) was responsible for keeping us in the right position on the potter's wheel. What an unfair pressure this must have put on a young husband, father and leader. In the unseen realm my expectations will not have been helpful as he desperately sought to be an agent of God's love and power in our community, the spiritual head of our little family. God has in the intervening years gently and consistently taught me that nothing and no one can be tolerated as my primary motivational passion, other than himself.

Towards the end of a year apart we decided we were ready to

renew our vows. Nick had said he was sorry, had got part-time work and had been going to church regularly back in his hometown. Looking back I was on a mission. I organised the redecoration of much of the house and we ordered a new bed. I had a new ring made; I booked a weekend away for the two of us after the simple ceremony and arranged childcare. I said I no longer recognised our original wedding date in July and wanted to have the new date in March as our anniversary. I put Nick's general lack of enthusiasm for detail down to the fact that he was recuperating and saw myself as lovingly relieving pressure.

It mattered to me to establish a clear marker between what had been and the fresh start. Nick never felt quite the same but went along with the plans. At one point he said he was fed up with all the coming and going and would happily have just come home. Sometimes I longed for him to be more engaged and intentional but I told myself that he was in recovery and had had his fill of public declarations. Believing it was understandable I pressed on.

We invited half a dozen couples that had prayed and loved us through the troubled years and had a simple gathering in the lounge of my parents' home. Andrew led us through renewing our vows. Our friends were delighted and thrilled for us. Excited that their prayers were answered. The boys had a sleepover with friends and I confirmed the booking for a romantic night away.

I was apprehensive about being together physically for the first time since Nick had admitted adultery but knew I could be brave and longed to endorse him. I thought it would please him if I took the initiative but I was deeply hurt when intimacy seemed to be of minor importance to him. I tried to hide my confusion; we had been apart for a full year by then and I longed for him. I knew he had had one-night stands whilst I inhabited a sex-free zone. It hurt that he didn't seem as keen as I was to cement this new beginning. I concluded that as we rebuilt trust the rest would surely follow.

One day, discussing our future, Nick expressed a desire to begin his own business. He is artistic and had developed a flair for interior design through his retail work selling floor coverings and furnishings. I really wanted to rise to the occasion. I longed to pass what felt like a huge test. It was as if he were asking if I was serious about trusting him, not least because the venture would involve asking to borrow money from my father...again!

I reasoned with my inner self that to be living with Nick at forty, with him full of regret and resentment over a missed opportunity for which I may well be blamed, would surely be far worse than living the adventure of starting a business together. I convinced myself that the financial errors of the past need not be repeated. Over the years, every now and then a payment had been forgotten or a bill overlooked. Sometimes a final demand would appear and the phone would be cut off. If these events were meant as warnings I failed completely to be alerted. Together, surely we could set things in place to safeguard the new plans. I was certain we both felt determined not to repeat past mistakes.

We enrolled on a small business start-up course run by the local authority, duly received our lump sum and with thousands of pounds on loan from my father the business was launched. When the inner voice whispered caution I told myself 'faith is action'. I loved Nick and felt I should be able to demonstrate that I had confidence in him. I was so keen to demonstrate belief in him I didn't allow myself to express doubt. As we began to rebuild our relationship I was sad at times. Close up, he felt more regret and irritation about the exposure of his unfaithfulness than concern for the pain he had caused. There was something unspoken in the air, a subtle pressure on me to accept that the past was past. In fact I needed reassurance.

I told myself I could be mature about the whole thing; time would heal but I failed to discern the old independent spirit lurking as I tried to squash doubt about the absence of the fruit of genuine repentance. I told myself I needed to put my best foot forward. I was a conqueror and had two sons who needed their father. I can only say that I did what I thought was the best for all of us at the time. I was convinced that God's purpose must be restoration, that us being back together living and loving in the church community would be what brought the most glory to his name. God would surely enable me to be the wife Nick needed in that season of his life. They say hindsight is a great thing but even looking back after decades I don't have revelation. I just know I did my very best within the circumstances to live out my faith, trying to be a good mum and wife.

Sam and Nathan were delighted that Daddy was not living at Gran's house any more. The separation had been presented to them in part as being a result of Nick's work being too far away. They were aware of the new business venture and enjoyed clambering under the stairs amongst the rolls of fabric and carpet that steadily accumulated there. The brutal truth is that within six weeks of the happy day, when we promised each other so much at that informal gathering in my parent's home, the lump of lead had returned to my stomach. Nick was quite clear that my job was to trust him and that did not entail questioning his phone calls or inquiring as to his whereabouts. I was to prove my trust and forgiveness.

One day, after a call I realised had been from 'the other woman', I suggested that if any future calls came he could consider hanging up and refusing to engage in conversation. He announced that he had no intention of being rude to anyone and would not be told what to do. I was desperate to know how to manage my own emotions and move the marriage forward. I gently proposed the idea that we might benefit from some extra guidance and we arranged to visit the husband and wife team that Nick had seen regularly for a period of time during the separation. I was very nervous but I reasoned that Nick would be far more comfortable with counsellors he already had relationship with than talking with a more local person. I didn't know the couple that by now were his friends. Taking a deep breath, peace enabled me to trust God and I decided that driving across the county would surely be worth it. I must find a way to manage my bruised emotions and the disappointment better. With a general air of 'I can't really see the point but if it will make you happy' Nick drove us to the appointment.

I listened as my husband complained to them that he didn't feel I was really prepared to trust him. They in response explained that trust is earned not commanded and that once broken, in the way it had been in our relationship, it had to be very deliberately re-earned over time. They said Nick had a responsibility to prove himself trustworthy. Relief fluttered in through the window, hovered briefly and then the front door slammed behind as it flew straight on down the street. Nick was cross and irritated. He was furious that he was expected to take responsibility for creating an environment where I could learn to trust him again. He had been demanding that I trust him, as an expression of my love for him, and I think this was the first time someone other than me verbalised clearly that he was responsible for the actions that had destroyed trust. It was certainly the first time he appeared to hear what was being said.

I think this was the point I understood with a jolt that although Nick had publicly apologised, asking the church family to forgive him, he still in his heart nursed the conviction that his actions had been necessary, that he had not had a choice. Clearly there was an aching gulf between this perspective and the humble acceptance of responsibility that could bring understanding of the pain and suffering caused to others. As Nick drove angrily out onto the by-pass I pondered how I could ever feel safe again. It seemed clear to me that if a person could not accept the reality of the consequences of their actions on others, there was nothing to inhibit them from repeating the actions. I think this couple could have helped us but they didn't say what Nick wanted to hear. We never went back.

As behaviour patterns began to revert to a now all too familiar rhythm, darkness rolled in. Nick began to be out for prolonged periods of time. He would regularly 'pop' to the video shop after supper and not return until the early hours with no explanation offered. We limped along attending church and attempting a display of normal life. Nick, a deeply creative, artistic man deprived of serving his community in the way he was passionate about, suffered.

He encouraged me to maintain contact with those who represented strength, security and stability as he steadily withdrew. Maybe (good old hindsight again) at some level he recognised what he was not able to give. I was at the end of myself and so greatly in need of understanding that giving it was impossible. We co-habited and with enormous effort maintained a semblance of normalcy for our sons. All the while, in the hidden recess of Nick's heart wound, the seeds of offence that were planted, fed and watered (that could have been healed and released if pride had stood aside) flourished. Acid tendrils from the taproot of bitterness multiplied to impact all Nick's attitudes. His perspective on everything and everyone was tainted by this deep invasion of his spirit. This process meant I increasingly felt I was living with a person I didn't know, but when I tried to talk about how I was feeling anger rushed to meet me. Every day was a battle and I focused on holding my ground. I began to sense a deep pressure building in Nick, like an abscess; it wasn't worth pursuing any issue too deeply because eventually toxins would spurt out over me and it could take me days to recover. I needed all my energy to maintain daily momentum for the boys.

During this time it was made clear to me that I should 'lighten up' and be more fun to be around. Memories of days when Nick had enjoyed carefree times with Millie cast a long shadow. He frequently challenged me, 'Look, the most important thing for me is that we just have fun, that's what really matters; to have a laugh.'

It was spelled out to me on a regular basis that I took life too seriously. I had battled constantly in the long months, which eventually proved to be those of the main affair with Millie, with the inner conviction that I was just no fun to be with. Tentacles of despondency squeezed the walls of my chest as patterns of behaviour steadily reappeared, constricting the flow of life and love from my heart. I felt a sickening pressure to somehow produce or be the entertainment each evening until it almost became a relief when Nick 'popped out' and didn't come back. Working towards the business producing sufficient income, Nick retained some hours in the store where he had been working. But it was across the county and with the journey seeming to take him longer and longer it became increasingly clear he was not coming straight home.

One day while loading the washing machine, I silently prayed for guidance and I could see I had a choice. I could walk away now or I could remain. I sensed God saying he would be with me in either choice. I reasoned it must be best for the children to have their father around for as long as possible and made the decision to stay. Another decision which seemed best at the time. Certainly I was far from being able to accept that the relationship was over. Imagine the trauma for the church. Having just publicly started a fresh chapter we were the answer to many prayers. Looking back I don't think I would do it any differently because I could not.

I was desperate. I was watching a horrific landslide in slow motion as Nick, my marriage, life as I knew it were steadily slipping further and further away. In a time of worship, crying to God for help and mercy he showed me a picture of a large rock in the middle of a tumultuous ocean. The boys and I were standing on the rock and Nick was thrashing about in the water some distance away. I wanted to jump in; I am a qualified lifesaver and I could rescue him. My pyjama bottoms lay in a soggy, shredded, useless heap; there was no throwable life belt. God showed me I could not protect and nurture our sons *and* save their father. He made it clear he had placed the three of us on the rock and to move from it would be disobedience. It helped that God showed he was fully aware and demonstrating he was in control but it didn't feel like it. I could not leave the rock without risking my own life and abandoning two defenceless boys. I was greatly distressed but this picture helped me to hold still. I daily wrestled with the subtle temptation to compromise in various areas, to co-operate with the pull to meet need in Nick's life. I was accused of being too black-and-white in a grey world. I considered trying to be more light-hearted; perhaps I was too intense and therefore boring. Maybe I should just not care so much about things. The small amount of self-esteem I had recovered was steadily eroding under the relentless waves of criticism and undermining. The rock picture was a warning to choose to remain in the safe place of God's purpose for the children and me at that time.

Feeling utterly wretched and helpless I could only watch and pray. I prayed alone, with friends, with Andrew and Sue, with the counsellor but nothing seemed to change the course Nick was on. I somehow managed to get up each day and I'm sure prayer prepared me for what was ahead.

5

Guiding Hand

I maintained some kind of momentum for three years but by then I was flagging and those close to me were concerned for my health. The endless ride aboard the sapping roller coaster of emotional challenge had almost taken on the guise of normal life. And then one day I was hit by a realisation. After a tricky conversation with Sam, trying to explain away another situation where Daddy had said one thing and done another, a thought circled. Finally lining up it came in to land on the runway of my mind. As it taxied towards the terminal I couldn't divert the truth. I could no longer say or even dream that I wanted my sons to grow up to be like their father. As this reality settled I experienced a giant wave of nausea.

The business venture had spluttered and died some months before. I was acutely conscious of the money my father had put in though he never brought up the subject. I was increasingly aware of a sense of disappointment. My parents had longed for Nick to succeed but their sadness never manifested in criticism or recrimination. I was distressed about the clients whose carpet remained under the stairs, their invoices never submitted. By the time it all came to light an in-depth review of what exactly went wrong was never an option so I don't know how Nick really felt. It was agony for me because I longed for him to realise his dream of being an interior designer. I was positive it need not have gone wrong. I knew I could give support on the administrative side and man the office phone when he was with customers; but very soon the old thing of wanting to do it all himself had surfaced and Nick made it clear he saw my contribution as interference. As calls and inquiries built up, letters left unopened and bills not paid, I felt hamstrung. I could see what was happening but had to accept I was powerless. It could have been a very successful venture but came to a messy end. Afterwards, Nick did a few odd jobs but seemed to lack motivation. He wondered about returning to the police force but when the forms arrived he sat me down and said that if I asked him to he would sign and return them. I was very wary of being held responsible for him being unhappy in the future. I felt from a human viewpoint it could be a good stabilising decision. As Nick talked I silently prayed for wisdom and then I explained that I would thoroughly support him if he decided to return to the force, but that it was not my decision to make. He did nothing.

Nick was distant and seemed distracted most of the time. The gap between us widened daily as he procrastinated about finding employment, organising finance or just planning family time. The anger that simmered below the surface erupted all over me if I attempted to voice helpful suggestions. Any hint that seeking outside help together or him alone if he preferred, met with venom that tainted the atmosphere for days. Longing for calm and anxious to protect the boys I tried to summon energy to keep life stable for them. Frequently I retreated to the home of one of my friends and often spent time with my parents. They were amazing, never suggesting I should handle things differently. Occasionally, mentioning a work possibility for Nick, they expressed longing for him to find fulfilling employment but recognised I had no influence. I swam often in their pool and it was some time after my father had died that Mum mentioned he had worried about me silently weeping through my lengths. I talked as openly as I could with them about life in general but found it hard to share deep feelings. I didn't know they were anxious for my health.

I don't really know where Nick was much of the time; it was just increasingly clear that he didn't want to be with us. I held on to the belief that nothing is impossible for God and with so many older, wiser Christian people in our wider circle of friends I remained convinced that Nick would turn to one of them for help. I was focused on surviving the constant bombardment of signals – that I was unattractive, inadequate, outdated in my perspectives, dull and generally just not worth being around – all from the one person on earth to whom I wanted to matter. When we did have conversation about a possible job, a bill that needed paying or maintenance on the house, it was like torture because Nick would say what he thought I wanted to hear, 'Yes, I will sort it, do that, be there,' and nothing would change.

It was as if he had a mental paralysis. Any hint from me that we could seek help he perceived as critical and antagonistic. We had always shared an exhilarating ability to see the funny side of things but now all attempts at humour or affection were shunned. The vice of an existence without laughter, held me in a relentless, life-sapping grip.

A friend who wasn't in the church but lived locally invited Nick to assist with the local Scouts and over time he took on responsibility for the Cubs. Mysteriously the escapism this offered seemed to generate energy for the task. As his skills and affable nature came to the fore he became very popular. Nick was never happier than when messing about with ropes, building fires or calling poles and canvas into line. I was glad he could be in an environment where he felt appreciated but it didn't resolve any deeper issues and over time the adulation he received from adoring mums compounded his conviction that I was responsible for the deterioration of relationship on the home front.

My parents and their marriage style had been a strong role model for us both. Nick's father died when Nick was in his early teens, having been a dominant figure in the family. We had both slipped into the conventional mindset of the man being very much the bread winner and manager of finance and administration. I aimed to hold up the domestic end. Years later, I realised these expectations had fostered a desperate need in my young husband to be seen to be in control and coping. Insecurity bred pride until asking or even acknowledging the need for help became unthinkable. My father was a brilliant accountant and had always been in charge of all things financial. I presumed my husband would do the same.

Whenever a red bill arrived it made me anxious. It created tension between us because I had never been overdrawn or in debt and it seemed somehow dishonourable to me. Nick was always saying he was going to put things onto regular payments to prevent it happening but never managed it. I felt a sense of shame when the phone was cut off and friends would ask if we were having a problem with our line. I minded that Nick seemed to shrug it off and I think I felt strangely vulnerable but couldn't find a way of expressing it that didn't feel like accusation to Nick. It seems unbelievable in today's culture but it never occurred to me to take over the administrative tasks; I wasn't earning. I think just getting up every day and sustaining some momentum for the boys was all I could manage at this stage. Then one afternoon, whilst playing a board game with the boys, we needed scrap paper for recording our scores. There was plenty of scrap paper in the bin. The clock stopped as I unfolded the discarded letter retrieved from the waste-paper basket in the study. It was from the Woolwich Building Society and stated that our mortgage payments, now being some months in arrears and no response having been received from previous correspondence, legal action would be taken forthwith. I was numb with disbelief.

Nick said all the right things about being in discussion with the Woolwich, about getting work lined up, about having the situation under control. But in the moment I read the letter something in my spirit shifted and fractured. I had worked really hard at believing the best, that Nick was deep down still wanting us to be a family. The seismic realisation that our children could be rendered homeless as a direct result of Nick being too proud to talk about it, meant I took action. I visited the building society. They assured me that they had had no communication from my husband but that in these situations it was always beneficial to keep them informed. (Nick's style was to hope that if he procrastinated long enough a problem would just go away.) I explained my husband was looking for work and that we had every intention of keeping up payments. As I drove home I wondered how long I could go on. If something as significant as this had been hidden what other debts might there be?

A few years previously, when Nick had given up his salaried job in the police force to pursue his pastoral role, my father had lovingly bought us a car on the condition that we paid so much a month into a named account. The intention being that when we needed to change the vehicle, funds would be in place. I think he wisely discerned that saving money and structuring finance could be a challenge and saw a way to help us help ourselves. I was stunned to find that my husband had robbed both himself and us, and emptied this account rather than talk to me about the pressures. I wondered briefly what on earth Nick had been thinking. We negotiated some delay over mortgage payments but with no funds and no predicted income our bargaining power was minimal. I felt sick whenever the phone rang. Anxiety successfully triggered my old recurring nightmare. It featured the daughter I had never had arriving on the doorstep and asking for her father. Prowling fear haunted my restless nights. Inner misery churned and swirled as I went through the motions of normal days and nights. I was crying to God for intervention.

Then in the middle of the year we received an invitation for the four of us to visit my sister in New Zealand, for a family Christmas. Somewhere in the turmoil of all that was going on we had been burgled and instead of replacing jewellery with the insurance money

I floated the idea of purchasing plane tickets. I felt a tiny stirring of hope. Maybe a holiday together, somewhere totally new, would help. Nick said he would wait till nearer the time before deciding where to spend Christmas and indicated he was quite happy for me to plan to go for a few weeks; just that he might make a shorter visit. Initially surprised by his reluctance, as he had always loved the sun and any adventure, I began to pray in earnest about the timing of the trip.

Thoughts whirled as I struggled to find wisdom. I came to see that if Nick had some time quietly, the house to himself for a while, perhaps healing might come? But no, being physically apart for more than a few weeks couldn't be good for any of us, could it? The questions niggled away as the summer term unfolded. I prayed long and often for God to reach into Nick's life and draw him back. A door had closed and I no longer had access. Things felt hollow where once we had valued each other's perspective and judgement. Perhaps the boys and I being away would create space in which he could think about what work he would do. July arrived and the school holidays beckoned.

So the boys could feel as if they were on holiday, whilst not wanting to abandon their father who said he did not want to make any plans, I set up our old caravan in a local farmer's field and took the bikes. The location being less than two miles from home meant Nick could drop in for barbecues in the evening and grandparents, living only thirty minutes drive away, could take advantage of some vicarious outdoor living. Days were spent happily helping with the sheep, making the fire and exploring in the woods. Sam and Nathan enjoyed being in a completely different environment but I was still within easy reach of my faithful, supportive network of church friends.

Moving out of the tension at home I began to enjoy a level of relaxation, which released some energy. I felt able to make the days fun for the boys. Soothed by nature, thinking became easier. As I asked God to let me understand what would be best for the timing of the Christmas trip I began to entertain the thought of extending the time away. Initially taken aback, as I prayed the idea grew rather than diminished. I quailed inside at the thought of being apart from Nick for any period of time. For the healing of any relationship people surely needed to come together, not be apart? Was I mishearing God? Or could he have a supernatural purpose in my being physically out of Nick's world for a time? If so, how long? A month? Six weeks? Definitely not months.

I spent time walking alone with God, as the boys pedalled on ahead. Always the question of the trip hovered; was it me or was it a God idea? If it was a God idea, that was hopeful because he would have a purpose for the time. If he was going to do something big in Nick's life maybe I would need to be away for a while. I had an impression about a time frame of six months but hastily pushed it aside. One day I would feel brave and hopeful that this thought must be from God. He probably wanted me out of the way so he could do a miracle in my husband's life. Then in the next moment I would be appalled I was even contemplating such action. What would my parents think? They wanted the marriage to succeed as much as I did and I felt certain they wouldn't sanction my not persevering at home. The inner voice continued to whisper 'six months' when I took time to listen but how could I ever tell my church family I was taking a long break? It would surely seem as if I was giving up or, worse, punishing my husband. Increasingly I felt I could see that if I took the boys and gave Nick a real break from the demands of parenting and the expectations of our relationship, he could take stock. I would need God to make it clear and to give me peace about such a big step. My thoughts churned. In reality: six months? A person could turn his life around…maybe it *was* God? Given time Nick could consider the future and decide if he really wanted a wife and the associated responsibilities of a young family.

There were lots of great walks from the caravan and one in particular led through a field of stubble. It was one of those where the footpath just meandered like a sheep track across the big field. It was only visible because the soil was a slightly darker shade of gold than the stubble and it was impossible to see unless you were standing ready, as if to walk on it. From any other angle it just blended in. This bit of the track was not visible from the caravan and walking one day I sensed God whispering that I should be prepared; this is how it would be with Nick. He would be making his journey, God would be working in his life but it would not be visible to others, in particular me, until he was almost back to the 'caravan', us as a family. I felt I was being warned not to expect evidence in Nick's life but to simply believe. It seemed like a promise to me and I recorded it in my journal and still gently remind God about it from time to time.

Then one Sunday at church Andrew spoke about Psalm 139, where it says that God holds our hand. He commented on how we commonly think it is our responsibility to keep a hold of God's hand. He told us about when his little boy was learning to walk, how he reached up to hold his daddy's hand. He pointed out that actually it was he who had a firm grasp of his son's hand, so that if he stumbled or tripped the child would be prevented from falling and hurting himself because of his father's firm grip. I felt some comfort as he explained that that is how it is with God; how so often we make the mistake of thinking it all depends on us keeping a grip on God's hand when actually God has hold of our hand. Later that night, as I hopped into bed in the caravan, I prayed letting God know that I was still thinking I should go away but not making any plan until he let me know it was *his* idea and not mine. Before settling to sleep I decided to have a look at the Psalm from the morning's talk. I read,

> *If I settle on the far side of the sea, even there your hand will guide me, your right hand will hold me fast. (Psalm 139:9–10)*

A peaceful kind of quiet settled on me, like a friend putting their jumper round my shoulders on a chilly night. A twinge of excitement. God had spoken. I would go to New Zealand. I felt the word 'settle' implied more than a few weeks' holiday but what? And that still left my parents. They were an enormous support for both myself and the boys. I couldn't disappoint them.

The next day my father arrived at the caravan unannounced, which was unusual. He left my mother in the car, approached the caravan and asked me if I had time for a little walk. He gently explained that they had been chatting and praying about my situation. He wanted me to know that if I should feel at any time that to go away for a spell could be the best thing, he and my mother would wholly support me. They wondered if I should perhaps consider extending the planned Christmas trip for say, six months? Dad was not at all given to sharing what he thought God might be saying in this direct manner; we were both awed into silence. We stood together, stock still in the middle of the field as the Holy Spirit watered the seed God had planted. I couldn't speak but hugged him. A peaceful reassurance enveloped us as we walked back to the caravan. God was showing me the next step. Being apart would be hard but God must have a purpose so there was hope.

Since going any further than New Zealand means you are already on the way back to Europe it definitely qualified as 'the far side of the sea'. I made plans and booked return tickets. I told Nick gently what I was thinking. I think he was a bit surprised. I had never hidden my desire to be with him and we both knew that taking the boys on my own and for so long would be a big thing. I assured him that I had prayed much, felt clear about the time frame and would book flights back exactly six months from our departure. (Which I did...to the day.) He didn't vigorously try to dissuade me, he didn't rant and rave about my wanting to take the boys. I think he knew a sense of relief and maybe smelled a new freedom. (Many months later there were rumours that caused me to think perhaps he was already exploring opportunities with grateful Cub mums. I don't know.) I know I felt a peace and confidence about the plan not being my idea, which gave me strength. A part of me hated to take the boys away for so long but it seemed Nick was no longer able to think of what was good for them. Through the gentle reassurance of family and friends I became convinced that two young boys needed at least one healthy parent who was able to put their needs first. My intention was to give Nick space and time to decide if he was going to find work, if he really wanted the responsibility of a young family, if he could ever be happy in a monogamous relationship, if the God he had preached for years was a closed chapter.

It was a grey November morning as the car pulled away. I looked at my street, the familiar driveways, the village store, but I saw nothing. The price of obedience seemed very high. Yes, I was going to see my beloved sister. Yes, I wanted my sons to be able to grow up in a peaceful, affirming atmosphere. I wanted to be faithful to what I felt God had said to me so clearly. BUT could he really be asking me to abandon the man who was a part of myself just when it seemed he most needed comfort and support? Every cell in my body was numb. I had asked a friend to whom I was not too close if she could take us to the airport. I couldn't risk being with anyone who might express emotion for fear I may break down and not get on the plane. I had to hold it together for the boys and duly switched to autopilot. Flights home were booked for exactly six months later. Completely believing this dramatic step was because God needed me out of the way to do his miracle was all that propelled me through check-in, security and onto the plane.

'Even there your hand will guide me,' it says but seriously, 11,386 miles from home? Yes, seriously. It was tough. A local school agreed to take both Sam and Nathan for a term in the New Year. We arrived in Auckland a few weeks before Christmas and in that part of the world all things academic take a long break over the hot months of December and January. Once the routine of term began I spent most afternoons alone with God sobbing, listening for him and wondering what was going to happen. I played worship music and remembered what Mrs Cowman had written in *Streams in the Desert*. I pictured myself tied to the mast of an old ship which was being battered by a raging storm, powerless but still afloat, at the mercy of the tide but still breathing. It may have looked as if I was holding on tight to God but he was just keeping his word. He was doing the holding. My sister Heather continued to work, worship and have friends over. She generously included me plus two boisterous nephews in her life whilst making room for all that God might be doing.

The boys loved the relaxed lifestyle (I learned years later that shoes had been carefully secreted on the route to school so that the barefoot culture enjoyed by the locals could be shared) and God brought Steve into their lives. Steve, a big-hearted, gentle bear of a Maori man was a friend of Heather's from church and a regular visitor. Pillow fights, water pistols, rough and tumble, ice cream and movies generously poured out on my sons with lashings of unconditional love and acceptance. How like God to meet needs that I just could not summon the energy for. Over time they learned to respect and trust Steve. Their delight was hardly containable when a year later friendship blossomed into romance and their hero became their uncle.

We missed Nick terribly. The boys and I made regular phone calls to him with extended chats over Christmas and on his birthday. After a few weeks I gently probed, asking how he was, wondering if he had any work ideas. He was non-committal. He needed income. Debts were mounting. The bank would not wait forever. Various friends from church were in contact and several extended invites for meals or dropped food in for Nick. He didn't pursue any of the relationships. After we'd been away a couple of weeks, my mother went to see how Nick was. She found him merrily serving coffee and chatting in the garden with several mums from the school gate. I later learned he had let it be known that I had upped and left, that I had taken his children with me and that he didn't know if I was ever coming back. I think that would tug any young mum's heartstrings, particularly as the father in question was tall, dark, handsome and a dynamic Cub leader!

6

Painful Obedience

Returning to England I was devastated. All the problems were worse not better and our lovely home was under imminent threat of repossession. I couldn't really believe what I was doing, all by myself. We had been away exactly six months and wonderful friends had met us at the airport. When we arrived at my parents' home my mother produced the keys. I was to be a tenant. I was a single mother. A one-parent family.

In the final few weeks in New Zealand it had become clear that all the reasons that had triggered my departure, far from being resolved, had escalated. It didn't make any sense to move the boys into the turmoil of a house being repossessed, a parent with his life out of control and the emotional chaos of inevitable separation. I had completely believed that given space and time without family commitments my husband would take stock, decide he did want a family, renew his relationship with God and find healing. I was profoundly wrong.

Nick had lost his way and with the bank threatening to claim our home he had reluctantly agreed. We had no choice but to put the house up for sale. It was shattering. Nathan had been born in the house and Sam had learned to climb in the willow tree. Nick had left his work in the police force not long after we moved there. This had meant he could be fully available to pastor those in the local church that by then were our family. God had amazingly provided finance for the original purchase. We were meant to be there. It was our calling to demonstrate God's love and his way of doing family, to the community, long-term. We were born to live, love and serve in that place and now…the wreckage of a ruined relationship littered every room.

Because I had felt so convinced that the stimulus to take the enormous step of leaving Nick alone and travelling to New Zealand had come from God and that he intended a positive outcome for our family, I didn't suddenly think I had been mistaken. I was appalled that Nick did not seem to have come to a place of realisation and numb with disbelief that he still viewed himself as a helpless victim of circumstance. I felt very small inside. How could I have thought that application of faith on my part could shift the mountain of rubble and debris that seemed to have buried who we once were? The dream of being a source of life and hope writhed and choked in the dirt of immorality and deception. I was mystified. I had stepped out in obedience and gone away utterly convinced God intended it for good and then he still seemed to be saying 'not yet'. I was no less convinced that restoration was on his agenda. How could it not be? What other outcome could show his glory? I knew from our phone conversations before returning to England that more time would be needed. But the actual losing of the house, our beautiful home and the stark reality of being back in the familiarity of Sussex yet inhabiting the uncharted terrain of being both a tenant and a one-parent family, was isolating. I felt like an alien trying to discern the expected behaviours of a distant universe. I wrestled to get to grips with my new world. It must be that God's process needed more time to unfold. I had come this far; I was certain he must have a purpose in what appeared to me to be a delay and I turned to him daily asking for the resource I needed to keep believing.

As the boys and I set out for our new life a huge rainbow appeared in the sky behind my parents' home. A symbol of the promise God made to Noah that he would never again flood the earth. I sensed a whisper, 'Never again. You will never walk that path again.' I felt unreasonably encouraged. I took this to mean that whatever unfolded in the future I would never again be living with someone who betrayed me.

We had never lived in a flat. On the second floor, it was completely unfamiliar to us to open the front door and face stairs. Being upstairs the living room was light with glimpses of Worthing seafront between the buildings across the road. I tried hard to be positive and I was very grateful to my mother for going to the trouble of contacting our letting agent who was the son of one of her friends. I had felt desperate not to move in with my parents because I feared I wouldn't have the courage or impetus to move on. Rental properties in the area were in high demand and initial lets of twelve months rare. It was amazing the flat was available, affordable and the landlord known personally to the agent. This meant he accepted us as possible long-term tenants and allowed my mother access prior to our arrival. The flat gave us independence but nothing was familiar. It was filled with someone else's furniture. There was a cloying, salty smell of damp carpet that no amount of 'shake n vac' could mask. I had to go through the ground-floor flat's courtyard to reach the shared garden and felt far too self conscious to ever use the washing line. We had strange beds and the noises of people we didn't know laughing and loving echoed from below as we drifted off to sleep. I yearned for the familiar comfort of a life now evaporated but stability for our sons had to take priority.

I thought it must be best to remain within our local area for schools, friendships and especially to make it as easy as possible for the boys to see their father regularly. I still believed God was lining up a miracle. I prayed and received prayer for healing at every opportunity. I felt raw. Rejection was absolute. Deep in my soul I was wounded by the shattering betrayal of the love of my life with a woman I had seen as a friend. This pain compounded as the weeks ground by and incidents of my husband's one-night stands, lies, deception and a double life emerged.

Some evenings, after the boys were in bed, the weight of being alone with so much knowledge and the reality of total rejection overwhelmed. I would slip across the road to the corner shop and buy a bottle of cheap wine and one of even cheaper own-brand lemonade. Guilty about spending money on myself and ashamed of feeling so low I sipped away until I felt the edges of the pain blur and it felt okay to be vulnerable. Then I wept for all that could have been and fell exhausted into bed, grateful to have made it through to bedtime. I felt bad in the morning as God lifted me once more into the everlasting arms that carried me each day. I always said sorry but never felt condemned, only loved enough to get the breakfast, read a few proverbs and pray with the boys before doing the school run, often singing along with DC Talk or Jars of Clay at the top of our lungs for mutual encouragement. During those months a number of people said to me, 'Things are so tough and painful. You've lost everything; it is amazing that you are still able to hold on to your faith. How have you managed it?'

There were days, when the boys were in school or with Nick and everyone around seemed full of purpose, it felt as if God's presence in my life was the only thing left and therefore of immeasurable worth. It seemed to me I was still clinging to the last branch on the tree and my very life depended on not letting go.

The days were demanding as we had to work on sorting and emptying the house in anticipation of a sale. After dropping the boys at school I would arrive in the area that had birthed so many dreams with fear grinding my stomach. The large skip was visible from the bottom of the street. A foreign object. A siren that blared the demise of us as a couple. Nick and Hazel slowly, deliberately being swallowed and dumped. Erased. Every drawer was loaded with memories, each cupboard spewing out hollow tokens of what might have been. Decisions about what to keep, what to throw out and what to give away drained me. I felt so pinched by the process all that remained was a shadow. Constantly Nick's anger prowled, accusing through clenched teeth.

'It's your decision, Hazel. It doesn't have to be this way. You could just come home. The boys want to.'

His total belief that he was a victim of my cruel decisions quietly bled the days of all colour. Such was Nick's ability to live in the moment that he wondered if we could have just one last night together. I clung feverishly to the rock picture of long ago and yearned for the battering to be over. Arriving one morning, in the grey shadow of the hollow spectre of a home that had once harboured hope and life, I faced another grim truth. I could not co-habit with what was going on in Nick's life and remain healthy. Living apart until he regained understanding or some balance in his life was actually essential. Just until he had resolved the issues that at this time seemed more important to him than anything else.

Years earlier the boys and I had memorised scripture walking to school. A favourite had been from the Old Testament in the book of Deuteronomy.

> *The eternal God is your dwelling place, and*
> *underneath are the everlasting arms.*
> *(Deuteronomy 33:27 ESV)*

This truth literally sustained me hour by hour because my hope of survival was dependent on letting God take the weight of my circumstances. Each time I felt the burden of a decision or the pain of another conversation I consciously reminded myself to 'hand it over'. As I chose not to agitate over the thing I experienced peace and pictured myself being carried in big strong arms. A divine embrace in which I could quite literally make my home. So much felt vulnerable and transient but in contrast something that is 'everlasting' doesn't wear out, weaken or give up. As life has unfolded this truth means I can make wherever I live or stay 'home' because, wherever I am, my actual 'dwelling place' remains utterly constant.

Two had become one when we married. I felt completely tainted. Damaged by my husband's choices. It was as though I had been dragged into relationships and connections without my knowledge or consent. A wretched feeling gnawed away at me, a feeling that we had not just been the two of us in times of raw intimacy. Even though we were living apart I sensed that his choices and relationships still had an influence in my life. I cried to God that he would somehow cut me off, set me apart, give me a safe place so that I could be healed and protected from any ongoing immorality and deceit.

My parents had a lovely home in the Sussex countryside and the door was always open. Now a parent of adult children myself I have more insight about the pain they experienced but their love, acceptance and encouragement never waned. This supported me as I fought to offer stability for my children. They and other close friends had made it clear that a bed was always available and I decided it was the right time to practise being kind to myself. On the darker days, when I felt the hot breath of despair on the back of my neck, I would make it a treat for Sam and Nathan to have tea and a sleepover away from the flat. In terms of coping, I think I expected more of myself than God or those close to me did. I was often struggling and feared that I was letting God down by not managing better. All along I think he just wanted to embrace and encourage me. I learned to graciously accept the offered help and stopped telling myself it was weakness. I recognised it was a tough season and getting through the best possible way was the priority. I remember even back then praying to God that if there was any way that sharing my pain in the future could encourage or strengthen another, I would be available if he would only show me how. The love and support of my friends and family made a difference every day. I can't bear to think of others in such unhappiness with no hope.

A few weeks after returning from New Zealand and moving into the flat, I was sitting by the pool at Mum's enjoying coffee with a dear friend. I shared my struggle to feel free and healed of the pain whilst knowing God's purpose for me must be wholeness inside. I talked about wanting separation from the consequences of my husband's sin but finding I couldn't shake off the strong sense of connection. Annie and I had prayed, laughed and cried together over many years. I knew she loved us both. I didn't want to be around those who mouthed off about my husband's failings. Love doesn't die just because someone slips off the pathway. I greatly appreciated those who exercised control around the issue; Nick was still the father of my children. Annie held my gaze as she dropped God's bombshell.

'Have you thought about divorce?' she asked quietly but not hesitantly. 'I think you should consider it as an option now. I think it could be God's way of making the final separation.'

I felt physically winded and the weight of her words settled like ice in my chest. My mind was spinning. This surely could not, just could not be…God. He wouldn't ask that of me.

'Anything, Lord,' I screamed inside, 'anything to be well and free but you cannot ask me to take a knife and deliberately murder the hope of restoration and the love that still remains and could yet be rekindled.'

Everything in me recoiled but the still small voice would not be silenced. I heard, 'This is from me.'

Divorce!? God hated it, didn't he? It was final, wasn't it? But surely if God intended a future for us together, serving him, there couldn't be any point at all in beginning a legal process. Divorce was when a marriage was totally and utterly over. He couldn't want me to divorce Nick. Everybody knew we were Christians, albeit Christians having problems. In my mind that was a million miles away from being a divorcee. How would the inevitable shame of divorce help the church's profile? In today's culture it may sound naive in the extreme but I can truthfully say that my belief in restoration was implicit. The possibility of divorce simply had not featured. In all my conversation, thoughts and prayer the emphasis had been on anticipating a better, richer future…together. Divorce is not even mentioned in my detailed journaling up to this point.

So, I had an answer to my prayers and it seemed it was not up for discussion. Divorce was not an option that had entered my head. I mentioned before that I had no friends who were divorced. This wasn't a strategy on my part; my married friends were all committed and enjoying their marriage relationships. I knew *of* people who were divorced; I was completely pre-occupied with how and when God was going to intervene in our circumstances and draw Nick back into relationship, first with himself and then, naturally, with me. Divorce was a major 'end of the road' step that people who didn't understand

God's love for them resorted to, usually in order to gain large sums of money to spend on a new love. How would it be in any way conducive to restoration? I had never considered it.

The summer days continued to dawn but inside me a winter chill took hold as the enormity of the idea of 'killing' my marriage sunk in. I knew if it really was a step God was initiating then wholeness could come no other way. I asked him to please make it clear and help me not lose hope. On June 23rd my reading in *The One Year Bible* was from Acts 15 and James is speaking to the council in Jerusalem about some of the conflicts of opinion. I was crying out to God each morning and so long as he whispered something in my ear I could manage to get up and start the day. Over time he gently affirmed my path with reassuring readings about him having a future and a hope with the promise of peace and joy. My thoughts wandered to my parents, as June 23rd is their wedding anniversary. My own painful memories hovered, so many broken promises. In verse 16 James quotes Amos, an Old Testament prophet: 'Afterwards, I will return and renew the broken contract, its ruins I will rebuild and I will restore it.'

I was stunned, relieved, excited and filled with anticipation. God was giving me a promise.

'Afterwards'…after I had initiated the process? After I told Nick I was divorcing him? Possibly even after the divorce? No, God wouldn't need me to actually go through with it if he planned to 'renew' the relationship, would he? As time passed I could begin to see the obvious sense in taking action. To cut myself off from Nick's damaging choices, somehow I would have to separate myself from the deep connection of our marriage vows. But restoration was promised and I was certain God could independently heal me and set me permanently apart from the implications of any relationships or actions in my husband's life. Hopefully God was doing things in a hidden place so that we could be restored soon. He spoke to me from Proverbs 3:5–6 about trusting in him with all my heart and not leaning on my own understanding. I tried to point out that divorce is final, public and inevitably painful. He showed me that those were the exact reasons I needed to take the steps. By now years not months had passed since I had been seeking healing.

By 'healing' I mean a permanent release from the pain of rejection, a dissolving of the mound of disappointment and an end to feeling debilitated by the conviction that I must be profoundly unlovely and therefore inadequate as a woman. If God was saying this was his answer, that he was 'making a way where there was none', what choice did I have? He is absolutely sovereign and totally supernatural. He was drawing me to engage with him and co-operate in a process. I could only hold on to the belief that, in some way I could not begin to see, obedience would facilitate answered prayer. Abraham and his journey of faith seemed to regularly crop up in my readings or in sermons. I was heartened as I read that God stepped in at the last minute to prevent the sacrifice of Isaac. I decided that initiating the divorce process must be my 'Isaac' experience. I thought God was probably testing my willingness to be obedient. The inner belief that God was going to intervene and sovereignly prevent the final ending of the relationship I knew was his purpose for my life, energised me to keep walking as God unfolded the steps.

With a heavy heart I spoke to my parents and they were sad

but also relieved. I checked it out with close friends whose love and prayers were holding me up. Nobody suggested I wait or that I may be mistaken or reminded me that God hates divorce. So was I really sure? With one accord they agreed the step should be taken for my and therefore the children's protection. Back then I was blissfully ignorant of the rigours of the divorce process. I didn't imagine that the distress and indignity of queuing for blood tests and rectal swabs at a clinic for sexually transmitted diseases could ever be surpassed.

As the wheels of the divorce process began to turn I looked on, from the distance that trauma creates, through the smoky haze of disbelief. I watched as a person who bore some resemblance to me went through the motions. A name was mentioned, a phone number given, a call made, an appointment fixed. Then one afternoon a hollow woman got out of a car and guided by a friend walked woodenly to an office door. She noted the name of the firm of solicitors that seemed incongruously flamboyant, grossly blazoned across the window in flowery, gold script.

I stared unseeing across the desk. A dense cloak of humiliation engulfed me. I tried desperately to compute what the smartly dressed woman opposite me was saying, '. . . therefore, because you have lived together with your husband after he committed the initial act of adultery, it is not permissible in law to site adultery as cause for divorce.'

I was stunned. Because I had sought to forgive, taken my husband back after adultery and separation, renewed vows and redoubled efforts to make the relationship work, I was to be viewed by the law as complicit in his adultery. How could this be possible? How degrading. How shocking to be informed that in order to divorce my unfaithful husband, I would be required to compose a list of 'unreasonable behaviours'. These needed to graphically demonstrate the breakdown of relationship.

Whilst nurturing the dream of restoration and hoping for the best, I was obligated to launch what appeared to amount to a character assassination of the father of my children. Surely there would be another option; this could not really be happening. If divorce was the next step of obedience there must be another way; a way that did not involve deliberately, actively finding fault as if to murder any hope of a future together. Surely God would unfold something?

The story of Abraham and Isaac and God's last-minute intervention hovered at the back of my mind but in that moment seemed to keel over, like the target on a bar at the fair. The woman in front of me reiterated her statement and began suggesting acts of betrayal and deceit that could be sited as cause for marital breakdown. I felt a desperate need for fresh air, made my excuses and fled.

7

Slippery Slopes

If you don't need to be royalty to claim *'annus horribilus'*, the year in the flat would have to be mine. As weeks rumbled on I knew I had to take control of my own circumstances. During the months living in New Zealand with my sister I had felt stricken inside. I had struggled to convince my sons that their father was not unhappy to be on his own, whilst feeling appalled by the enormity of my own actions. Returning after six long months suspended out on the limb of faith it was unthinkable that Nick had not chosen us. He inhabited a broad place where illicit sex beckoned and God had shown me I could not compete. Being apart had been agony but it always had a fixed time period and sharing life in a new culture had offered plenty of fun and distraction for Sam and Nathan. The weight of being apart from Nick had been substantially lightened by the certainty of an ending.

Time now yawned endlessly as I groped towards an unknown future. How blessed I was that my parents were in a position to be generous and had covered the first few months' rent. I churned inwardly and debated at length with close friends and family the pros and cons of going back to work. I had previously completed a 'Back to Nursing' course and I wondered about the possibility of part-time work whilst dreading making a decision that could result in my not being there for my sons. I made the huge decision to apply for state benefit. Nick sometimes said he wanted to contribute to bigger items the boys needed, such as school shoes, but his input was not consistent and I needed stability.

I was unprepared for the process and completely taken aback when the lady from the benefits office visited me at the flat. She stated that to qualify for help I was required to sign a form permitting the Child Protection Agency to 'go after the boys' father for money'. I felt cornered, pressured, as if I were being asked to set the dogs on someone behind their back; but she made it clear that without my signature there would be no money. I desperately wanted to be independent of my parents who had been so giving over the years. I wasn't naive enough to think that I would manage totally without help but I wanted to do my best to support us and it was explained to me that assistance with paying the rent could also be available. It took some weeks but eventually payments regularly came through and I rose to the challenge of shopping and cooking with economy in mind. Nick took my choosing the official route as a personal assault. He was angry and hurt all over again. Trying to sort things out between us was hopeless. Consistency and faithfulness were not his strong points and I was really working to get things onto an even keel, so there was an element of relief for me as the state took over. I felt it was important for Sam and Nathan that they knew they were my priority and that I was there for them even if it meant we had less.

The rooms in the flat were spacious with high ceilings and I daydreamed often about what fun it would be once Nick could live with us again. We settled into a routine where the boys would go and spend the weekends with their dad. Nick appeared keen to have them. His life was empty and I thought it must be good for them to maintain as much contact as possible. I felt hollow and unhappy as they left. We should have all been together at weekends. Happy families seemed to be everywhere and it didn't get easier. My parents and close friends were an invaluable source of comfort but they were all married, happy and inhabiting a different planet. I had to battle not to agree with the voice of resentment as it whispered in my ear that I had the grind of the school week with homework and chores, whilst Nick had all the fun time.

Looking back I think I was trying to make something exist that did not. However much time and space I made available, if Nick's heart was not towards loving, including and bringing healing into his sons' lives, it was futile. There was evidence that he was totally preoccupied with his own pain but I wanted to give him the benefit of the doubt. I wanted Sam and Nathan to think the best of their father. I never told them the whole truth. I didn't criticise him to them: I was thinking we would all be together again in the future. Sometimes now I wonder if I was too protective. Is it more or less painful to be let down as a grown man? If the greatest thing a man can do for his children is love their mother, then Nick betrayed them too. If a hero falls perhaps it is better faced.

When the boys returned with stories of being sat in front of various screens whilst Dad slept or did chores during the weekends I struggled. I knew the statistics for absent fathers, how the pain of constant goodbyes usually became too hard, with visits becoming less and less frequent until they dried up altogether. I was anxious for that not to be our story and it is to Nick's credit that he pressed on through the grief of constant separation to remain in the boys' lives. Perhaps unwittingly I was feeding my sons to an insatiable need in Nick's life since time has proved him unable to establish meaningful relationship that has endured. I did what felt like the best thing at the time. On days when the pain was slightly less raw and I could cope with his physical presence Nick would come in and see the boys to bed.

There had always been exciting chemistry between us and in the vulnerability of so much wounding I recognised a need to be on my guard. I had read that over 90 per cent of separated, even divorced couples continue a physical relationship. We were both mourning the loss of so much that had once been beautiful. Sometimes Nick would linger once the boys were asleep. We just sat side-by-side drawing a form of comfort from each other's presence. Every nerve in my body was on red alert, and I can understand how the comfort of familiarity and the relief of intimacy with the person who has been the centre of your world, could seem alluring. We both felt rejected and wounded but for my part I knew to yield to any physical urge was not an option. An entry in my journal at that time reads,

When I am aching to creep to where Nick is at night I recognise the battle is not with flesh and blood. Also, I am desperately longing for the comfort that a relationship of mutual trust and respect can bring, not just a quick

bonk! Stay awake, woman, and realise that what you yearn for and need does not exist. Only trouble, turmoil and emotional damage could possibly materialise through physical contact. Will it all ever be unravelled, understood, healed?

The last time we were intimate we were still in our own home. It was a few weeks before I left for the six months in New Zealand. It was a night that left me scarred. Desperate to somehow reach what was falling over the cliff in front of me I recall flicking an internal switch. The tender foundation of trust was shattered but the chemistry between us remained compelling. I found my husband physically very attractive and I knew that for many people sex was simply just that: sex. Maybe I had done my usual thing...been too intense, expected too much, convinced myself that what we had was special, unique even? If I could just let go and immerse myself in pleasuring him maybe he wouldn't feel the need to be with others. I was soon going away for six months. I wanted to make one final attempt to reach the man I could no longer find. The night that ensued left me dazed and bewildered. Deliberately surrendering myself to unbridled passion I was catapulted into unknown territory. The next morning I felt fearful as I recognised the level of compromise to which I had sunk. With no tender communication, respect or affirmation providing a healthy hammock of safety I had abandoned myself to self-gratification. To say I was profoundly shocked by the power of my own actions would not be to overstate the case. Up to this point I had fully respected and lived within the parameters promoted by Dr James Dobson in his book, *Love Must Be Tough*. My nocturnal behaviour completely contradicted my commitment; the one to respect myself enough not to be intimate with my husband whilst there was no genuine, honest conversation between us. It felt to me that the bleak spectre of his unfaithfulness, which seemed to have retreated in the scorch of passion, returned with jubilant companions in the early chill of the new day.

As I walked the boys to school that morning I felt wretched. Dug out. Something inside was marred and whether or not sex without emotional commitment is normal for a percentage of the population, I felt utterly violated. Recognising I had debased whatever may have remained of the strong, glorious, tender intimacy that had once been an integral part of our marriage, I burned with shame. I walked numbly, feeling I had put myself up for sale and been bitterly short-changed. It was raw; absolutely clear to me that for my own sanity it must never happen again. At no time was that night discussed and three months later I left for New Zealand.

The unspecified time frame and the aloneness of the flat represented an uphill climb beyond imagining: enormous. There were blessings. The flat was only a street back from the sea front, which made for great picnic opportunities. Friends could drop in easily though parking was a challenge. The carpet continued to smell as if it had once been under sea water for a period of time and no amount of plug-in air freshener prevented the dank, salty aroma from clinging to the inside of your nose. A muddy animal undertone hinted at the possibility of a previous tenant having ignored the 'no dogs' clause. Nathan had always been keen on the idea of a pet, something to look after. Keen to say 'yes' whenever possible to two troubled young men, I began to look at our options.

By the time the boys were born Pickle, who was a liver and white Irish Springer Spaniel, had been very much a part of our lives. They had played and romped with gusto until a malignant growth got the better of her. The hamster chapter that followed had not ended well when we went away for a few days. Separation anxiety rendered Haffertee completely hairless. The kind friend minding him hardly fared much better. Coping with the stress of knowing how much his little furry friend meant to Nathan was costly. The final passing of Haffertee brought many weeks of sticky ointment and sad inspections for hair growth to a close. After a respectable amount of time (which amounted to three days in child speak) Nathan had announced that, Haffertee being irreplaceable, what he had always really, really wanted was a snake. His mother filed this thought in the 'too hard' basket and pressed on.

Sam had shown little enthusiasm for a pet of any kind and began to have days where he needed coercion to get out of bed in the mornings. A week where he was at school every day became a victory. I was worried. Previously of a sunny, inquisitive disposition he was often withdrawn and rarely expressed enthusiasm. Despondency became the tone of life. I was so thankful that Andrew was willing to spend time with him, encouraging and motivating Sam to get up, go to school and have hope. I was out of ideas but he would come and sit on the bed talking and encouraging Sam for hours when all I could do was withdraw and weep for the heartache and pain I could not resolve. Sam had been the apple of Nick's eye for the first few years of his little life and the searing loss of the father Nick had been inflicted a deep wound. Nathan appeared to embrace life and I was thankful but appearances can be very deceptive.

The boys returned to their original school. Although it meant a fifteen-mile round trip twice a day for me, I felt a quiet sense of achievement at having managed to keep them near enough to resume both familiar relationships and after-school activities. I felt blessed to have a reliable little car and prayed constantly, as I drove, for the restoration of our family. I loved the area of rolling countryside we drove through each day and began to feel a strong pull. I felt we would one day live off to the right of the A24 and was excited when a friend told me of a Christian landlord who owned land and a number of properties in that area. When I called the estate office to inquire, his secretary assured me that nothing was available. Tenants were seldom moving because families were welcome to remain long term and, the rents being reasonable, they did. There was a considerable waiting list. I still requested an interview with the landowner believing God may step in. He was kind and sympathetic about my circumstances but only confirmed his secretary's doubts about a property becoming vacant. I asked to have my name on the waiting list and the secretary gently put her hand on my arm as I was leaving saying, 'Do stay in contact, my dear, you just never know,' which gave me hope.

She and I were to have many exchanges on the phone over the next few years.

The clear sense that Nick and I had originally moved to the area and thrown ourselves into the community life of the church because God wanted to do something significant never waned. Restoration is what God is committed to so surely, in the unseen realm, he was bringing Nick back to himself and then we would be re-established to love and serve together. I continued to believe that God would step in to prevent the divorce actually going through. I had been totally obedient just like Abraham and the reward would surely be a glorious reunion, thus demonstrating God's power to all.

Each day I persisted with determination to read and pray, casting myself deliberately into the promised everlasting arms. Pearls of wisdom from Mrs Cowman's writings and words of encouragement from the Psalms complemented comforting promises from Isaiah. I felt held by God and relished a certain inner stillness. I experienced a deep pool of resource growing inside me and each day, parched and weary, I could crawl to the edge and drink. Hope remained.

I began to recognise that the fact that Nick and I came from quite different backgrounds had significant influence on how we were living. God showed me a picture of our lives as trees. In October 1987 there had been an incredible storm, described as a hurricane, which swept through large parts of southern England. I will never forget opening bedroom curtains to view a whole new world of devastation. Our street was completely blocked by enormous fallen trees. It looked as if a giant in a fury had rampaged through relentlessly uprooting and throwing aside oak and beech, bins and sheds. The wind had simply sucked out of the ground anything in its path.

With a heritage of praying relatives and a hunger for daily prayer time the roots of my life were down very deep in the soil of God's word and sustaining presence. It was as if the tree of Nick's life had sprouted rapidly, tall and lean in leadership. It towered above his peers laden with gifting and skill with words. When the storm hit, his life was top heavy, lacking the crucial underground support network of far reaching roots. God showed me how it is vital that the root system of a healthy tree spreads out wider and deeper than any growth that is exposed above the surface because this is the life-source and strength of the tree. Only the weight of a vast, well-established root system underground enables the sustaining of life. It is a life of hidden intimacy that produces the strength that will keep the tree standing when storms crash in.

When Heather and Steve were married, our home had long been sold and we had been living in the flat for about seven months. They decided to have their main wedding in New Zealand as that was home and then a second 'blessing day' in England. My parents generously paid for all of us to be at the big day in Auckland. The event was still some weeks away when the snake conversation resurfaced. Thinking the idea could possibly diminish (indeed longing for same) I promised that we would talk about it again on our return from the wedding trip. At Christmas, which is high summer that end of the world, we travelled to New Zealand for the wedding. Heather and Steve both now in their late thirties had nurtured their relationship over several years. Excitement was high. Heather had not had a previous serious relationship, always believing God had someone special in store. She has not been disappointed.

Such was the love of the newly-weds for Sam and Nathan that they invited them for an enormous adventure. They planned the first few nights of their long-awaited honeymoon in a luxury hotel in Auckland and then proposed their nephews join them for the second half of the holiday. It was to be spent in Disneyland. Travelling to England to celebrate their nuptials with the many family and friends who could not travel to New Zealand for the actual wedding day, America would be en-route. The family time together leading up to the big day was precious. New Zealand weddings follow the same style as in America where the bridesmaids and groomsmen stand facing the congregation throughout the ceremony. I had to be very brave. Standing in my bridesmaids dress at the front of the church, haunted by the clock of my divorce proceedings ticking, I experienced the ceremony as though watching a film with someone who looked like me in it. Fortunately people do cry at weddings.

Sam and Nathan were thrilled as the course of true love unfolded. We returned to England and the boys informed me that they preferred life when we were all together. Once the newlyweds returned home to Auckland the boys began praying each morning for Heather and Uncle Steve to move to the UK and set up home with us. This urgent prayer journey was not discussed but Uncle Steve was often on the phone. He assured his nephews that he and his new wife were praying for them and regaled them with stories of life with their much-loved auntie. He was unaware of the seed of hope that his unconditional love had sown in the hearts of two young nephews.

Another seed, one I had fervently willed to shrivel and die, stubbornly produced a tiny, new, bright-green shoot and it became clear that the issue of Nathan's pet could be deferred no longer. To this day, the supernatural process that occurred enabling me to contemplate, nay, embrace the presence of a silent, slithering reptile in my own home, awes me. Somehow, possibly unconsciously driven by a sense that I must compensate my sons for the loss of their risk-taking, adventurous father, I went along with the idea.

The thing is, of course, snakes don't drop hair (best pet for allergy sufferers) or make any noise (perfect for flat life) and don't feed every day so they can be left for short spells here and there...ideal. The hardest part was living with mice in the freezer. Mice are bred deliberately for snake fodder and the frozen babies are sold in bulk packets. I never arrived at being comfortable with the feeding ritual that required the little rodent corpse to be suspended from tweezers, within range of the hungry Harry, until he struck out, wedging it between his jaws and then with slow peristaltic movements worked the defrosted morsel down into his stomach. I was ever grateful that the food arrived with all tails removed. The boys seemed both fascinated and comfortable with the performance so, suppressing my natural desire to shudder and squeal, I generously allowed them to keep Harry in his cage in their bedroom. That would be the cage that he was not able to get out of.

Unfortunately, if the latch on the trap-door style opening to the aforementioned cage was not securely fastened, escape was indeed possible. It was an unsuspecting friend, having kindly offered to baby-sit one evening, who brought this design flaw to our attention. Kindly venturing outside her remit she lifted the laundry-basket lid to drop something in and found one other family member awake in the flat. Her ensuing yelps of panic soon changed that state of affairs. She sprung back sending the laundry bin, at this point still containing the unsuspecting Harry, flying. Two willing little helpers swiftly threw themselves into tracking down the errant reptile. The offer of minding the boys was never repeated. The day that Harry went to 'Show and Tell' at school is fondly remembered and for a pleasing time Nathan's street cred went through the roof. Corn snakes don't grow too large (we were told up to about the width of a small double bed) and can live for as long as twenty-three years in captivity, so Nathan felt there was potential for a happy and lasting connection.

Traditionally, corn snakes are not aggressive but over the next few months it became apparent that Harry had broken with tradition. One day, casually sauntering up to me as I cleaned the bath, Nathan explained that he was feeling the weight of responsibility. He solemnly announced he had decided that we should take up the offer of the pet shop owner and return Harry. I became very busy at the plug end knowing a broad grin was not the appropriate response to such a weighty decision. Nathan returned to his homework. I exulted in the power of prayer, even if the answer were delayed.

On a bleak morning in February the Decree Nisi arrived. I opened the post in bed with my wake-up cup of tea. I called my sister in New Zealand and we cried together as I read out the stark words of the decree over the phone. God whispered to me through Mrs Cowman's entry from *Streams in the Desert* for that date. I copied it into my journal.

February 1
'This thing is from me.' (1 Kings 12:24)
'Life's disappointments are veiled love's appointments.' (Rev. C.A. Fox)

My child, I have a message for you today; let me whisper it in your ear, that it may gild with glory any storm clouds which may arise, and smooth the rough places upon which you may have to tread. It is short, only five words, but let them sink into your inmost soul; use them as a pillow upon which to rest your weary head. This thing is from Me.

I would have you learn when temptations assail you, and the 'enemy comes in like a flood,' that this thing is from Me, that your weakness needs My might, and your safety lies in letting Me fight for you.

Are you in difficult circumstances, surrounded by people who do not understand you, who never consult your taste, who put you in the background? This thing is from Me. I am the God of circumstances. Thou camest not to thy place by accident, it is the very place God meant for thee. Have you not asked to be made humble? See then, I have placed you in the very school where this lesson is taught; your surroundings and companions are only working out My will.

The writing style was old fashioned even then but the clarity of the message left no room for discussion. God was saying plainly that I wasn't imagining his leading; I wasn't required to understand the why or how but my part was to accept my situation as from him. It didn't suddenly make everything all right but I was humbled and reassured by such a direct communication.

I reasoned I probably only had a maximum of six weeks, then, before God would bare his arm and turn my circumstances around because although this bit was from him and I was walking obediently forward, *actual* divorce couldn't possibly be his ultimate intention. In the following weeks I hugged myself to sleep at night, mentally re-running the part of the story where God 'stayed the hand of

Abraham'.

I felt not hopeless but hollow. Nick had at last signed what was required. He had been deeply hurt by the list of 'unreasonable behaviours' I had drawn up and was very angry about losing his home. Once debts were settled there was little to play with so he was in an unenviable position. I did also spare a thought for my girlfriend Millie. I heard she moved to a different town and set up a home that she had dearly hoped Nick would share with her and her little girl. I never saw Millie or her husband again though it was years before I stopped having jelly legs due to the fear of bumping into one of them in the supermarket. Too many spoiled lives.

I consoled myself with the thought that the Decree Nisi now gave God six weeks to work his purpose in the situation. Gloomy and grey, the weather felt entirely appropriate to the content of my post and I went to visit my mother. Later, after coffee together, she was driving into the town when a driver pulled out of a side road right in front of her. I was driving some ten minutes behind and making my way back to the flat when I came upon the ambulance and recognised, with a jolt, that the wrecked vehicle on the verge was hers. Thankfully Mum was in much better shape than her car. Not a day I will forget.

The six weeks between Nisi and Absolute came and went with no change; no knock on the door from Nick saying he was sorry, he understood what pain he'd caused and did not want to lose us. The Decree Absolute arrived in the middle of March and the thick fog of grief rolled in. I was witness to a death but there could be no funeral; indeed each weekend I was required to visit the open grave. I hardly knew how to keep going.

8

Go...Where?

I continued to feel that, in the absence of any other clear instruction, it made sense to remain in the familiar geographic area of West Sussex. The flat had only ever been a stopgap, a breathing space in which to make a plan. I tried to find a place for us to live back over the South Downs which we were crossing each day on the school run. I was optimistic we could find a home within walking distance of schools, Cubs, church, etc. but time after time the door shut in my face. Even a perfect little bungalow that backed onto the school playing fields, which seemed to me ideal, was a 'no'. Many landlords were wary of tenants who were in receipt of benefit and made their decision without even meeting me. I couldn't help feeling that I was somehow a second-class citizen. These landlords judged me without a hearing and I was sure if they would only meet me they could be reassured. It seemed I wasn't worth being considered as a tenant and this only compounded my sense of dislocation.

One Sunday evening, longing to hear God's voice, I returned to the church where we had originally met Andrew, when God brought him into our lives as 'encourager'. The talk was around the story of Jesus healing some people and then sending them to 'show themselves' to the local priest. A lady went to the front and shared that she felt God was saying to someone present that he was healing them and that they had a step of obedience to take which involved a 'going'. I was at this point praying specifically about whether to remain in the area or move away and, as she spoke, I sensed God highlighted in a particular way the part where it says, 'in *going* they were healed'. I went forward for prayer and later recorded this in my journal with a prayer I wrote saying I was willing to go wherever God showed me.

. . . quite an emphasis on 'going', Lord, is my full healing in that? I trust you and wait for you to unfold the pathway.

Within two weeks the agent was in contact to give us notice that the landlord would be unexpectedly returning from overseas and wanting to live in his flat from July. We prayed together each day after breakfast, the boys continuing to petition the Lord about a new life with Heather and Uncle Steve and me entrusting the coming move to him.

With no clear guidance as to how the 'going' word may be fulfilled I continued on the track of moving nearer our old haunts. Working on the principle it's easier to move a rolling stone I pressed on but kept the possibility that God may have something new at the back of my mind. One of the strong pulls to return to the village where we had been living before New Zealand was our connection with our church family. We travelled a twenty-minute drive from the flat to worship with them, clutching the continuity and searching for love we had always known. I spent every service silently weeping as the pain of intimacy lost rolled in. The acceptance and warmth of God and his family colliding with the stark reality of the rejection that had invaded every cell of me, stung all over. Lost dreams and fractured friendships hovered. Nothing was as it had been.

In spite of the weight of sadness my sense of belonging remained strong and I clung on, thankful for some continuity in the strange new world I now inhabited. I loved the atmosphere of hopeful worship and was grateful to let it hold me for a while. The thought of branching out somewhere new didn't feature because I was focused on trusting for restoration. Grief dulled everything but familiarity provided a strong anchor and it was strangely helpful to be with people who loved Nick. A number of them offered him hospitality or attempted to maintain contact but he was illusive. It was hard, hearing he had refused a supper invite or, worse, accepted it and not managed to turn up. But I was grateful they cared. Many people in the church had been blessed by Nick's teaching and love and I was thankful he wasn't being criticised. I held onto the hope we would be reunited and believed that God would use any demonstration of his consistent love to draw Nick back to him. A number of those in the church had known us since, as a newly married couple, we had begun travelling across the county to visit the church. Now as a single mother and ex-pastor's wife I felt like an ugly spot on the face of the radiant church we had been so happy serving. I wore black clothes for months feeling such a failure I didn't deserve the beauty of colour. Why did I keep on going? Church and the people there were the only constant in my life and I did know that 'feeling' something didn't make it truth. God had clearly called us to this group of people years before. I felt that I needed him to communicate specifically if he had a new plan.

Behind the scenes tragic unrest was percolating. A man of influence in the church (years later his own adultery and addiction were exposed) became critical and angry. He grumbled to others, stirring up dissent by complaining about leadership decisions. He felt strongly that Nick should have been treated differently. Presumably he was desperately fearful of exposure, which created urgent need for a diversion to thwart that possibility. With no prior warning in a church meeting one terrible week he initiated a vote of no confidence in Andrew as the leader. This culminated in a dramatic change of leadership and suddenly what felt like the one remaining constant in my shifting world became fragmented and very uncomfortable.

Unspeakable pain and the inevitable fallout of shattered relationships left many numb with disbelief but things said cannot be unsaid and there was no going back. The heat of the refiner's fire burnt white-hot and those tested found all they could do was curl up beneath the safety blanket of truth for fear only a pile of ash would remain. For Andrew and Sue the gulf of searing loss was all enveloping. Somehow the fruit of the prophetic word in Jeremiah, faithfully delivered by a hesitant friend some years before, enabled me to offer comfort and support. I recognised that because the words had taken root in me they were true and I could reach out in spite of my own circumstances. I hope I have not withheld words or pictures that may prophetically strengthen others. We need to love others enough to take the risk if we feel prompted.

I realised also in this period of shattered hope and unfulfilled vision that God had made himself more real to me, a tangible presence, teaching me I was to be dependent on him above all other relationships. I was learning that although friendship was valuable and being part of a church community important, I was to trust him with the full weight of my life. Healing came over years as he lovingly kept me out of my depth so that I remained abandoned to his love at work in my life. Love that changed how I view things, how I respond emotionally and influences every area of my life and character. From time to time the 'riverbank' in the distance looked like a tempting place of safety but I would remind myself there was no discussion. Safety was not an option since I had pushed out into the mainstream of God's love and there was no going back. The Holy Spirit adventure became life itself.

Was it really time to move away? Were the property applications failing because all along God had another purpose? How could all the promises and prophetic words about the whole county coming to God ever happen now? I took my Bible and went up onto the South Downs where I loved to walk. God had been speaking to me from the story of the children of Israel, about the importance of his presence and how the people only moved on to the next phase of their journey when the cloud representing that presence moved.

I read aloud the prayer I had written about being willing to go wherever God showed me. Rereading what had been said in that Sunday service about 'in going they were healed' was reassuring; the timing of the word gave me confidence that God was showing me that he was initiating us 'going' from the flat. I was still often asking God for healing and was prepared to embrace whatever method he chose. Surely I must be right in thinking that to remain in familiar surroundings would be best for the boys? I spoke it all out loud as I walked and asked God to show me if I was looking for a home in the wrong area. There would still be a few weeks of the school term left after the landlord returned and I wanted the boys to be settled to enjoy that time.

I've never felt wholly comfortable with the idea of 'sticking a pin' in the Bible and claiming divine guidance as a result. There were those in my life who thought I should loosen up (I was never first in the party queue to pin the tail on the donkey) but life with a broken heart is a pretty serious business. However, these were desperate times so asking God to speak to me I slowed the pace and opened my Bible. It opened in Joshua. In chapter three, under the heading 'Crossing the Jordan', I read,

Then you will know which way to go, since you have never been this way before. (Joshua 3:4)

I knew immediately we were to move out of the area but had no idea where.

Anticipation shivered in the pit of my stomach. Awestruck, I knew God to be saying he had a plan. I hadn't found a new home because I hadn't yet looked in the right place. I had been focused on returning to the familiar but now God said it was to be a place I had never been. Praying out loud as I walked I agreed with the Holy Spirit that I would follow his lead and as I asked him about the immediate future my caravan came to mind. Over the next few days I had a growing peace about the possibility of using the caravan as an interim home. It was summer, we loved the outdoors and I found a farm local to the school with a small campsite and a stunning view. The farmer agreed that if I had not managed to find a house in time, we could stay on his land for a few weeks before regulations meant we would have to move on. It was such a convenient spot. I just hoped a few weeks would be long enough.

The sense that we were to leave the area grew steadily and I found something in me rising to the challenge of a fresh start. It didn't need to be too far away, just somewhere I had not lived before. But where? I prayed, writing my thoughts in my journal. I was beginning to notice how much is said in the Bible about waiting and patience and God always having a purpose in seasons of life even when nothing appears to us to be progressing. It was very heartening and I was thankful to look back on my written record of things God had said and showed me. How easily things are snatched away by the next life event. I strongly advocate the practice of keeping a spiritual journal. Recording words and pictures from God and having them as reference has strengthened my faith and consistently encouraged me as so much is fulfilled and transformed over time. If I hadn't consistently written things down since that initial leaving of the riverbank, much of the detail of my story would be lost.

In my mind we would finish the summer term with me house hunting whilst the boys were in school. Once the academic year ended we would have a little break and then use the end of the summer to move into our new home before the boys started at what would obviously be a new school. The big question was where? Thinking about geography and where I had previously lived, a pattern emerged. I had been born in Kent not far from the border with East Sussex. Our family had moved over the border when I was twelve and after my training years living in London, Nick and I had settled as newlyweds in a police house in Crawley. Sam was born in our next home in the ancient market town of Petworth. With parents and friends living in the string of villages between Shoreham and Midhurst I wondered how we could go to a place that was unknown to us, without being far away from the much needed support of family and friends. Across the border into the next county surely couldn't be on God's agenda. It was important to me that it was not a long journey for the boys to see their father, but it felt huge to be thinking about a whole new area.

I kept praying and listening. I walked miles, pouring my heart out to God telling him aloud how much I loved the South Downs having lived all my adult life in sight of them. I know he knew already, but drinking in a certain reassurance from the constant presence of their ancient undulations had become vital to my well-being. I felt I had nothing to lose by being honest with God. Allowing the current to carry me along in the middle of the river it seemed we were more intimate and increasingly that no detail was too small to invite his involvement. One day, passing a small shop not far from the flat, the postcard stand caught my attention. I felt a lurch in my tummy.

9

Over The Border

The postcard that jumped out at me featured a map. It was royal blue with the county border marked in dark green and place names in red. I recognised the familiar outline of West Sussex. A strange sense of anticipation crept over me and my skin prickled. It was bizarre. Each place I had lived or that had some significance for us as a family was clearly highlighted in bold capital letters. The left-hand edge of the card showed the border of West Sussex with Hampshire and the only place name on the card that was outside Sussex was Petersfield. My heart rate increased and I knew God was showing me something. I bought the postcard, took it home and spread out my map of southern England.

I was staggered as I realised that Petersfield was the same distance from my parents' home as I was in the flat, just in the opposite direction. It was the nearest I could possibly be to my familiar support network and yet be in a 'place I had never been before'. Studying the map more closely I followed the line of the South Downs and tears came as I registered that Petersfield was another old market town (Sheep Street in the centre so named because years ago the sheep were literally driven down it to the market square), nestling into the foot of the hills I loved. On the card the small town was surrounded by swathes of green indicating acres of open countryside. The main road, the A272, was clearly shown running almost directly from my parent's village to Petersfield. I was very excited and chatted and prayed with family and friends who were praying for me, asking God to let me know clearly which direction to go.

Over the next couple of weeks a quiet confidence grew in me and I was increasingly sure about the decision to move west. I told the boys God had shown me that we were moving into Hampshire. Initially excited they then asked how far it was from the rented house where Nick was living. I explained the drive to their father's would be a little bit longer and we agreed we would pray for a house that was easy for him to get to. They were reassured and we began praying for a home and church where we could settle. I had heard of a lively Christian fellowship in Petersfield and resolved to pay an initial visit alone on a weekend when Sam and Nathan would be with Nick.

One Sunday morning in early May, feeling rather intrepid, I drove across the border into Hampshire. A broken road sign caught my attention; it said, 'Welcome to Hampshire... good quality of life.' It seemed an optimistic note even while intimating that council maintenance may not be quite up to standard. I had made enquiries and learned that the Petersfield Christian Fellowship met in the local school. This would be the school the boys would attend if the move went through as anticipated. I felt shivers of excitement as I sat in the car park and prayed again for the spiritual growth and healing of my sons. They were my priority so a church committed to nourishing and supporting their young people would be a great bonus. I was encouraged on entering to see groups of people dotted around the hall praying together before the service began. I thought this could be an indication that God was being invited to influence the morning's proceedings. Prayer, or conversation with my heavenly Father as I increasingly saw it, was becoming the backbone of my relationship with God and I wanted to worship with others who craved his company.

We started by singing a song called 'Faithful One'. It's a song about God's love being our anchor and our constant hope in the storms of life. The lines of this song had become something akin to a personal mantra in previous months as I sought to gain energy from listening to praise songs that I didn't have the strength to sing. It so happened that the Sunday morning in question featured the dedication of a baby born to a family in the church. The speaker used the illustration of a sunflower and talked about ideal conditions for growth. I felt excited as the talk focused on conditions for healthy development, the need for appropriate soil, positioning and care, with emphasis on the desire of the church family to meet those needs. It was clear that the church was concerned to provide an environment that facilitated growth, particularly for young people. I was heartened also to see that the youth were clearly represented in the band of musicians.

After the service one of the women chatted to me making me feel welcome. I explained I was praying about the possibility of moving into the area. She positively 'lit up' saying she loved finding places for people to live and if I'd like to pop home with her she had a copy of the local paper with accommodation for rent advertised. When we got there I learned she was the wife of the speaker and she thrust the sunflower seedling, which had been used as the visual aid in the talk, into my hand. I guess, being intimately acquainted with the issue of my short-term memory loss, God thought I would benefit from having a physical reminder. It worked because as I mulled and prayed in the following days having the actual seedling was concrete evidence, reminding me of how God had spoken to me. It was an encouragement on days I was tempted to think it was all too hard and was especially helpful as I explained what I was thinking to the boys.

With six weeks of the academic year still to run I began making visits across the county border looking for a house we could rent. I was optimistic that God would provide accommodation within the time frame so that we could move from the flat to our new home. The agent said he had a house he thought might be appropriate. It sounded far from perfect to me because I felt it was a big hurdle that the house was being let 'furnished'. The landlady was going to work in America for a few years and didn't want to bother putting her worldly goods into storage. I could relate. In light of my own experience, with things I rescued from our house not fitting in the flat and having to be stored, I wasn't unsympathetic. But even new to the role of tenant as I was, it was clear that unfurnished rentals could be considerably cheaper. The time frame didn't sound ideal either as the house wouldn't be available immediately. I nearly told the agent it wasn't worth bothering but nothing else was in the offing and my dear friend Sue suggested we at least go and look at the outside.

How often I hesitated over the first step only to find that once I started walking God made a way. I had been very reluctant about going away and staying with my sister but God opened a place for the boys to be in school, brought Steve into our lives and began preparing me for the next step. I had been unconvinced about not returning to our home after New Zealand but as I trusted and opened my mind to the possibility, the flat was provided. I was unsure about the idea of waiting in the caravan until the end of term but God had showed us a beautiful place to park if it should become necessary.

Sue manages to be positive and enthusiastic about all kinds of situations she views as completely unenviable for herself. By that I mean that she has an amazing ability to co-operate with what she sees the Holy Spirit doing in another's life. This is a very powerful gift and an amazing strength that, through her generous friendship, has helped me maintain momentum and hope through many situations. I never in my wildest imaginings pictured life as a tenant...ever. Living in the property of a stranger with someone else's furniture and never knowing when I may be required to move on; not the ideal for someone who likes to 'have a plan'. Sue and I had had lovely homes a few minutes' walk apart and had been expecting to share life, working together in the church community, for many years. I was still slipping into church on Sundays and wondering if there was any hope of restoration and Andrew being reinstated as leader. We were still reeling over the loss of church and community lifestyle. Pastoring and teaching the people had been Sue's passion and she, with Andrew, had made what they understood to be a life's commitment. Yet in spite of her own disappointment and grief (rejection of Andrew as leader and related unresolved issues increasingly inhibited her ongoing involvement) Sue was a constant support. She recognised God's leading in my situation and encouraged me. I valued this more than I can say.

The agent informed me that the landlady was passionate about her garden. He explained she would probably want to pop in on her annual visits to the UK. Yet another thing that indicated to me that this probably was not God's place for us. Since my fingers are anything but 'green' my plan would have been to keep things under control and then have a pre-move blitz to restore all things growing to as near their original state as possible. This couldn't be God's place for us because I could feel my stress level rising just at the idea of regular inspections, possibly unannounced. The great friend that she is, Sue gently insisted coffee in Petersfield couldn't do any harm and praying together outside the house could be a helpful first step. We've indulged in considerable amounts of coffee and prayer together over the years, both to pretty good effect.

When I got back to the flat after that first conversation with the agent, I picked up the Petersfield church news-sheet that I'd collected on my Sunday visit. A couple of things caught my attention. Firstly, there was a quotation that read, 'Obedience hews the path for prophecy's fulfilment' (I noted this quote in my journal but not the reference so its origin is unclear). This seemed generally encouraging and reminded me about the prophetic word from the story of the lepers. As I pondered, it increasingly looked as if my 'going' was the 'obedience' that would lead to the promised healing. I was conscious of what I had read about the place we were to move to being 'a place you have never been before' plus the specific area that seemed to be so clearly highlighted on the postcard.

Secondly, there was a bungalow advertised for rent. It was in a hamlet just on the outskirts of Petersfield and sounded hopeful. Maybe if the owners were church members with a second home the rent might be within my range. Also, there was a caravan advertised for sale. My father, observing that the caravan was and probably would be featuring increasingly in our lives, had generously offered to help me purchase a new one. Not brand new. Granddad had been dead for several years by this time and the little caravan I had inherited was the one that he had kitted out for himself and Nana to pootle up to Scotland in each year. It could safely be described as 'facility free' and was nearing the stage of its life when it would no longer be considered roadworthy. I don't know that my dad had ever towed anything in his life and up to this point I was completely dependent on the husbands of generous friends who happily moved the caravan for me. My decision to master the art of towing so that I could be independent in terms of holidays with Sam and Nathan, plus stories of my attempts to master the skill probably precipitated his offer. The original caravan was very heavy. The one on the news-sheet ultimately proved to be a different layout to the one I was looking for. Eventually, when we did find one to buy, progress was such that we gained two feet of living space and a lighter van. I inquired and the bungalow was already let.

But with the quotation, the house and the caravan all in the one news-sheet it did seem that God was indicating that he was on my case and, although rather dubious about this particular house (for my part), Sue and I duly set off one morning. Petersfield seemed to be a happy blend of old and new with the dark wood, gabled frontage of a gentleman's outfitters nudging up to the trendy glass-and-chrome atmosphere of Ask Pizzeria. Some areas retain cobblestones underfoot and there was a shiny Waitrose with big car park softened by large leafy trees. The one-way system took me a few visits to master but proved essential when the A272 summer holiday traffic rumbled relentlessly through.

Keeping all options open, we first viewed a couple of rather dingy terraced houses that were available. I felt disheartened but remained determined not to just settle for something because of the timing. I knew a stint in the caravan may not be ideal but if waiting a bit longer were going to mean a really nice place to live it would be worth it. The house the agent suggested might be the most suitable was in a quiet cul-de-sac in which there were only a couple of dozen homes. Most of them had beautifully manicured lawns and bright borders bulging with spring flowers. My gardening skills to this point were more of the wild and woolly variety. I wasn't at all sure that I would fit in.

The house at 12 Russell Way had a cherry tree on the front lawn that was laden with blossom. The spreading branches formed a canopy that spread over most of the grass. The tree and other shrubs obscured the view from the street into the lounge. All I could see were the crowded flowerbeds. How much would it cost me to replace all the plants if they should die whilst I was in residence? My first impression was that it must be rather dark inside. Sue, on the other hand, pointed out that the house was ideally situated for the boys to walk to school and shops were nearby. With a recreational lake across the road that was surrounded by woodland, she anticipated hours of fun for boys on bikes or with fishing rods. There was ample room on the drive to park a caravan and still have space for a car. We prayed and she encouraged me to contact the agent to arrange to go inside for a look. Having come into Petersfield on the main road we got the map out to find an alternative route back to Sussex. What I registered as we studied the route made me gasp.

As we poured over the map, thinking about driving around the lake the opposite way to the one we'd come, there, clearly marked, was the border between Sussex and Hampshire. Coming in from Sussex the very first residential street on the map as you entered Hampshire was, Russell Way. Pulling out of the junction to begin the journey back we turned right out of the cul-de-sac and within thirty metres we saw the sign for West Sussex sitting on the county border. What this meant was that if we lived in that house we would be living as near as humanly possible to the familiarity of West Sussex with our family and friends *but* also be in a totally new area, 'a place you have never been before'. I was completely in awe of God's clear leading. However, there was still the issue of the furniture and the rent to navigate, presuming of course that the inside of the house was appropriate for our needs. When I called the agent it was a week or so before we could view the interior.

Meantime, I was feeling overwhelmed about choosing a new caravan. Nick had always taken the lead in big things like buying cars and I felt intimidated by the task of looking at caravans. I'm sorry to say I let myself be robbed of the joy of choosing by being completely anxious. I was really nervous about learning to tow. I don't know if the kind friend who taught me suffered sleepless nights. I was worried about not making the best choice. Did we need a water pump? I was used to operating a basic foot pump. We surely didn't need a flush toilet but then a modern cassette style sounded too easy. Hardly like camping at all. Just a bucket of cold water with frozen milk or freezer blocks had always sufficed. What if the fridge leaked gas fumes or simply wouldn't light? Then there was the issue of spending such a large sum of money. Yes, we would save money on holidays, and the caravan could also double as a spare room if the need arose but 'hook up'? (This is the term applied when your caravan has the facility to be connected to mains electricity.) It was all very confusing and I felt desperately alone. Mum was a great support coming to look round various yards and forecourts but I would have to make the final decision. I narrowed it down to two possible vans and then after a sleepless night (apart from the hours I was on a nightmare drive towing not one but two caravans down a narrow mountain road with hairpin bends) I got up, went to the sales yard and bought one. I know it was supposed to be a treat but for me the experience polarised the fact that any decisions large or small were now my sole responsibility. I never felt lonely in the 'abandoned' sense because God's love and the belief that he knew every heartache and detail gave me strength each day. However, the raw absence of Nick made my chest hurt and it felt enormous to be preparing for future holidays and trips for a single-parent family that I wished wasn't my own. A few jobs needed doing inside the caravan. This gave me a few days to let the idea settle and begin to enthuse the boys about the plan of taking it to Petersfield for a long weekend in the following half-term break.

Although I sensed that the house in Russell Way could be God's place for us I didn't know how the timing would unfold. The landlord wanted to move back into his flat and there was still just under half a term left of the school year. One weekend we packed up the bulk of our possessions and put them into storage, collected the new caravan and set up home on the farm campsite I had found on the edge of the Downs. I had been anxious about managing the caravan without Nick but as I began to learn I knew a delicious sense of achievement and freedom.

The flat had been God's provision but I felt relieved to be moving on. It had begun to feel a bit like living in a graveyard. So many endings. So much sadness. Each time I saw Nick I felt I was being made to stand gazing again into the open grave of our marriage with no shovel and no means of closing the hole. I concluded that the 'let no man put asunder' line from the wedding ceremony had been crossed and this agony must be the result. Raw grief would swamp me with each visit as any small scab forming over the wound was savagely knocked off. I had two innocent sons; they had no choice and were in no way responsible. I could only keep walking and praying.

In the caravan we had a comfortable awning which offered extra living space, West Sussex as our back garden and more cycling tracks than we'd ever dreamed of. It was only a few minutes' drive to school and friends dropped in regularly. This style of living had its challenges, not least when one of the boys managed to break his arm doing bike stunts, but a canopy of peace and the soothing balm of being surrounded by natural beauty brought a measure of healing to us all. Clearly this was only a short-term solution but the freedom from overheads, the need to eat simply, keep rubbish to a minimum and live clutter free in a small space, created an uncomplicated rhythm of life we all savoured. I made time each day to bring the question of the next step to God, thanking him for being so clear and making provision.

We had access to a little shed-style out building with a simple toilet and basin in it. Chickens roamed free and we began to find eggs on the draining board in the washroom. I had been reading a story in the Bible where God provided food, shelter and eventually a husband to a young woman called Ruth. Enthusiastically I decided that the eggs were being laid and left as a demonstration of similar thoughtful provision. The boys were delighted that God could meet a need in this specific way. Sadly, jubilation was short lived. You can imagine my mortification when going to clean my teeth a few days later a large notice greeted me; it was stuck to the mirror with Blu Tack. The scrawled message read, 'Thou shalt not steal. The wages of sin is death!'

To this day I cannot understand why they didn't just come and say, 'Hey, would you mind not picking up the eggs, please?'

I felt like a criminal. I've no idea if they were Christians or not but using the scripture to get at me made me feel terrible.

I had booked to see inside the house in Russell Way and returned with Sue. I didn't want to raise the boys' hopes. When we went to look around the landlady had already left and I was surprised to discover the house was completely empty. The agent explained that before leaving for America there had been a change of plan. The landlady had decided that to cut her costs she would stack her furniture in one of the downstairs rooms and lock the door. The room in question was a large square space that had the appearance of an extension. It wasn't a conservatory but perhaps a previous owner had had it built for an elderly relative who could no longer manage the stairs. It had windows but all blinds were down. I was surprised but had been praying for an unfurnished property and there was still an ample lounge/dining area with separate kitchen. I presumed this arrangement meant the rent could be negotiated and felt a frisson of excitement.

Every room was light, airy and appeared freshly painted but best of all the back garden had a post-and-rail fence, beyond which we looked out onto rolling countryside. A couple of large fields away the ground rose up and banking away from us, right there, were the South Downs. I knew it was our new home. Sue was beaming. There were three comfortable bedrooms. The master bedroom was freshly painted in my favourite colour, a fresh aqua green (the shade that some people see as duck egg blue), had a stunning view straight out onto the downs and something I'd never had before, a modern en-suite. Standing at the window I felt the healing power of nature reaching out to me. Over the next few days my mother and the boys came to see the house. We all liked it and I offered the agent a rent that was more than I had been paying for the flat but with generous help from my parents would be manageable. We were excited but holding our collective breath. Nothing was definite. When the agent rang me a few days later to say he had shown someone else around and they had offered a higher rent I felt weak. He graciously said he could wait a few days before any final decision. We prayed and chatted with my mum and dad. They loved the house and felt it would be a great place for us to live, so generously stepped in again. The agent said if we could pay what the others had offered we could have the house. We were overjoyed and the move date was set.

The next thing was to look at schools. The church met in the only state secondary school in the town and I duly got in contact to arrange a visit. Finding that the head of year who came to show us around was also on the leader team of the Petersfield Christian Fellowship only encouraged us all that God was leading. The boys seemed relaxed. Sam would have been changing schools anyway since West Sussex had a system involving three years in a middle school and he was just finishing his third year. Nathan appeared fairly ambivalent but happy to go with the flow. There were spaces available so we got the uniform list and agreed to return in September.

I stewed internally on how best to leave the church. In the wake of that fateful meeting, when any meaningful leadership role had been wrenched away from Andrew and Sue, an interim group of leaders had reluctantly stepped in. They were now holding the reins while the church prayed and wondered about how to move forward. Plenty remained unresolved and my emotions churned and broiled. I couldn't begin to face any kind of formal goodbye. I gently explained to Sam and Nathan some of what I was feeling and assured them that we would remain in regular contact with their friends. Then on a blue Sunday morning like many others in June, we quietly left as normal after the service. We gingerly picked our way through the ugly rubble of more shattered dreams on our way to the car. I was too numb to cry.

The summer term ended and details of the tenancy for Russell Way were confirmed so we said our goodbyes, loaded up the caravan and trundled into a whole new chapter.

10

By Still Waters

It was a time of enormous change. Situated in the quiet cul-de-sac, No 12 was literally just across the road from a sizeable lake. Happy days with bike rides, fishing and exploring filled the end of the summer break. Neighbours were elderly but kind and there were no complaints about a caravan on the front drive. I was savouring a new sense of anticipation. In the week we heard from the agent that we could have Russell Way I had woken in the middle of the night thinking about the house and recorded later in my journal,

I felt a strong impression that I am to write there.

I had been keeping journals of my faith journey with God for over ten years at this stage and had found revisiting things he had shown me or spoken to me really encouraging. I had written diaries with varying degrees of continuity and relished the writing and receiving of letters but 'write'? As I pondered I wondered if God meant pressing on with more of the same, write to someone or something more specific.

I was meeting a friend for coffee. Jilly was working for Youth with a Mission and travelled a lot so we made the most of chances to get together when they arose. We always had lots of news to catch up on and although she was sad for me, for the boys, for the church and Nick, she was always encouraging. She urged me to continue believing that God had a purpose in all that appeared to have gone wrong. I brought her up to date with how God had unfolded the way for us to move to Petersfield and how incredible it was that we were living just over the border with a stunning outlook onto the downs. She suddenly leaned across the table. 'You should write a book, Hazel,' she said.

I held her gaze for a few moments as I sensed a small sprouting of the tiny seed God had already planted in my life. I now understand far more than I did at that point about the conditions needed for the healthy germination and growth of spiritual seedlings. How the Master Gardener of our lives, usually in a hidden, protected place, will tend the seeds. If left undisturbed and unseen, in due season they quietly begin to grow tiny roots and eventually vigorous shoots develop into strong fruitful trees. Under his wise husbandry and pruning, what God cultivates in our lives will contribute to our character becoming an exponential source of blessing, in both our own and the lives of others.

Two things on either end of a spectrum happened quite soon after this conversation that, though born out of naivety, had serious impact. Firstly, driving back into Hampshire one day on the main road from Sussex I noted the original broken road sign had been replaced. It read, 'HAMPSHIRE, you are now entering Jane Austen country.' I'm not sure what would qualify as a delusion of grandeur, bearing in mind I hadn't even put pen to manuscript, but the thoughts in my head, whilst wowed by God's ability to use my environment to encourage, were possibly not those of a completely humble spirit. My week took on an ebullient undertone, which probably contributed to the second incident. This involved me unwisely confiding in a friend who I knew to be a published author that I thought God may be asking me to write a book. Maybe I was unconsciously seeking a kindred spirit as I dared to picture myself wafting, quill in hand, to mingle with the upper echelons of creative society known as 'writers'. The tender seedling of God's purpose was rudely uprooted and shaken long before it was ready to be potted on. All due to the power of the spoken word as my friend's declaration filled the car.

'You can't just write a book. It doesn't happen like that.' And I didn't.

There were occasional notes in my journal about promptings to write and a longing that was so strong it hurt, for God to use my circumstances. If in any way he could help me share my story to strengthen and bring hope to others I wanted that. But it was fifteen years before I sought specific prayer about that conversation and summoned the courage to start. I learned a big lesson. The comment was in part true but if the seedling of the dream had been nurtured in the soil of my spirit for longer it may have been mature enough to withstand a discussion. At that time it was far from ready for the exposure so I had made a quiet agreement inside with the negative statement, even though it contradicted the whisper of God. Obviously one couldn't just write! What was I dreaming of? How powerful the weapon of the tongue and the influence of words we speak. The seed was pushed in deep and buried itself in a place of safety.

As a family we had for some years enjoyed the summer highlight of Stoneleigh Bible Week. This camp started as a relatively small gathering for church families in Sussex who got together to learn and enthuse about applying teaching from the Bible to the way they were raising their families, doing their jobs and establishing churches. There was great teaching, brilliant activities for the children and young people, and the shared joy of being under canvas. The event had grown until it was held in the massive agricultural centre in Warwickshire and to accommodate numbers the programme was repeated over two weeks. There were nearly twenty thousand of us attending and the idea was to go with those from the same region to create networking opportunities. The explanations about the fundamental truths of Christianity and the teaching on how to express our faith as it was lived out in New Testament times had been life changing. We had initially attended as the four of us but the group grew as we invited friends and family to join us each year. I missed a couple of years feeling it was just too hard to be in an environment where I had known such hope and fun with Nick. However, singing passionate praise to God with thousands of others was always uplifting and I looked forward to returning that summer. Although there was plenty happening around the time of the move I just decided we could take our time over unpacking the last boxes and finally sort things in our new home later. We focused on preparing the caravan and all we would need for the week away. I was really looking forward to going.

Nick seemed genuinely pleased that we had a nice place to live and coming across country the journey was only a few minutes longer for him. I quashed a niggling suspicion that in some sense he was relieved that we were no longer in his immediate area. I was very conscious he was struggling financially and emotionally. He made no secret of the fact that he didn't particularly like where he was living which made me aware of how blessed I was in such a beautiful house. I think I felt obligated to try and believe in the best motives, especially since Nick continued to talk about the fact that he believed we were meant to be together. He was renting a house through someone he'd met in a pub but it was on a rather bleak housing estate and he seemed very low. Sam and Nathan worried about him and talked about how much he slept when they were with him for weekends. Nick continued to like to linger when he was collecting the boys. Sometimes he stayed a while after he dropped them home and they had said goodnight.

In this season I began to resent any affectionate overtures, such as the offer of a hug in greeting. Nick's touch increasingly left me churned up and he was talking again about the possibility of returning to the police force, which could have offered an income, accommodation and stability. I wonder now just who he was trying to convince but a favourite statement became, 'I want to be with you in the future, I want us to grow old together.'

It hung in the air, a hollow echo as he drove off to resume an independent life that I knew less and less about. As time passed I was confused and frustrated by how a person could appear so convincingly to want something but have no apparent ability to start to bring it into being.

I believed Nick wanted what he said. Obviously I wanted it to be the truth but there was still much to untangle. Rather than face responsibility for his actions, which might have led to change, he had told friends that the divorce was what I wanted and because he cared about me he was just accepting it. It was as if he believed this absolved him from any action. I was completely talked out. The injustice of the circumstances was so enormous and Nick's conviction that he was the victim absolute; discussion was pointless. I just kept on believing God would do a miracle, meet Nick and help him see the dark alley he was heading down. I reread the promises and words of encouragement recorded in my journal. I regularly asked God to remove the hopeful feelings and longings for a future together if they were not from him. I prayed for Nick and tried to encourage him that there was hope but he seemed to have taken on a mindset, a steel helmet of hopelessness that nothing could penetrate. He genuinely believed his version of events but being with him it felt as if he was under the influence of an incredibly powerful spell. I wondered if there could be a risk he would hear God at Stoneleigh; it had been a place of such blessing in the past and I felt sure the boys would love to have him around. Even I could see the invite was a bit of a long shot. Nick declined. I struggled to accept he was a broken man and I couldn't help him.

I can see now that two important things were being exposed though I was too close at the time to focus. If there was a drama, such as the car breaking down or one of us being ill, nothing was too much trouble for Nick. I was grateful but began to understand that these occasions were about Nick enjoying, even needing, to be the hero. What his sons needed was a consistent, loving presence offering wisdom and stability but that was just not on offer. It needed to be a crisis because Nick could manage short, extravagant gestures that showed him in a positive light. Secondly we had fundamentally opposed attitudes to tackling difficulty. If we needed something and couldn't afford it I would begin saving, a few pence at a time. Nick would think it wasn't worth trying to save. If the journey of a thousand miles (our reconciliation for example) begins with the first step, I believed we could move gradually towards the destination; even dolly steps would mean we were beginning that journey towards a shared future. Perhaps Nick had given up and was going through the motions of a person struggling on. I did not discern that. I think perhaps he was waiting for a rescue crew to fly in. But hope lived on in me and I continued to long for him to want to change his situation enough to reach out for help.

My sister Heather had been to Stoneleigh Bible weeks several times before emigrating to New Zealand and she was very keen for her new husband to share the experience. They decided they would come back to England for it. Heather announced her plan to come for some of the summer holidays and they kept the fact that Steve was also able to get the time off work a secret. We all knew it would be a fabulous surprise for Sam and Nathan. The newlyweds duly arrived and blissful days were spent showing them our new home and enjoying time together. We prepared for the Bible Week. We had always tried to invite others to camp with us and the caravan would become a hub for endless hot chocolate and late-night chats.

When the day came Heather and I set off to arrive at the campsite early and set things up. We relished a few hours relaxing in the open air before the showground filled up. We treated ourselves to a cold lemonade shandy with ice from the new fridge (what luxury) and took time to anticipate what God might do in our lives. The boys came with us and Steve was due to come in the other car a bit later in the day. This proved to be my first real insight to the possible tensions within a mixed-race marriage.

Steve's dad was a full-blooded Maori gentleman and New Zealand's population has a high percentage of those whose family roots are in the Pacific Islands. Steve has lovely dark skin and thick black hair leading my mother to enthuse about the possibility of chocolate grandchildren. My sister is a completely natural, nearly white blonde with blue eyes and skin that blushes at the very mention of the word 'tan'. Actually all three of my siblings are blue-eyed blondes who when lined up for head-and-shoulder shots as toddlers could reasonably be perceived as triplets. I take after my father's side of the family: a brunette with hazel eyes. There is a definite 'native' flavour to the way they do life in New Zealand and, it still being early days in their marriage, my sister was on a steep learning curve. She was on tenterhooks most of the day as she awaited the arrival of her beloved. He was bringing her bags and their tent, which in her world would need to be erected and bed made ready before things kicked off with the evening meeting for which she wished to be prepared. I think Steve's phone was switched off. He quite literally went 'walk about' for the day and eventually arrived just before dark having driven the scenic route taking in all the old buildings, cathedrals and places of interest it offered.

Steve had had a wonderful day in his own space and felt thoroughly prepared for a week hearing from God and living cheek by jowl with hundreds of others. Before marriage he had been alone a good deal, relishing time to think and pray. He read volumes. Heather, who is totally sanguine, processes every thought and feeling out loud. She proceeded to do this when Steve eventually arrived at the camping ground. Once her blood pressure had returned to normal she helped her husband to see that a phone call explaining he was taking the scenic route would have sufficed. He pointed out that she hadn't spelled out the need to have their tent established and beds made up in order for her to enjoy the first meeting. Meaningful conversation was had and harmony restored. Heather recharges her batteries via social contact. Steve has helped her learn to sit and read a book without giving a running commentary; with films there is still a way to go, especially if the story has an element of suspense!

After a great week we returned home and the others flew back to New Zealand. Spurred on by such a happy time together, my sons renewed their prayer efforts petitioning their heavenly Father to act so that Heather and Steve would actually move to England. We were a few more months into Petersfield life when their prayers were answered. Married for just over a year Steve and Heather had been praying and asking God for direction. They decided their desire to care for and support their nephews was a Holy Spirit prompting. They called and announced their intention to come to England to share life. They were bowled over when the boys declared this was a direct answer to their prayers. Jubilation in our house knew no bounds. They lovingly expressed the desire to support me as I struggled to get to grips with the role of solo Mum that had been so violently thrust on me. They wanted to offer any stability and love they could which might sustain the boys as the teenage years beckoned. Initially they said they would put everything into storage and come for twelve months. We were all very excited and thanked God often as we looked forward to their arrival the following year.

Those first months living in Petersfield were special as we enjoyed meeting new friends and the boys got used to a different school. The church seemed poised to experience more of God and the people were very enthusiastic about getting connected in the community. I was still completely believing that to be reunited with Nick was God's purpose for me; I was mindful of the promise from Amos about a broken contract being renewed and I remained sure that this related to our marriage despite the fact that nothing looked less likely. I felt God must have a purpose that had yet to unfold for me in this chapter. As I prayed, asking him to show me his agenda and the time frame, I was inspired and challenged by a sermon at church about the significance of Jesus accomplishing what he did in just three short years of public ministry. I felt the period of three years was being highlighted.

There was also a fair amount of talk in the particular group of churches that Petersfield was connected to about God 'leaning in' to speak to his children and his word being 'life'. This had certainly been my experience when I had known that a separation was the only way forward. It had felt totally beyond me but because God had spoken audibly and I had recorded it, I was able to obey when my world fell apart and initiate separation. That step had led to where I found myself now. Because I had heard 'the audible voice', I'd taken real strength and comfort from a sense of God knowing, knowing fully my circumstances. I had felt reassured when there was every reason to panic. I experienced his presence in a way that helped me to face my husband's sin with a calm authority. I had found that within the warning when he'd said clearly, 'There is no other way,' was hidden the promise that he was present. Though often alone and desperately sad in those following years I never felt abandoned by God. That didn't mean the weight of sadness about what might have been wasn't crushing but it meant I kept on breathing. I felt the devil had assaulted our lives and that because Nick had been in leadership the enemy had targeted him. Not that being in leadership had weakened him; more that being willing to be on the frontline, in the spiritual battle to see people around us and ultimately the whole region we lived in enjoying God's loving presence in their lives, had placed him in a conspicuous and vulnerable position. Sin creates weak places in our personal armour so it is wise to expose it to loving friends and receive support before the enemy fires. In the flat, years later, the strong sense of God speaking again through the verses in Amos, felt like promise seeds in the soil of my life. Over time they were developing extensive root systems that held the soil of my faith firmly together in a deep place.

I felt drawn to connect with other women and began going to a prayer group. As we invited God to speak to us one of the ladies there felt God flashed up a picture on the screen of her imagination.

She described a picture of a monkey putting his hand into a jar of nuts. The monkey wanted to walk away but was hampered by his clenched fist. The neck of the jar was too narrow so he could never be free unless he released his grip on the nut. I worried. Still aware of how far from 'whole' I was, I wondered, could I be 'holding on' in a negative way to hopes and aspirations relating to Nick that meant I couldn't be completely free? How, I wondered, could I hold on to God's 'Afterward . . .' promise in Amos and still live completely free, enjoying the liberty and wholeness that Jesus died to give me. The weight of misery, as the boys were growing up without their father, was sometimes suffocating and I was yielding to the solace of a couple of glasses of wine in the evening to dull the edge of the pain. After a couple of weeks stewing on the 'monkey jar' I finally prayed one night, 'Lord, if that Amos scripture with the promise of restoration is not really you, please just take away the conviction and let me be released from it.'

The next morning my dated devotional reading began with the word 'Amos . . .' I felt that as there are so many words and names in the Bible that a paragraph could begin with, God was not releasing me from my commitment to believe that restoration of my marriage was his intention.

I had heard about the year 2000 (three years hence) being a year of jubilee. This was also referred to one Sunday at church, with an explanation about slaves being given their liberty and captives being set free. I made notes and later as I prayed and mulled over what I had written, I began to have a strong impression that I would be in Petersfield for a season of three years before the next change. I have often found that God whispers to me about seasons. This has meant that however dark it feels I have a sense of moving through. In this instance I felt energised to think that I was probably facing a season of three years on my own. I didn't doubt that Nick and I would be worshipping side by side in the future but I was recognising that even once Nick was reconciled and reconnecting with God, it would be wisdom to allow a considerable period of time for the rebuilding of trust. Meanwhile, I felt sure that God had a reason for my being in Petersfield at that time.

Sam and Nathan were building friendships and enjoying their respective youth groups. It was refreshing after the previous church sadness to be among those longing for God to reveal himself and praying for his supernatural intervention. I was reading a book that had been reviewed at Stoneleigh that year. Jack Deere titled his book *Surprised by the Voice of God*. He writes,

> **When God speaks to you most clearly, it usually means you are going to go through such a difficult experience that later you will need to be absolutely certain that God had spoken to you. In fact the clarity of the voice may be the main thing that gives you the power to endure the subsequent testing. The audible voice comes when the divine ministry about to be performed is extraordinarily difficult to accept or believe or when the task about to be undertaken is so hard that it will require clarity and the assurance of an audible voice, to endure and complete the task.**

After reading about the way God seemed to line up 'divine appointments' in Jack Deere's book I felt challenged and excited. Maybe God would do the same for me and guide me into some special encounters. These were conversations and meetings that God initiated in Jack's life with people who already had questions, prompting them to want to know more about a God who loved and about the Christian life. Maybe he would give me messages for others or show me things about their lives they hadn't told me so that when I shared them they would understand the power of God. It happened often for Jack. Maybe God would show me how to pray for a sick person and they would get better. Desperate to see God moving in people's lives I decided I could give a morning a week to being out in the community and available.

As I prayed about it the bench outside Waitrose came to mind. So I decided that on Tuesdays I would fast, pray and be on the bench. I had decided not to tell anyone about this but the first week the only person to come and join me on the bench was a lady from church so I decided to ask her to pray for me. You know, so that I would be ready and anointed to heal the sick and see captives set free. The following week it was a bit busier. A middle-aged lady, pale and rather drawn-looking sat down. Rummaging in a grubby canvas bag she relit the cigarette hanging from her mouth and then opened a brown paper bag at the neck. I realised she wasn't sitting for a sandwich and chat when she raised the bag to her lips and took a big gulp. Reluctant to chat she moved off.

Richie arrived soon after. Mid-twenties and dressed mainly in black PVC with greasy hair, sporting three nose rings, he wanted to chat. Forty minutes later we had covered the fact that his brother had died a few years previously and then, because his father had followed within a year, Richie had been on nerve tablets since he was fourteen. He explained without pausing for breath that he'd been through approved school, regularly saw flying saucers and was a firm believer in the Bermuda Triangle. My journal entry that night read,

I brought you in whenever I could, Lord, but you didn't seem to be already working in his life and he had no sense of need.

(I was just learning about communicating the gospel by co-operating with the Holy Spirit rather than delivering The Four Spiritual Laws with fervour.)

Thinking back over the encounter I felt terrible realising my parting shot of, 'I'll pray for you, Richie,' sounded more like a threat than a promise.

I really believed God might do something supernatural and show himself to be the answer to specific need in a stranger's life.

One of the other ladies in the church came to my home for a cup of tea and pressed me about what I was doing on the bench. She clearly thought that I was OTT (over the top) and explained that people in the church had been fasting and praying for years and were convinced God was about to do something; the inference clearly being that outsiders breezing in to pray on benches was definitely not required. She went on to say how, in her experience, God is often teaching something in situations where we sense him ask us to step out and then nothing appears to happen. Whilst I wasn't about to accept that God 'sets us up' on a regular basis I did receive his whisper about teaching and agreed with him that I would stay signed up for the course! The following Tuesday I was ill and then the next week the leader's wife asked if I would help with a Tuesday lunch group she ran for the unemployed, so I felt released from the bench. Who knows if the original nudge was God or not but I maintain I'd rather err on the side of being too keen to obey than be found to be dragging my feet. It can be embarrassing at times but so far, to my knowledge, nobody has died of embarrassment. There are multiple stories of God doing exciting healings and demonstrating divine love as people take the risk that they have heard from him.

Nathan and Sam listened to the music of a Christian band from America, called DC Talk, and we heard they were coming to do a big concert in the north of England. We had old friends from the church in Sussex who had moved house near to where the stadium was and we planned a trip. At that stage I was used to being the passenger on long trips. Nick always liked to drive. I tried to see it as just another drive but with all the motorway exits and Birmingham to navigate, I felt sick. We decided to set off really early and we had provisions and games packed. I felt completely indomitable roaring up the M1 at dawn. Even though the music at the concert was so loud it made our chests hurt (we moved to the back row of the auditorium for the second half), it was good to see old friends and the sense of victory, arriving safely home after a great weekend, was worth it.

The glory was short lived on my part as the caravan needed moving ready to be towed again the following week and I could not manage it alone. Still programmed to need Nick I called him and he willingly came over and helped; well, he did it really. He never seemed to mind and never mocked me for thinking I could be independent. Even with all the prayer for healing and release and although I no longer felt that his choices had power to impact me in the same way, the whole 'two becoming one thing' was deeply ingrained. I communed with him mentally all the time wondering how he would manage a situation, what he would think of my choices, how he really saw the suffering of our sons. One night I awoke to hear noises and became convinced we had an intruder. It was two in the morning but Nick still responded to my whispered panic and came. It turned out to be an electronic alarm running flat that had disturbed me and then the other noises of the night just lost all perspective as I panicked.

The chemistry between us remained strong and I still prayed much about resisting the longings I had for physical contact. One night after he had brought the boys home and they had gone to bed, Nick just fell asleep on the sofa and I quietly prayed over him in tongues, probably for my own protection as much as his. I wondered again if it was actually possible to ever be really free once you'd married someone and been completely vulnerable with them. By this time Nick had begun to look physically different: his skin was very pale and he was often unshaven. He smoked much more and never spoke of anything in a positive way. I worried about how he was with the boys at weekends but they still wanted to be with him when the opportunity arose. He would sometimes come to parents' evenings and events that might impact the boys' lives but nothing about being together felt normal. I read in Ezekiel about life coming into old bones and a new

heart replacing a stony one and wrote the verses out for Nick, praying
they would bring some hope.

The first Christmas in Petersfield loomed. Old memories and
hurts hovered very close to the surface and both boys got a bout of
flu. I had felt part of my contribution to church life could be a banner
that hopefully would enhance the school hall but also our worship
together. It was exciting for me as I prayed, first for the idea and then
for helpers and then had something to be working on, in a creative
context. Previously I had been quick to discount myself from such
projects. I offered my services a day a week in the church offices to
clean and help out generally. I felt increasingly enthusiastic about
being able to stimulate and encourage others to pray. I approached
the leaders offering to host some regular nights of prayer where we
could practise praying for longer periods of time. I was longing to
experience more of God's presence and see him answering prayers.

The boys continued making new friends and were bravely positive
about our new life. Both continued to have days where they appeared
pale and listless. Nathan particularly had less and less enthusiasm for
school and wondered if he could have a dog? I longed for him to
have a pet he could cuddle. I explained that it wouldn't be like Harry
but much more demanding. Realising I would have to be the one in
charge of house training, I suggested he think about the responsibility
it may be for him and assured him we'd think about it in the New
Year. Running it past my mother resulted in a vicarious unfolding that
was rather wonderful for us all.

11

Deeper

The festive season made me acutely aware of the lack in my own life as families and couples talked endlessly about their plans. At church I was struggling with the way the initial rush of welcome had subsided. It had whittled down to rather skimpy Christian hugs; a hug with as little body contact as possible. There were several women keen for me to pray with them on a regular basis but they didn't seem to know how to include my broken family in picnics or outings. I think it is much the same fifteen years later as the church struggles to see where women with experience in relationship but living a single life fit in. I felt as if I had a label on my back: 'I'm free.' Men were wary and women even more so. What the label actually said was, 'I'm living in a sex-free zone but am safe, plus, I gain great comfort from the sincere embrace of a man who is made in God's image and willing to venture into my personal space.' Even sitting in church I felt waving a placard stating, 'I am not after your husband!' might have helped.

John and Penny being the exception to all the rules became great friends. John was a great hugger and took a real interest in how the boys were doing. I asked them if they would like to eat and pray together regularly. I established with the Lord that the boys and I would exercise hospitality just as we were, a one-parent show, sometimes sad, often struggling but hungry for God's love to expand in our lives through relationship. I encouraged the boys to choose who they would like us to invite. We found it a great blessing to have others around our table and I felt the urge for late-night wine diminishing. Please don't misunderstand…I love wine! It's just that it became clear to me that while the Bible says, 'He has given me the wine to make my heart rejoice,' I was guilty of using it to dull the edge of my pain. This can not only make us vulnerable to addiction but offers the enemy opportunity where God wants our default position to be leaning into him for comfort. I was encouraged that my offer to host nights of prayer was accepted and I began to ask the Lord about format for the year ahead.

A week or so into the New Year Nathan approached me in the kitchen. His expression was earnest. 'Mum, I'm hoping you feel ready for us to have a puppy now we're settled. You did say you were thinking about it?'

Grandma had always wanted her own dog but my father was adamant he did not, so my mother embarked on the puppy search with great enthusiasm and generously said she would like to fund the new addition. Nathan had mild asthma and I had multiple allergies so a poodle seemed the obvious choice and we learned they come in several sizes. Standard are the largest then miniature and the smallest is a toy. Delighted at the thought of a pocket-sized pet (me silently rejoicing about what else would be pocket sized and therefore easy to clean up!) that could still run for a ball and be cuddled, we opted for the smallest. We located a breeder and visited the litter of new puppies. Nathan chose a small black ball of fluff and we began the wait for him to be big enough to join us at home.

I felt rather despondent during January and summoning enthusiasm for the year ahead was hard. Both boys caught a particularly nasty flu bug. In spite of the puppy to look forward to it seemed the 'newness' of everything finally caught up with Nathan. He began to experience headaches, tummy-aches and flu-like symptoms on a pretty regular basis. He would go white as a sheet and lie in bed limp whilst complaining he had no energy. Around this time I was reviewing my options. Having worked as a nurse for some years before becoming a parent I had attended a retraining programme prior to the divorce, which could open up work opportunities. I prayed long and hard and observed other single mothers in the community. It was obvious to me that I would not be able to work, particularly shifts, and be available to the boys for the unexpected. If things were ticking along, they were both happy and at school, then fine but if one of them was sick or struggling, how would we manage then? We were still grieving. Each in our own way. I felt that by being fully available, being 'present' I could offer focused support. I was able to sit up late into the night when one or other needed to talk, without anxiety for the next day's shift. If extra appointments with school or doctor were needed I would be free from the stress of requesting roster changes. I made what felt like a rather lonely decision at the time but I have never regretted it. My parents were constantly generous and supportive but I was still keen to be as independent as possible and set myself to manage the challenge of budgeting. Benefits and allowances had to be applied for and adjusted as circumstances changed but they gave a level of independence and meant consistent income.

I was concerned about the boys and the recurring need for time off school but felt that if they were allowed to feel their pain and process the grief it would be better in the long term. Many of their peers seemed to be chivvied through life fitting in one activity after another, leaving no time for thought or questioning. I believed that a calmer pace with me not focused on a career could create opportunity for Sam and Nathan to experience a greater wholeness. My worst fear was that the divorce would somehow scar them for life. How could it not? Nathan was desperate for Branston, as he had named the little four-legged addition, to be old enough to leave his mother and come to live with us. I found this patch particularly hard because historically the start of a New Year was a time of great optimism and celebration. Goals would be set and direction for the year charted with great enthusiasm. Now I struggled to keep my head above water long enough to see land on the horizon. I woke each day aching with the effort.

Nathan, by this time twelve, had seemed particularly resilient. When things had fallen apart and the initial separation happened he had been four years old and about to start primary school. For many months I stayed in his room till late evening as he cried himself to sleep. He had been dressing himself and organising his own little life quite efficiently for over a year when the separation happened.

He'd enjoyed several sessions a week at playschool and was ready for the stimulation of 'big school'. Despite the turmoil in our world he managed it. But behind closed doors he no longer dressed himself and needed lots of extra support during the year Nick and I were apart. Then within months he appeared to be through into a new place. I felt I couldn't quite plumb the deep waters of his inner world.

As we had neared the end of our six-month stint in New Zealand I talked to each of the boys about the possibility of not being able to return to the physical building that was home and the probable need to live somewhere else. I particularly dreaded bringing up the subject with Sam as he remained fiercely loyal, often becoming defensive if it was intimated his father found it difficult to be reliable. Nick was his hero. Knowing Sam to be a sensitive young man who had already expressed concern about his father being left alone in England, I thrashed around internally trying to come up with an appropriate way of explaining why we could no longer live with his adored father. 'Deceitful, adulterous, backslidden, no longer wants us' were clearly unpalatable. In the end I felt that at twelve Sam had some understanding of 'girlfriend, two-timing and dumping'. I think I needed him to understand it was not my choice the marriage ended even though I initiated us being apart. As we swam in the sea together one day I explained that because Daddy had had a 'girlfriend' we would not be living with him on our return to England. I admitted I was very sad about this, feeling honesty was important, and explained it was nothing that he or Nathan had done, that Nick still loved them, we both did. I felt absolutely wretched. Sam went very still in the water. Big brown eyes just stared as the sky tumbled into the sea and his world was changed forever. The idol crumbled. Sam didn't ask any questions.

A few days later on a long walk in the bush, I asked Nathan how he might feel if Daddy could not live with us anymore and he simply responded, 'I don't really mind where Dad lives, Mum, but I would like to see him regularly.'

He was ten years old at that time and his maturity shocked me. I think in the months of anguished crying during the original separation and the pain of life being so out of control, something significant in the core of who he is shifted and it has dictated how he manages disappointment.

I was reading about the life of Elijah when the agent forwarded a letter from our landlady. In particular I noted how God led the prophet to the widow of Zarephath. (It had caught my attention that three years elapsed before God spoke again.) The letter informed us that our landlady had decided she would not be returning to live in her house again for three years. God reminded me I had previously written in my journal that I sensed him drawing me into a three-year commitment to Petersfield. I took encouragement from the fact that I felt this confirmed God had a particular purpose for us being in the church there and that it would unfold soon.

In the meantime I continued to promote contact between Nick and Sam and Nathan whenever possible. I had always held a quiet belief that Nick had been brought into our family for a purpose, one that would heal and bless his life. He loved my parents and had been welcomed as a son. Our backgrounds were quite opposite with mine being studded with generations of praying Christians and a comfortable education in an all-girls private school. Nick was the youngest of seven and his father had a history in the Navy, then was ill and difficult at home until he died when Nick was just thirteen. I was struggling to see how that belief could possibly play out now.

My parents generously shared their chalet in the Alps and the layout being on three levels meant guests could spread out. When it was suggested that the chalet could provide opportunity for the boys to have a holiday with their father included, it demonstrated my parents' prayerful longing for restoration. As the rawness of being a broken family in the festive season dissipated, I was again filled with hope that this could be the year when Nick would allow God's love to meet the need in his life. Optimistic that being part of a family group would relieve any awkwardness and knowing that if I could manage it the boys would love us all being together, I prayerfully decided to invite Nick. He immediately accepted the invitation with no apparent compunction. Looking back it is surprising that he didn't feel too awkward to accept but I think his mindset remained that of victim and he really felt he was 'owed'. He could never resist the snow. As a family we continued to pray and long for his restoration believing it must come.

As January became February the spectre of the planned ski trip loomed large on my horizon. How would I manage to be around Nick but not 'with' him? What planet had I been on when I had thought it a good idea to invite him? I felt fat and ugly in the aftermath of Christmas, increasingly aware of my body and what it was not. During the original separation I had felt so wretched I couldn't eat properly for months so had inevitably lost weight. Nick had expressed hearty approval. Because he had had his main affair with the luscious, lithe body of my aerobics friend, I felt I could never compete. I dreaded being seen as lumpy and plain ugly.

It had been graphically revealed to me that this was an area of spiritual warfare in my life and not just low self-esteem or a family trend for comfort eating. Years previously, on the morning of the day we had renewed our vows, I dressed and got ready in the bedroom at home. Before driving to my parents' I stood in front of the mirror knowing I was in an outfit smaller than any I had worn, and that I was in great shape from walking and swimming regularly. As I looked at my reflection I sensed a presence, like a cold draught of air, and the image in front of me expanded, much like those mirrors at the fair. I knew that what I was looking at was not real, was a distortion, and in that moment I recognised how powerfully the enemy uses this area to undermine and imprison women. I shuddered and prayed aloud declaring that it is the truth that sets us free, the truth that I am made in God's image and I am beautiful. In the years that followed, this revelation helped me withstand the barrage of undermining that assaulted my life as relationship deteriorated. I knew fat revolted Nick. (I wasn't fat but the point about warfare is the enemy lures us to a place where we see only the all-engulfing negative perspective that he is promoting. That's why there is so much in the Bible about the value of a healthy mind and Holy Spirit inspired thoughts.) This knowledge hung over me as the trip approached. I don't mean Nick was going to have opportunity to see any part of my anatomy at close quarters and I was only size fourteen but it easily felt like twenty-two in light of the rejection I'd experienced. It was still a few weeks until the holiday.

In this season I was feeling very anxious and uncomfortable in my own skin and the old battle raged in my head. I particularly feared ongoing scrutiny by Nick if we spent time together. Around this time I was out walking with a friend who relishes controversial debate but when the statement 'I actually see orgasm as worship' hung in the air between us, I squirmed.

My initial internal response to recoil was predictable. As our riverside walk continued though, I wondered…what if God wanted to show me something new about intimacy with him? Was I at risk of missing potentially liberating truth because of preconceived notions about holiness? Over the following months I pondered. I prayed and read my Bible.

Scriptural evidence that God is passionate, desires to meet needs, intends me to know Jesus as, among many other things, lover, husband and friend, is abundant. Indisputable. So where does that leave a single person? In this instance a woman who has received a deep wound in the area of her sexuality? Is this an area that is just too complicated and sensitive for God to heal and restore? I was certainly inclined towards trying to forget the conversation and the challenge it raised, to just press on with the stuff of every day. But over time, alone with God, I began to risk. If God made me the way I am and loves unconditionally he must think I'm okay, see me as attractive even? So if I have rubbish thoughts about my looks or my body what might their source be? God created me a sensual being with the potential for arousal. Wholeness being high on God's agenda for people, single people included, it would seem unlikely that he would overlook the key areas of sensual need and desire. That's without even looking at the recognised health benefits of orgasm. These range from stress relief to longevity to decreased risk of heart attack. I began to see that the main hiccup in this area of physically appreciating my body, looks and sexuality is imagination. I think my taking pleasure in how God has made me, to be glad about my physical form, specifically my womanliness, my unique curves, pleases God. Being thankful I am female is honouring God's handiwork. Being glad and thankful... both are elements of worship.

A sanctified imagination cannot be beyond God. If the Holy Spirit is enabling us to realise the freedom that Jesus died to give us, then our minds, thoughts, dreams and daydreams are surely included? In the Old Testament much of being acceptable to God was about doing what was required but after Jesus sent the Holy Spirit everything changed. My life on the inside is important. My heart posture and my thought life matter. It is possible for my thinking to be renewed, so God can give me his thoughts. Receiving forgiveness I am a daughter of God, in that moment without sin (otherwise it would only be partial forgiveness). What if the moment can become two, three, ten? The perceived 'sin' in self-stimulation is surely not about touching our own bodies but all about what is going on in the mind. We can learn to receive thoughts from God and please him in what we do in other areas, why not this one?

I practise trusting the Holy Spirit and when praying for others or asking God for wisdom I have found he sometimes puts a picture or impression in my mind that conveys a message. I began to ask him to do that for me, a picture message as it were for myself. Inviting him to teach me and control my imagination I felt nervous at first but collaborating with what I felt was truth I made positive statements about myself out loud. I think bringing stray thoughts about previous sexual encounters under the releasing, cleansing power of Jesus' name is wholly doable and the Holy Spirit can bring healing and replacement mind images. Sensuality is God's idea. You might play beautiful classical music, moisturise, listen to love songs of worship, light a candle, have a bath; any action that promotes beauty is appropriate in creating an atmosphere for intimacy. I encourage you to set aside time to linger in Jesus' company, talk to him and ask the Holy Spirit to grow the intimacy you crave as you deliberately imagine being physically in his presence.

I've really tussled over whether to even mention this area but the nudges to do so won't go away. Being misunderstood is inevitable. Wherever you look healthy attitudes to body size, shape, weight and definitions of sensuality are under attack, accompanied by skewed relationships with food. The spirit of our culture sustains vicious attempts to demean, distort and enslave. But God has created the option of a Holy Spirit collaboration that liberates. Divorced women may be particularly vulnerable because having sexual experience (which may need Holy Spirit healing) they know at some level what they are missing and often battle painful rejection. Guilt makes a mockery of the cross so I encourage you to risk freedom. Walking in the woods, curling up with a good book or savouring the sand between my toes, embracing the truth that the Creator of it all delights in who I am, sees me and utters a 'phwoah' (it's been in the dictionary for some years now) is mind blowing. Comprehending that the Divine Heart skips a beat over me has been transformational in my life.

Still hesitating over including this section God reminded me that long before I put pen to paper I prayed regularly for the ability to bring hope. If anyone facing similar circumstances could be encouraged or gain a shred of hope from my telling my story I would love that to happen. At the time I think I was picturing being invited one day to share something in a house group or women's meeting.

Anne Lamott, in her book *Bird by Bird*, shares the perspective that 'If something inside of you is real, we will probably find it interesting. So you must risk placing real emotions at the centre of your work.' To read this, just as I am telling myself to delete this section reasoning it is so personal that nobody will relate, felt significant.

12

Then We Were Five

The church in Petersfield encouraged members to go to a venue in Marsham Street in London and a series of meetings were being scheduled for the year. At this time there was much excitement around the events occurring in a church in Canada. Ripples of supernatural activity seemed to be spreading over the world as people experienced the person of the Holy Spirit in new ways. There were meetings starting around the country, intending to inform Christians about what was happening and also to share the experience in teaching and worship. A number of us were praying together and longing to see more supernatural evidence of God's presence; not just in our own lives but believing that God would heal sickness, restore broken relationships, break addictions and generally invade our communities with the power of love to transform life. The reports were that this was happening in other places and we were learning that the Holy Spirit responded to earnest seeking. Travelling to London seemed a small commitment in light of the possible gain in our spiritual growth and understanding of how God could move in our lives and town. Since saying yes to the Holy Spirit in my own life it seemed the more I learned the hungrier I was for his presence. Any risk of something powerful being deposited in my life, causing love, love that could influence change to become my default setting, had become irresistible.

Then one Sunday I woke early having had a broken night. I'd been up in the early hours and written 'Now is the time' on the pad beside my bed. I was asking God over my first cuppa of the day what that might mean, time for what? I began to feel a sense of calm as I pondered once more the sense I had of making a three-year commitment and I wondered again if the year 2000 was going to bring great change in my life. I wrote down a number of things I had felt God prompting me to do, such as initiating seasons of prayer and fasting, making the banner, engaging with neighbours, contributing in worship and serving in the church office. I also had a specific list of people with whom I could pray regularly and build friendship. I felt that at the end of the three years I would need to be ready for something big to change and willing to put down anything more public I may be involved in, such as leading singing or heading up any groups. I was already thinking that if Nick and I were being restored in that season it wouldn't be appropriate for me to have any profile.

I arrived at church that morning to learn that a team from the church in Toronto, Canada were actually visiting and would be leading our time together. Being among those who prayed for others often in services I was blessed to be able to pray for several people, and then one of the visiting team who was Korean approached the microphone. He said God had given him a picture to share. I wrote his words in my journal.

I saw as we worshipped a huge creature, a beast with long sharp talons and big pincers, it looked similar to a giant lobster. It seemed to me that this was the spirit of separation and the pincers showed me the pain and suffering people are experiencing through separation. Grief.

He had my attention as he continued.

Then I saw two trees: one was a small white tree and as it grew its way was blocked by a huge dark tree. The dark tree seemed to grow bigger to obstruct and overshadow the light tree. I saw a house and a window opened. There was light. Not harsh and strong. Gentle light. As the small tree moved more and more (the smallness here spoke to me of humility) in grace and freedom it began jumping and it jumped high and was hopping backwards and forwards over the dark black tree. The dark tree then changed into a Christmas tree and as the white tree moved completely in the freedom and grace so spots of white from the smaller tree appeared as decorations on the Christmas tree. Then the two trees fused and became one white tree. This is speaking of reconciliation, that there is to be a reconciliation.

I was bowled over with the conviction that God loved me so much he would bring someone across the world with a specific message that demonstrated he knew the detail of my life and was going to answer the longing of my heart. It seemed clear to me that the love and openness of my family and my longing to reach out to Nick were the little white tree and the dark tree represented the sadness and negativity in him. The key words – 'separation', 'grief' and 'reconciliation' – were so pertinent they were as flashing neon lights to me.

I began to feel more peaceful about the forthcoming ski trip. It had seemed like a good, even God-inspired idea at the time when I had invited Nick to join us, with some other old friends, for a few days over half-term. As it drew nearer I wondered at my own madness but Nick seemed to be calmly moving towards the holiday without misgiving and this word helped me to see the time together as an opportunity to splash God's love over Nick's life. Just like in the tree scene.

God is so faithful. We had a peaceful week together on the snow managing to make it fun for Sam and Nathan. I can't recall much detail and think that must be to do with the level of 'coping' that was necessary for me to emotionally sustain a peaceful atmosphere whilst sharing the days with Nick. I was feeling more comfortable in my own skin. Since the unexpected riverside conversation God had been gently teaching me to appreciate my own body, to see myself as he sees me. This increased my confidence. Whatever Nick may say or think, I felt increasingly attractive in my womanhood. The loyal friends that had agreed to come along had generously maintained contact with each of us and there had been no element of 'taking sides'. The happy memories and shared family times that were woven into our history created a buffer zone of love and it was really helpful for me that they were able to be themselves, teasing Nick and generally infusing the atmosphere with fun and laughter. My parents were amazing and kept the homefires burning in the chalet whilst the rest of us ventured onto the piste each day. In all the years Mum and Dad never had critical outbursts about Nick, although they understood my need to sometimes. I can't imagine how painful these years were for them. With both my brothers busy with lives based overseas Nick had actually been another son to them and their own loss was great.

The beginning of March was truly springtime for us that year as Heather and Steve confirmed they would come to England mid-summer and planned to be with us in time for the annual trip to Stoneleigh Bible Week. Naturally our landlady had to be informed of the proposed additions to the tenancy. With some daring I approached the agent about the possibility of her moving her things so we could have use of the locked downstairs room. I thought it would be perfect because it had external access and would potentially give Heather and Steve more privacy. I knew I was pushing it because the original agreement had stated 'no pets' but after some discussion she had agreed to a small dog that did not shed its coat.

We prayed and waited. Amazingly the answer came back as a 'yes'. It was also the month Branston came to join us and he and Nathan became firm buddies although we all loved his woolly antics. The new arrival soon decided his favourite sleeping spot was under Nathan's chin and he was great therapy. He arrived on March 3rd. That was the date Nick and I had renewed our wedding vows six years previously. I thought how gracious God is when he does that thing of overlaying a happy event on the anniversary of something sad thus depleting the power of grief.

Having a new puppy was great fun but not enough. The clouds rolled in again for Nathan. As weeks crawled by the wisdom of my choice not to work was affirmed. Nathan grew more and more unhappy. He became quiet, pale and withdrawn. His response to any question relating to preference for food, activity or time frame became a shrug with, 'I don't mind, Mum, you decide.'

He frequently complained of headaches, suffering what presented as viral symptoms. Naturally he was grieving the loss of family life and missed his father but he couldn't vocalise this and countless visits to the doctor, plus appointments with various people at the school, did not produce a pathway that brought any relief. He would seem to go along happily for a week or two and then all the symptoms would return. On one harrowing occasion he was off school for nine weeks by which time I was fielding threats of home assessments, psychology reviews and criticism about lack of discipline. I was feeling desperately inadequate and out of my depth but I knew Nathan wasn't faking anything and sensed there was an underlying stress. I continued to pray for wisdom, for healing for him, and I asked God to bring into our life anyone who could help uncover any issue that needed to be resolved. One day I gently asked questions around the topic of bullying and eventually Nathan reluctantly admitted that there were indeed boys at school who picked on him.

At primary school back in Sussex, Mrs G. had one day summoned me for a chat. She explained that Nathan was her most exasperating pupil. He had boundless energy and was always fiddling with something. Never comfortable sitting still he would wriggle and fidget, sharpen his pencil, study passers-by and regularly ask to be excused. Whenever challenged with a question about the lesson content, however, he could tell the class in detail what it was his teacher had been explaining. She was very frustrated and I didn't know then what I know now about learning styles, fidgeting and how high Nathan's IQ is.

Now twelve, Nathan admitted that returning to class after nine weeks, he had come top in a science test. He had received a 'doing over' in the lunch queue as a result. In desperation and with no solution up my sleeve I asked him one day if he felt moving to a new school might help. In a quiet voice he said, 'Could do, Mum, but no point really; I would just take all the problems with me.'

On moving into the area I had prayed much about our choice of GP (General Practitioner) and had not been disappointed on the occasions we had needed to visit the surgery. I chatted with my parents who expressed concern. I spoke to the school but understandably Nathan didn't want a big fuss, wearily telling me he could handle it.

Lovingly my father spoke: 'Darling, if ever you feel that a change of school would be of help to Nathan I would be very happy to fund that. I don't want you to feel that there are no options if things at school don't improve for him.'

A constant source of gentle support and wisdom, often relayed through my mother, Dad provided an anchor. His wise counsel was always infused with hope. I don't know how those years would have been without him. Now a parent of adults myself I can only guess at the pain both he and my mother suffered as I shared my hope and convictions that God was going to step in and perform a miracle on my behalf by causing Nick to have a change of heart. They supported me but I suspect in private they longed for me to 'face reality' and have a fresh start, perhaps with a new, stable man.

I found special holidays like Christmas and Easter, anniversaries, even Bank Holidays really hard. It felt to me as if the whole world were revelling in family time on these occasions and I felt raw. I wasn't really looking forward to Mothering Sunday. The previous year Father's Day had just left me with an overwhelming sense of how terribly we had let our sons down. How could they possibly grow up whole, with a deep understanding of God's love for them when the people they trusted most had not managed to sustain a loving family environment? Sam had been in bed at home for the two weeks leading up to the Sunday and Nathan was struggling. The doctor told me they were both suffering from post-viral syndrome after the rotten winter flu bug. It became increasingly clear to me as I read around the subject, that the grief of the divorce caused a stress level within their bodies, which in turn compromised their immune systems. In recent years there has been plenty of research into the impact of stress and much more is recognised regarding its physiological impact. Sam and Nathan continued to get every bug going and took ages to recover.

I was relieved. John was leading the service for Mothering Sunday. His style of leading was particularly gentle and the gathering felt like a journey into God's presence, as opposed to the experience of being led on a route march through a leader's prepared agenda. His emphasis was always on expressing our love and thanks to God with a refreshing openness to a change in the direction of the meeting if he sensed God prompting him or the atmosphere shifted. As I walked to church I felt pain relating to Nick's unfaithfulness come strongly to the surface. Later in the morning a woman shared a message from God about him wanting to heal things from our past. I sensed God touching me as I stood at the front. I held my hands out palms up in front of me, as an indication of my longing to receive from him. I had struggled with a wrenching loss over how the intimacy and physical love that had been pledged to me when we married had been quite literally sprayed over the county as Nick's seed had been sown far and wide. Even though we had moved to a new area I regularly experienced a deep apprehension that someone may knock on my door one day and announce herself as the daughter I would never now have. Fear lingered for some years; fear that if it happened I would not be able to control my reaction; fear that if Nick had fathered a daughter the grief of my own lost opportunity would be unleashed and the whirlpool suck me deep into oblivion.

As I stood at the front of church, distress, which I had pushed deep down because the weight of it threatened to overwhelm, began pushing up to puncture and explode through the cling-film veneer of bravery I had neatly arranged over the surface. As I accepted prayer God gently showed me that each sperm belonged to him, that each expression of affection was rightfully his before it was mine and that his loss in it all was great. Healing came as instead of turmoil and groaning I experienced being cocooned in peace and reassurance. Tension melted from every muscle. A deep comfort settled inside me; my breathing became relaxed and normal. I felt a deeply sad, negative atmosphere leave my life and it has never returned. God patiently let me see that by clutching, to try to hang on to things long gone, I was harming myself and that a possessive 'holding on', even if only in thought, was delaying my being able to experience emotional healing and the freedom it offers. I was finally able to see that only completely relinquishing my grip would bring relief. God had already shown me that unforgiveness or being angry with another person simply gave them a hold over me, which then had a negative influence in my own life. That is the complete opposite of the release of wholeness and freedom that come through releasing the situation or person to him. But this deep issue, of the other half of me actually having intercourse with others and my need to relinquish this pain, had taken time for me to recognise and on that day God set me free and did some more healing. The fact that it was Mothering Sunday caused me to feel especially targeted by God's love.

The next day a lovely lady from church called Mo, came to see me. She said she had been praying for me and shared some verses from the book of Joel 1:4: 'What the locust swarm has left the great locusts have eaten; what the great locusts have left the young locusts have eaten.' Also from Joel 2:25: 'I will repay you for the years the locusts have eaten.'

She brought with her wine, bread and oil as symbols of God's promise of an abundant and fruitful time ahead. We broke bread together and Mo prayed for me. I was blessed and encouraged. As she left I marvelled again how the word 'in going they were healed' felt more and more true as God gently led me on a journey to wholeness.

13

Hope Deferred

In May Nathan had a hammock for his birthday. It did me good to see him reclining with a book, blissfully suspended between two trees with Branston often asleep on his stomach. Together we were counting down to Heather and Steve arriving. The boys soldiered on and Sam was settling well into new friendships. It was going to be exciting living all together, and having the downstairs room unlocked would mean the boys wouldn't need to share a bedroom. I would be pleased to be downstairs if the happy couple preferred the idea of the en suite. If it would afford better privacy they could opt for downstairs with the cloakroom and use one of the upstairs bathrooms. I was relaxed either way.

I tried to eat sensibly and get enough rest but couldn't shake the fluey bug I had now picked up. Recurrent chest infections took me to the doctor but I was so depleted even antibiotics seemed to have no effect. I was reading in Daniel and noted that again the period of a three-year training was significant. I was feeling challenged about praying and fasting; this was partly to do with the sense of a stronghold, something that was bigger than him, in Nick's life. I read about Jesus telling his followers that sometimes people were not healed and set free when they tried to help them because 'this kind only comes out by fasting and prayer'. Perhaps Nick might need someone to fast and pray on his behalf. His perspectives were so changed and he was totally convinced he was the victim of circumstances. It did feel to me as if he had been taken over by a kind of 'insanity', like what had happened to Nebuchadnezzar in the Bible. None of his thoughts or expressed ideas related at all to the person who had encouraged me to entrust my life to the Holy Spirit and embrace the adventure. Daniel 4:34 says, 'At the end of that time…I raised my eyes towards heaven and my sanity was restored.'

I knew God could do it again. I was sure he wanted to.

In addition, with much talk of revival at church, we were being exhorted to earnestly seek God. I fasted and prayed and began to gather others as we longed for God to reveal himself powerfully in the town. I should probably explain that when I say 'fast' I don't mean anything as heroic as six weeks with no food at all, impressive though that would be. I mean consciously going without something in order to demonstrate to God that hearing him, understanding his perspective and having him transform me from the inside, is the most important thing for me. Most often I would have drinks all day and then a light supper but in some seasons I would eat only rice and vegetables for days or weeks. Sometimes over a prolonged period, crying to God for his intervention or perspective on a situation, I might quietly cut out tea and coffee for a number of months so that in a private place several times a day I would be reminded to turn to him. The time not spent shopping for, preparing, cooking and eating food, not to mention clearing up, soon builds up and using it for extra prayer or worship builds a kind of inner spiritual reservoir. It worked for me by praying and asking God if I should fast. I would wait and then act on the thoughts that came into my mind. Over years this process has definitely and mysteriously helped me to know God better. Sometimes it may be in a specific time of need or battle. In other seasons I decide on one day a week to eat only an evening meal. Then as an act of discipline I pray and read the Bible, or a book about doing life the way Jesus did, when I would normally be eating breakfast and lunch. Agreeing with a friend to fast and pray together, asking God to unfold his purpose in certain situations and our lives in general, has also been a strengthening and exciting process.

Sam was fourteen in June that year and we managed to have a good day. When he had been born in our own bedroom in Petworth it was the most amazing experience. I really felt Nick and I had laboured together. We were passionate about the idea of natural home birth and he was fully engaged in supporting me in a long and demanding labour with no interventions over nineteen and a half hours. The sense of togetherness and wonder was incredible and I felt completely cherished and cared for.

Now I experienced waves of raw abandonment washing through me as memories came. I understood the boys' longing for Dad to know all about their lives but it wasn't easy for me when the lines blurred. Inevitably they wanted to invite him for special occasions.

It was clear they felt a weight of concern for his happiness if time spent alone with him was prolonged. Hosting things like Father's Day in our home meant the boys could relax and let the adults carry any 'atmosphere'.

I felt I needed to remain at a safe distance emotionally for my own well-being, but it didn't prevent me longing for Nick to experience God's love and rediscover hope. Sharing life with Steve and Heather made it easier to include him in things like birthday meals. There was always someone chatting and Heather and Steve remained supportive of the boys whilst being careful to leave space for Nick to have whatever input he wanted. I think as Nick continued to grope his way through, living in places he said he didn't want to be living, doing jobs he disliked, we in a sense propped him up. It's true I was acutely aware I had a comfortable home and the joy of sharing life with Steve and Heather and our sons. He seemed to be very unhappy and as far as I knew he was much alone. I continued to be convinced that restoration was God's plan and all my decisions were taken through the filter of this belief. On Father's Day Sam invited Nick to come to church. I felt apprehensive about Nick appearing on the stage of our new church life but for all I knew this could be the time when he would suddenly see that there was a way back for him. I prayed that God's love would reach Nick through something that was said, sung or prayed and hoped I would be able to hold it together myself.

Over years Sam never gave up hope that his father would come back. Now nearly thirty he could be accused of being a 'glass half empty' person. It was very tough for Sam. For the first four years of his life, those commonly regarded as key in terms of attachment and emotional development, Sam was much with his father. Sam had a bond with his dad that Nathan never had the opportunity to develop and therefore never lost. This bond wholly coloured Sam's world. As Nick began to struggle and his principles were eroded Sam suffered. The dimensions of his world slowly changed and he found he could never manage to come up with the response his father required. He wasn't quite tough enough or daring enough. He was too sensitive and needed to develop emotional muscle. Sam pretty soon realised that even his best was never going to be good enough, and having to manage the terror of his father possibly dying from smoking the cigarettes he previously volubly condemned, had a profound impact. If at twenty-one the one thing that matters to you, the very thing you have been waiting for all your life, hasn't happened…how does it feel? In a moment of passionate caring, when all I longed for was to bring hope, I had shared with Sam that I believed God had spoken to me about us all being together again. Trusting and having faith are issues for him because he believed with all his heart and it didn't happen.

As I clung to God and the promise of restoration for our family he patiently revealed more to me about his way of doing things. He gradually taught me to understand his character. It is a huge challenge to fathom the depth of a love that is so profound it will not dictate; a love that will quietly stand in the wings whilst freewill wreaks havoc; a love that waits to respond to even the squeak of a shoe, worn by a prodigal turning in its direction. Omniscient and omnipotent but once rejected this love patiently awaits invitation. Freedom of choice may cost this love everything yet still the gift will not be rescinded or manipulated. I had experienced this love enough to know its overall intention towards me was good and only good. Therefore if the promise was delayed love must have a purpose. Unanswered prayer became the hammer on the anvil of my life, working out the answer to a much older prayer as I was pressed relentlessly deeper into God's dream for my relationship with him: intimacy.

On July 14th that year we would have been celebrating our eighteenth wedding anniversary. Nick phoned to say that he was thinking of me and that the day would always be special for him. I felt very sad because there was heavy resignation in his tone. I felt desperate for him to translate the positive feelings he expressed about me into action but they remained hollow sentiments devoid of any visible expression. Galvanised in part by the tone of the phone call I felt maybe it was time to reach out again. This tended to be the pattern.

In the past (several months into the season when Nick had been struggling to understand what it was that the other leaders intended when they suggested 'time out' from his pastoral role) God showed me a picture when I was praying. In the picture Nick was in a deep pit, like a well. It was too deep for him to climb out. Nick had to shout to attract attention and friends came, knotted ropes together and lowered them down. He had to accept and use the offered rope for his escape. I felt the picture was showing that Nick would need to ask someone he knew for help and then be humble enough to accept it. I felt a rise of hope on several occasions when he asked for prayer from anyone we knew. In the picture I wasn't one of the friends but as the years unfolded, if a particular meeting or family event had potential for helping Nick (as I saw it), I would ask God about whether to extend an invitation. I saw myself as venturing again to lean over the edge of the well to offer encouragement but I felt vulnerable doing it and always prayed for God's direction. There was far too much at stake to just act on my own ideas.

I heard of a particular service being held at a church that was reputed to be 'lively' in Winchester. The speaker was to be a man whose teaching had challenged and inspired us in the past. In my reading the day before, I read in Romans 4:17, '[God] who calls things that are not, as though they were'.

My faith stirred, I contacted Nick and invited him to meet me there. Incredibly, in the service there was an emphasis on the prodigals and talk about them arriving home in the coming year. Nick went to chat to the speaker afterwards and before we parted he talked to me about feeling worn out. I was heartened, wondering if this indicated he was 'coming to the end of himself' like the young man in the parable.

I continued to have members of Nick's family for meals and visits. He is the youngest of seven who in turn had expressed their disappointment and sadness about the divorce. They were not involved in church but commented that Nick had somehow 'lost his way'. Nick's mum in particular had been a constant source of love and showed interest in our lives. She made our visits special with lovely meals and presents. Once we were divorced I found it harder to be in her home, the place Nick had grown up and we had spent blissful time as courting teenagers. Instead she came to stay with us most school holidays and the boys loved playing cards and doing quizzes with Gran.

The next Stoneleigh beckoned and with it the long-awaited arrival of Steve and Heather. I continued building friendships in church and the local area, trusted that God was working his purpose out and believed he was on our case. The locked room in the house remained just that. I contacted the agent who said he was awaiting instruction from the landlady. I decided after praying about it that unless God prompted Nick to ask about Stoneleigh I would not invite him and he didn't ask. Sam and Nathan moved into the larger bedroom together and I took the smaller one so that Heather and Steve could arrive and be comfortable. We could all reshuffle once the locked room was opened up. Sam decided to go off to Faith Camp with his youth group and I saw this as a positive sign. As the rest of us set off for Stoneleigh I cried out to God for a measure of healing for Nathan. He went along to the gatherings for his age group and I longed for the vicious vice of grief to fully release its grip.

I found the teaching and praise times in the big meetings very strengthening and returned home encouraged; but that didn't dull the sinking feeling of returning to a life that was so far from any I had planned or imagined. It felt very hard to have to live with the great loss that resulted from the sin of others. I couldn't shake off the conviction that now life had fallen apart so completely, my only option was to settle for 'Plan B'. I still couldn't grasp how other parents, other mothers even, had been so willing to collaborate with Nick in destroying our lives; especially for two innocent boys. These thoughts ebbed and flowed as the wrestling match in my head rolled on. Does God have a 'Plan B'? How does that measure up against the belief that he loves me completely and only wants the best for me? If Nick was 'the one' and we messed up, will I always be an 'also ran'?

I was assailed by doubt. I feared that I had failed so badly I would just have to settle for my lot. Having embarked on the adventure, of a life lived in full sunshine under the dynamic influence of the Holy Spirit, it seemed now that the horror of grey twilight threatened. I had signed up and committed to pioneering. How would I ever be happy or able to fulfil God's dream of my life if relegated to the shadowy sideline? I was way too far down the road of 'Yes, Lord' to opt out and draw my own map. So trusting what I did know about his love and kindness and being less desperate for answers looked like my only option. Could God have more than one 'Plan A'? The anvil burned hot as I held still under the barrage of questions. What I did know was that God's intention in my life was for good. If I couldn't see or feel that 'good' it didn't mean it didn't exist. I needed to make a decision to believe what I knew about the character of God and not indulge in constant internal debate. Perhaps it was an issue of timing? One morning in mid August my daily reading in *Streams in the Desert* read,

> **The important thing about guidance with God is to stay in the place you know he has brought you to until the cloud moves on.**

This was alluding to the cloud being the symbol of God's presence with the Israelites, when they were wandering in the wilderness.

Later that same day I returned from the shops to find a letter on the doormat from the agent. It said that the landlady had changed her mind and would not be putting her things into storage to free up the extra room. I felt prepared by what I had read earlier in the day and thought, 'Okay, it seems we're on the move.' We chatted together and agreed we would ask the agent if he had anything else on his books that we could have a look at. We would pray for a property where Heather and Steve could have their own bedroom and bathroom and the boys a room each. A move would probably work out for the best, and the beautiful outlook and pretty garden in Russell Way had worked a measure of healing. To be living in a different region from Nick had been positive for me since I no longer worried I would bump into him in the shops or that he would be driving by. We gave our notice and when the move came there was an element of relief for us all. It felt as though the landlady had only ever let her home reluctantly; we found out that without us knowing she had returned to Hampshire and been around the garden. This was breaking the terms of our contract (she should have written to give us notice of any visit) and made me feel as if she didn't trust me. Her decision not to let us have the room clinched it.

We found a house available for rent in Love Lane. It had four bedrooms, one with an en-suite for the marrieds, and a separate dining room, lounge and kitchen. A downstairs cloakroom was a bonus as was a back door, which led straight out of a utility room into the small garden. All joy; the garden was low maintenance. An open fireplace was the icing on the cake. Oh, and the back of the house overlooked a large playing field. God knows that being able to see the sky from my living area greatly enhances my sense of well-being. Turning right out of the house a pretty walkway led through from the end of the road (another cul-de-sac) and made access to school and the town centre straightforward. On one side of the path the rambling hedgerow produced a luscious crop of blackberries in autumn and the other had football pitches. It was perfect for cycling, walking and rollerblading. The driveway was adequate with a space behind a hedge that suited the caravan. The driveway butted up to next door's driveway but the houses were detached.

Nick didn't express any enthusiasm about us all living together. At this time he had been evicted from the rather uncared for house he had rented. He had acquired an old caravan and had resorted to setting up home in the car park of the factory. (He had begun working there around the time the boys and I moved into the flat.) A neighbour had knocked on the door one morning not long before our house had sold, saying he'd heard Nick needed work and extra hands were needed at the factory. Nick probably wondered if Steve would in some way usurp his role as father of Sam and Nathan but Steve was always very careful and remained very much in Uncle role. Nick came regularly for meals and occasionally slept over in the dining room. The boys continued to visit him but his confined living space made it challenging. I was disappointed *for* Nick and also *in* him. I longed for him to be able to host the boys in comfort. They were growing up and time was passing. I was very frustrated that having a place where he could easily welcome our sons to stay just didn't seem a priority for him.

There was continued talk at church about revival and I was encouraged when God gave me a picture or a song to contribute.

Fasting and praying were part of life and meetings in the church building in Marsham Street in London began to be a regular feature. The leaders of Pioneer, which was the name of a group of churches, increasingly sensed a time approaching when God would reveal himself more fully in our communities. At these gatherings there would often be a speaker from somewhere in the world where they were experiencing more of God than was evident in the UK. Hungry to know more of God in my own life and keen to be part of anything significant he may be about to do, I went whenever I could. The leaders in Petersfield initiated a six-week period of prayer and fasting for the church. I thought times of corporate prayer could be beneficial and with their blessing I drew up a theme for our prayers each week. I offered to host early-morning prayer times at home Monday to Friday for the hour between six and seven in the morning and a small stream of people joined me in our living room.

For me this season was about aligning myself with the troops God had planted me alongside. We committed to motivating, encouraging and exhorting one another to see ourselves as marching forward into the purpose of God, whilst at the same time pushing back the enemy where he was attempting to infiltrate. I applied this to both corporate church life and at a personal level. I was fasting to demonstrate my ultimate longing to God that he would find he could accomplish whatever he wanted in me. I was hungry for transformation and longing for his love to be an obvious influence in my life and relationships. This included all ongoing contact with Nick and whatever level of relationship was to unfold.

The leaders sent a message to ask if unity could be the theme on one of the weeks of prayer. This was ironic because their reluctance to prioritise prayer times in the busy church schedule had left me feeling rather isolated. I felt cancelling other meetings and events would create real opportunity for us to unite in prayer. There were plenty of meetings on every week so if the prayer was going to be significant I felt prioritising was important. The young people were very enthusiastic about their Friday-evening slots and enjoyed coming to the house for breakfast on Sundays. By week four several of the leaders were facing challenges in their home situations or had health issues and I was tired. God gave those who came to pray a number of pictures around the theme of fire and there was a strong sense of him moving in our lives. We soldiered on and I was greatly encouraged reading about a situation in the Old Testament where God instructed a man to dig trenches. There was no wind or rain all night but under cover of darkness God caused the trenches to be filled with water. That must be what was happening; we were faithfully digging on in prayer and though it was not visible to us yet the Holy Spirit was quietly moving in to fill the church and change us. If that were his modus operandi then I could believe it was also happening in Nick's life.

As a church we supported a number of people serving God around the world. During the six weeks season of prayer and fasting, a woman who had an international role in teaching and discipling visited. She had been associated with the church in Petersfield for some years but her work took her all around the world and we hadn't previously met. We had coffee and as we prayed together she said she sensed God wanting her to warn me. She said I could be seen as a 'rescuer' and to be aware this was not necessarily the role God wanted me to play in people's lives. I noted this in my journal and asked the Holy Spirit to teach me, warn me where that may be happening and restrain me from jumping in to situations where he already had things in hand.

I began to understand that there may be times when it was God's intention that a situation or relationship be allowed to crash. His heart is for all things to be made new not that old things be rescued and patched up. Pre-empting God's work could inhibit the unfolding of his best purpose.

About week five, Nick who had been slowly beginning to speak about the possibility of changing his job, admitted he was in debt. This was a hopeful sign for me because up till now his victim mentality had been so well developed that he had not been able to assume control or take initiative about anything. He constantly spoke about being at the mercy of circumstances that, as he saw it, had been orchestrated by outside influences. He reasoned that he had no meaningful control or viable options. I prayed about whether to invite Nick to Marsham Street and did. There was a meeting scheduled on Saturday as the six weeks of praying and fasting ended. Nick accepted the invitation. I was trembling but hopeful as we sat side by side in the meeting. We sang one of the hymns that we'd had at our wedding and then the leader of the meeting prayed for people with partners or children who had stopped wanting to live God's way or were 'backslidden'. Nick made no comment. I felt God had his finger on our case and the peace of his presence accompanied me home. There was hope.

My birthday was coming up and it was the big 4-0. My sister rather conspiratorially informed me that I was required to pack an overnight bag. The night before my birthday we were sleeping at Mum and Dad's because there was a plan. It involved an early start. Obediently I did as asked and the next morning found me being poked awake at 5 a.m. to be bundled into the car. We had breakfast on Eurostar, sped under the channel and were in Paris by lunchtime. It was an amazing surprise. I had had no inkling of what was afoot. Dad had booked a meal at the restaurant that is actually up the Eiffel Tower and the icing on the cake was a great friend, who happened to be working in Paris that year, came to join us. I felt completely overwhelmed with treats and will never forget walking together in the rain along the banks of the River Seine. The walk took longer than expected. Mum and Heather still talk wistfully about the time in Paris when they were close enough to stick their noses out of the taxi window and inhale the scent of fashion but Dad's schedule left no time for fripperies such as shopping.

As winter set in Sam and Nathan worried about Nick in the tiny caravan. The sad shadow of living apart from him hovered but they loved sharing life with Heather and Steve. We continued to have various folk we wanted to support and encourage for regular meals, we made it a habit to eat and chat and then pray together. A number of people found this very strengthening and we saw God spilling out from the love we shared as a household. We encouraged the boys to invite friends home. It was agreed that Branston would benefit from company of his own kind and we duly chose another puppy. Nugget was the same breed as Branston but a honey-blonde colour known as apricot. He was the runt of the litter but grew into a rather rotund little dog whose temperament was anything but stolid.

Having bouts of eczema did little for his equilibrium, or mine for that matter. Branston was placid and affectionate. Nugget thought he was too, but the production of skin ointment for dogs could push him to attempting a little nip of human flesh. We could never fully discern if it was the need for him to wear the collar at such a tender age (one of those large plastic 'anti scratch' collars to prevent him from chewing himself raw when the eczema flared up) or the fact that he was inadvertently dropped on his head as a puppy. He had the same upbringing as Branston but there was always just that little air of temperamental anxiety that we never managed to help him overcome.

As the year drew to a close Sam seemed more settled but Nathan still had patches where the clouds rolled in and I continued to feel stricken at my powerlessness to make life better for him. I'm not sure, looking back, if I could or should have done more . . .

The church leaders decided that to stop most of the activities and see what God unfolded in the New Year was the next step. It was not a popular decision and the cessation of youth activities proved unhelpful for the teenagers. It was a time when we hunkered down as a household, supporting and encouraging each other. Steve and Heather were busy making adjustments of their own. Coming from New Zealand the lack of sunshine was a challenge and they both missed friends, family and the large thriving church they had sacrificed to be with us. Steve had heard God speak to him about his season in England being one of 'further training' and interpreting that as some further study, he began looking at courses. He had two degrees already and had had his own business in New Zealand. He had been consultant to the government and assisted in the overseeing of a complete revamping of the Housing Department in previous years.

In the lead-up to Christmas some old friends, who were in the heyday of their own voyage into church leadership, got in contact. They were leading a Christian ski holiday to Austria during the coming season and would any of us be interested in going? My mother thought it was unwise for me to consider going away with Nick. I think she was anxious that I was keeping my life on hold when there was no evidence that Nick was creating the framework for any future together. She had begun intimating that 'moving on' was an option since one of her friends had commented that I was still young and attractive. But I prayed about it and felt I wanted to take the risk. Time to venture to the edge of the well once more? I trusted the love and prophetic gifting of the friends leading the holiday and Nick was passionate about the snow. Maybe he could rediscover God in the mountains? The bulk of those in the hotel would be Christians so plenty of chance for helpful chat plus the evening meetings could give God an opportunity. The trip was several months away but maybe it would be the time when Nick would turn his life around.

14

Clouds Gather

As already mentioned I had sensed God speaking to me about a three-year commitment in Petersfield. The impression came strongly during the lead up to our first New Year in Hampshire, which was some months before Heather and Steve came to live with us. The boys and I had been living in Russell Way nearly six months by then. I had spent New Year's Eve itself alone with God and lit three candles as a sign between us that I was accepting what I sensed as his time frame. The following year was our first all together and I lit two. I wasn't wishing the time away but it felt important to mark my decision to cooperate with what I felt God indicating and take time to review all the things he'd said and shown me in the previous year. Early in January I went with friends from church to the next event at Marsham Street. I wasn't alone in feeling that momentum after the autumn season of prayer and fasting was lacking on our own church front. What next? Were we really going to see God move in power among us and in the town? What is your time frame, Lord? was the question we were all asking.

The man leading the gathering began by sharing a story. He spoke about the son of a prominent church leader who had abandoned his faith and walked away from God over a number of years but had been recently restored in his relationship with both his family and God. Then he told us about a worship leader who had come from America because he sensed God telling him to come and prophesy over London. This American had felt prompted to go and lay hands on Big Ben and he had prophesied, 'Now is the time,' pronouncing as he spoke over the cold, hard stone, that God was saying hearts were going to be warmed again. (When I got home I found that I had written those words in my journal exactly a year before beside some verses from Ezekiel where God promises that he will turn hearts of stone into hearts of flesh. I was hopeful that in a hidden place God had been doing that for Nick as family and friends continued to pray and he accepted the occasional invitation to be in church or come to a meeting.) The evening finished on an inspiring note with talk of the coming year being one of expansion and breakout. 'Be prepared to walk off your own maps' was the speaker's challenge. He exhorted us to believe the coming year was one when we would do things we had never done and see things we never thought we'd see. I wrote in my journal,

. . . write books we thought we'd never write???

. . . just because it dropped into my mind.

Some seeds take a lot longer than others to take root and produce fruit in our lives. Perhaps we are prone to think this devalues them. Since the speaker finished by quoting the words from Joshua, 'then you will know which way to go', which had been so important for me in the move out of Sussex, I felt excited to think that God had caused much of the evening to be so personally relevant. I confess that the times of really noisy prayer and the feeling that people were shouting at heaven sometimes made me uncomfortable. I've never felt the need to yell to get God's attention but hearts were longing for more of God's purpose to be unfolded and I know being a Christian doesn't make us all the same. I asked God to help me be more aware of him than the jangly feeling inside and decided not to let it deter me.

Steve and Heather were constantly supportive and encouraging but I struggled with disappointment because I had assumed we would be at church together. It was different for them. I felt that part of why God had taken me to Petersfield was to bring a contribution to the church. He had spoken to me about being willing to be a catalyst so I was prepared that people might not always feel comfortable when I was prompted to initiate. It was painful not to be able to share that journey as they held back, wisely waiting for God to lead them.

Heather and Steve were hungry for an environment that strongly reflected the structure and principles promoted at Stoneleigh and they were hopeful of finding that in a church in our area. Gradually they did make connections with certain people in my church and, in spite of an underlying sense that things could be done better, they came along. Steve quickly discerned if someone was being an unhelpful influence and identified a deep reluctance in the area of confrontation, which was inhibiting church growth. The network of churches that Petersfield was linked to was less structured than he and Heather were comfortable with and I did understand they wanted to be part of a church with what they saw as a broader horizon. They regularly visited other churches and caught up with friends back in Sussex where Heather had lived and worked prior to moving to New Zealand. They really felt that the organisation that hosted Stoneleigh had so much life and stability to offer that they wanted to align themselves with it. Their long-term dream was to carry the foundational truths and biblical teaching of the group called New Frontiers, back with them into the wider church in New Zealand.

Later in the year, despite his misgivings, Steve graciously shared his musical gifting and we had much fun singing together with friends in the Petersfield church. He was determinedly looking for work and also applying for study places in line with his sense of God intending this season to be about 'further training' for him. When we look back now we can see that God's intention clearly unfolded as Steve became involved in supporting and encouraging leadership in a number of churches. He developed gifts and abilities for building team and discerning issues that stunted growth but initially he had assumed the 'training' to be more structured and academically orientated. He faithfully pursued the process with the paper trail and interviews it entailed. He gained a university place on a course for the following academic year but by the time the start date arrived he was fully in harness on God's training programme and relinquished his entry.

Steve humbled himself in order to create income and, whilst awaiting a response from the Social Services Housing Department, he began a job in the post office in Petworth. The postmistress was an 'unusual' lady and although he completed more than a month of duties in the office and shop front there, she never paid him. In personal issues he is not a confrontational type but my sister and I were outraged on his behalf. Eventually his name came to the top of some pile in an office somewhere and after interview he accepted a job in the social housing office in Guildford. He drove up the A3 each day and arranged to work flexi hours to avoid traffic. This meant he left at dawn but was home for afternoon tea as the boys came in from school. I never heard Steve complain, or even intimate that it mattered to him, that he had to accept work on the bottom rung of a ladder of which he'd previously been top in his native land. He seemed genuinely delighted to be sharing life with us and unselfishly gave his time and energy to being available for Sam and Nathan. He and my sister were both in their late thirties and trusting God for their own children. That this never happened for them made their generous lifestyle of loving us so extravagantly all the more precious. Steve's income was the minimum wage, which at the time amounted to £3.60 an hour. The boys and I were entitled to some assistance with the rent and I had child benefit but there was still a shortfall in our monthly outgoings.

Heather had had a break of about eighteen months but decided to pick up the thread of her prestigious nursing career in order to swell the household coffers. Before moving to New Zealand she had trained as a paediatric nurse at Great Ormond Street Hospital in London. She had gained various qualifications equipping her to work with babies and children needing open-heart surgery and treatment for cancer. She had previously run a department but wasn't seeking that level of responsibility. She began to search for work in the area and ultimately covered various shifts for the local health authority, caring for children who were very sick but being nursed in their own homes. This involved working days and nights. We felt so blessed to be sharing life together and we prayed and chatted about how best to support the boys. They were now getting used to the idea of us being a household. I continued to be the hub of their lives but we ate together as a family whenever possible and Steve and Heather gradually engaged as we went along. Steve, for example, was far more help than I could ever be with science homework. He would often bring in logs and light the fire in the winter with willing helpers wherever matches were concerned. He or Heather often mowed the lawn or did housework.

Often in survival mode, and overwhelmed that Steve and Heather had so freely left New Zealand to be with us, I didn't really give any thought to how it may look to those in the community. It was only Sam mentioning one day that he didn't know anyone else growing up with their aunt and uncle that alerted me to the fact that what we had chosen was rather different. We chatted about how to make that seem as comfortable as possible. The boys were very happy for themselves but inviting friends home felt a bit strange, until we hit on the idea of pizza nights.

In complete contrast to me, Heather loves cooking. I read books but she devours recipes. It makes birthday and Christmas gifts easy and we all benefit from her love of cooking programmes. She loves to put into practice what was demonstrated. Our lives were changed when my mother gave her a much longed for bread maker. Not just because every other morning the waftings of fresh bread would creep upstairs to wake us but because the machine also made genuine pizza dough. We decided Friday nights would be pizza night and the boys invited friends. There still wasn't anybody Nathan wanted to invite home but Sam had linked up with several teenagers who lived in the area. We had great fun laying out rows of topping options and then making up our own pizzas before popping them under the grill. There were huge benefits to having Aunty Heather in residence. As I've mentioned, Heather wears her emotions for all to see and likes everyone to be in the moment, as she lives it. She is fun-loving and very upbeat in her approach to life, enjoying a good giggle. Sharing life with her is living in glorious Technicolor with the full benefit of surround sound. The 'mute' button is not an option; my sister needs to verbalise in order to process.

My sons were royally entertained. Having lived with me as I sought to manage my pain, remain positive and sustain momentum without needing to talk about it, they now lived in a state of permanent fascination. Drama unfolded as Heather demonstrated every emotion on the spectrum, always inviting them to share the ride. Life was never dull. It took me a while to adjust to the comings and goings, often at short notice, but I think I could easily have leant the weight of my life on Steve and Heather. Obviously as a married couple they needed liberty to have breaks away, pursue friendships and nurture their own relationship. God gently used those times to remind me that he was sufficient for any need I may have.

We grew in our respect and love for one another and I was thrilled for Heather. For years she had thrown herself wholeheartedly into her single life, successfully encouraging and inspiring others to do the same. She had been passionate for God as a single for over twenty years, completely believing that if it was God's best for her he was more than able to bring the right man across her path. She and Steve had built their friendship over several years before recognising they shared romantic inclinations and it was obvious that Steve's mission in life was to be the best husband possible. He openly adores everything about my sister whilst loving and respecting her enough to gently help her with those areas of her life she wants to change or grow. The love they share caused our home to have an aroma of affectionate fun that attracted others. I was in awe of how Steve seemed to be the outworking of a special kind of love. We had been living together for some time when things were feeling particularly tough for me. Nick continued to imply a future together was still what he wanted but appeared to be doing nothing about causing it to come into being. I cried to God for help and strength to go on and he whispered, 'I love you in just the same way Steve loves Heather.'

Just like that. This revelation caused a deepening in my relationship with God that continues to enhance my life.

Steve and I share a similar, rather dry sense of humour. We would sometimes tease Heather to distraction as she blustered that she just couldn't see what was so funny. Two nephews chuckling on the sofa only fed her frustration but laughter was common and healing was in the air. We spoke often about the more serious things and they were lovingly supportive of my belief that restoration was on God's agenda. Sam and Nathan continued to see Nick often and it was perfect to be able to plan for the approaching skiing holiday, knowing Steve and Heather could keep normal life ticking over at home. I was so thankful for the stability that was growing as Steve's quiet consistency infused our lives. He always encouraged the boys to spend time with their father and offered Nick friendship as from time to time he came for meals. I was grateful that though passionate about peace and stability for the boys, Heather and Steve also understood how important it was for Sam and Nathan to see their father welcomed into their living space. I experienced some relief, as it seemed the emotional load I felt was lessened because the others were round the table. The hollow ache of being just the three of us, a stark memorial of a once fruitful family life, eased.

Probably the boys felt 'safer' emotionally with us all together. Unable to express it they had begun to carry the weight of Nick's despondency, especially after times alone with him. Having other adults sharing life, who loved them unconditionally and who they knew to be wholly 'for them', diffused anxiety. The generous love Steve and Heather shared created a safe place for the boys to enjoy Nick's company. Heather really extended herself, relinquishing pain and disappointment. She and Nick had been particularly close and her wound was deep. Steve hadn't known Nick prior to their marriage and he was a strength and godly presence in our lives as we all struggled to recover. He consistently made himself available to Sam and Nathan.

Nathan had had another patch off school and the doctor spoke about him having outgrown his strength, as he was already very tall for his age. He spent time with our old friend Andrew, who had helped Sam when we had lived in the flat. Nathan appeared to feel more hopeful. Sam was flexing his fourteen-year-old muscles and we all knew about it as I sought wise ways of helping him keep his room habitable, deliver the papers on his round (ideally in the same week he received them), and collect ingredients for food technology the night before the lesson rather than during breakfast the day of the class.

When the planned Christian ski holiday came around I was nervous. But anticipating a positive trip I boarded the coach for Austria. In my time with God the previous week I had been challenged by reading some words Paul had written in the New Testament about the importance of forgiveness. He writes,

> *I have forgiven in the sight of Christ for your sake, in order that Satan might not outwit us. For we are not unaware of his schemes. (2 Corinthians 2:10–11)*

I was challenged again that if I didn't completely forgive Nick I was playing into the enemy's hands because it is as we forgive that we receive God's forgiveness. God was teaching me about spiritual warfare but what a lousy hostile tactic. If I hold on to even justified hurt and anger, refusing to forgive, this blocks my ability to receive God's much needed forgiveness in my own life, therefore the enemy's intention, my separation from God, is accomplished. I took deliberate time to extend forgiveness in prayer asking God to help me keep the lines of communication between us clear. I was also very encouraged to read words that I felt were prophetic from the New Testament in 2 Corinthians 1:11,

> *Then many will give thanks on our behalf for the gracious favour granted us in answer to the prayers of many.*

I knew many faithful friends continued to pray for Nick and I remained sure that the thing that would honour God most would be for us to have a glorious reunion.

I'm still convinced that God's nature is to restore. Even when something has gone painfully wrong or not worked out as planned, he is brilliantly able to cause living with the consequence to birth something good. Through my circumstances not 'coming good' as I perceived it, I have gained understanding about his great desire for us to offer our heart and will, to choose him whether or not life is going as we would like. I had much to learn about how the Giver longs to be loved and known for his own sake and about receiving unconditional love.

My fervent dream was for us to be united as a family thus demonstrating God's power to heal and restore. I can see clear opportunities where I think the direction of Nick's life could have changed; but how would life be today if God had magically made Nick do what I was sure would be best for us all? Do I want to worship a God who uses his power manipulatively to achieve what he wants or am I allured by the soft, loving, permanently aching heart of a God who draws me into a love relationship I never dreamed possible? This relationship involves cultivating intimacy, and loving the Giver takes easy precedence over any gift; even that of a renewed marriage. The concept that there could be an even more radical option for 'good' than our marriage being restored just did not feature in my perception of God's love at that time. I had no inkling of a wild romance unfolding, as clinging to the log of divine love I ran the rapids one day at a time. I had indeed embarked on a love affair: it bore little resemblance to my feelings for Nick.

By this time I did occasionally have thoughts about whether I could even manage to change gear and live in a relationship again but my heart was still towards Nick. We had agreed that we were not going on this trip as a 'couple'. Obviously we weren't sharing a room and I had long since stopped wearing a wedding ring. I was hopeful that we could have some easier time together away from familiar tensions. Perhaps we could have some meaningful conversation. He might see I could be fun to be with and that there was hope for a future together. We sat together on the bus but the general idea was to blend with the larger group as 'friends'.

I was appalled when the husband of the couple heading up the trip, stood at the front of the bus and welcomed everyone concluding, 'Great to have old friends Nick and Hazel along on this trip.' Christian circles being what they are, it was only seconds before a nubile gazelle came leaping lithely to the back of the coach where we had sat in the hope of being unobtrusive. I didn't know her but that did not inhibit her as she squealed with delight to encounter my companion, 'Hello, Nick, I thought it must be you when I heard "Nick and Hazel", but I'd heard you weren't together anymore.'

Did I mention this particular gazelle was blonde with china-blue eyes that gazed adoringly at Nick from a peaches-and-cream face? Subtlety not a strong point then. The journey was not enhanced for me by overhearing the same girl tell her travelling companion, with unconcealed relish, that she had in the past approached Nick about the possibility (I could hardly believe my ears) of him agreeing to be her sperm donor! Closing my eyes I consciously rebuked the enemy. I knew it was important to forgive and let it go. I mentally chalked it up as my first victory of the trip. Others who could not have failed to overhear were too polite to press us and as the holiday got underway we spent time separately, doing things with different groups, then meeting at meals though not necessarily sitting together.

As the bus rumbled on neither of us wanted tension and the connection between us remained strong. As the miles passed we chatted more easily. Clearly, it was a false environment away from responsibilities but it was good to find we could be together, share food and look forward to being on the snow. I felt God helping me emotionally and practically as the week unfolded. Nick was used to being the life and soul on such occasions and always found situations where he could help people out. He's a natural leader and enjoyed teaching what he knew so beginners trusted him easily on the piste. I hoped he would be encouraged and I was glad he came to some of the evening meetings. On the last night he even initiated the singing of a hymn, 'Great is Thy Faithfulness', one of the hymns we had sung at our wedding though I couldn't say if he was aware of its significance for me.

On the long journey home we talked. I felt very sad. We agreed that we wanted to be together but that there was a lot of baggage from the past. I felt wretched as Nick talked about wanting a future with me but he wasn't sure he could be with me because he said that for him it would mean living in constant fear, 'always anxious that you might throw me out again'. It seemed he was no nearer recognising what had actually happened as trust had been destroyed. I was acutely aware that he wasn't purposefully declaring that all ties with other sexual partners were severed. We were both teary as we said goodbye.

I missed Nick after having the holiday together and had to be firm with myself. The reasons we were divorced were real and they all still stood between us. I didn't really know what sort of lifestyle he was living. He had admitted to one-night stands in the past. I prayed about ways I may be able to encourage Nick that there was a future worth fighting for or believing in at least. I talked with him, explaining that if he felt he would like to live nearer and have more time with the boys, I would welcome that. He shrugged and muttered a list of reasons why that was unlikely to happen. Away from the emotions evoked by his physical presence none of the reasons were valid: not if he was serious about remaining engaged with our sons and was truly thinking of rebuilding relationship. The journey stretched uphill and long in front of us. I felt Nick was crippled by self-pity, unable to take any first tiny step into change.

15

Rock Bottom

I wrestled to keep the pain at bay. I was constantly shocked at how self-absorbed the father of my sons had grown. Up close it was as if the boys had become an optional extra in the whole scenario. Nick had wanted children more assertively than I, declaring he hoped for boys in order to train them to be little replicas of himself. As a new wife I had been daunted by the concept of motherhood. Now Nick could no longer see beyond his own disappointment about the hand he perceived life had dealt him. He remained vehement about his status as victim, regurgitating every dejected detail of how his life had been stolen from him. Constantly referring to the elders meeting as the 'brutal assault of friends claiming to be speaking the truth in love'. He also remained furious with my parents for not meeting his needs and berated our friends for not restraining me from divorcing him.

In the years that followed Nick stepping down from church responsibilities, one or two of the men from the original leader team quietly came and apologised for not knowing how to support Nick. They expressed concern that with hindsight perhaps the situation could have been handled more sensitively. Nick was driven by an insatiable desire for public recognition, that he had been misjudged and victimised. It coloured his whole outlook. He seemed blinded to truth and unable to recognise any personal responsibility for his circumstances. He was, in his own eyes, a helpless, mutilated victim. I was desperate for realisation to dawn, certain it would pave the way for restoration, firstly with God and then the family. Whatever I said, Nick could not be persuaded that people loved him and had acted with good motives. I decided a practical demonstration of love was called for. After much prayer I made what I saw as a big step towards him.

From time to time Nick started to mention again the possibility of returning to the police force. Surely this meant there was hope of some change. I wanted to demonstrate my willingness to rebuild trust and I offered to negotiate with the powers that be, to see if the Child Support Agency would consider relinquishing their grip. I saw this as a huge demonstration of trust. I explained that if they agreed to stop taking the money from his salary (which he bitterly resented) I would need him to commit to regular payments. When I raised it with him he said it all seemed just too much effort and he thought it wasn't worth the bother. I felt as though I'd had a slap in the face, but I knew I had done the distance emotionally and that my desire to show a willingness to believe in his ability to provide was sincere. It was another situation where he could say the right thing – that he *wanted* to provide – but actually taking a step towards it was just too hard.

Maybe Nick's perception was that it was some kind of test? Perhaps he was surprised that I would risk losing the income we depended on or he may simply have recognised he would never sustain regular payments. I don't know what he thought. I just know I was profoundly disappointed by his lack of response as I had misguidedly thought it might enhance his self-esteem. I never understood what he really thought about the idea.

I took on responsibility for a youth home group and a fortnightly Lent prayer and discussion time that brought people from all churches in the town together for a season. As the months ground on I began to absorb the fact that at this rate the boys were likely to be grown up by the time Nick was ready for the commitment of a stable relationship. I felt drained. Nothing really seemed to be changing on the church front. Nick continued coming and going but not appearing to take any initiative in his life and Nathan hit another sad patch.

I had in the past visited a conference centre which hosted retreat days for women who wanted to press into God's presence. The facilities were made available for the day providing plenty of 'quiet spaces'. I decided to return and found myself again in the room where I had cried to God as I wrestled with his word to me about going to New Zealand several years earlier. It was good to look back over the time, reread journal entries and clearly see God's loving direction. I had become aware that I was living each day trying to be very brave. Brave about the fact that my daily life was not only a million miles from what I had envisaged, but was tough as a direct result of the sin of other people in my life. I don't intend to imply that I am a sinless being. I wrote earlier about my unfair expectations, which retrospectively clearly classify as idolatry. Where I contributed to Nick's vulnerability I have repented. I'm desperately sorry for the pain experienced by our sons. I'm deeply sad that Nick was unable to reconcile with those he viewed as the culprits. It matters that he made choices that led to consequences that impacted everyone who shared his life. Those things are all beyond my control.

As best I knew how I was listening to God. I deliberately leaned into him, understanding I couldn't bear the weight of my own life without divine sustenance. I felt I had nothing of value to offer as a parent unless God's love flowed into and through me each day. I obeyed one step at a time, as I believed he was showing me. Given the time again I couldn't do anything differently because obedience was the thing, hour by hour, saving me from drowning. Obedience didn't save me from the consequences of sin but I was never alone. I never felt abandoned. I know that God doesn't initiate sin because he is wholly good. So had he allowed these wretched circumstances in order to teach me? I was reading in Psalm 139: 'All the days ordained for me were written in your book before one of them came to be.'

On that quiet day away I pondered the word 'ordained'. God doesn't cause sin so how were these days ordained for me? Was my life ordained and determined by him irrespective of others' sin, then? The word ordained means 'set apart, especially chosen, selected'. All those words are the complete antithesis of the idea that someone sinned and life spun out of control beyond God's reach. Or was this time 'ordained' for me in the sense that he knew in advance that the sin was going to happen so he used the opportunity to teach me and mould my life through it? Certainly the relentless rhythm of living with emotional pain exposed my vulnerability. I suffered the imprisonment of being completely unable to change my circumstances. I was powerless to relieve the agony of unfulfilled longing for my sons. This forced me to face my own weakness which over time brought me to see the truth of what Paul wrote in 2 Corinthians 12:9 when he claimed God said to him, 'My power is made perfect in weakness.' So it would seem that some experience of 'weakness' was always going to be necessary if my prayers for great strength were to be answered.

I had been reading about the prophet Elijah in the Old Testament and felt encouraged by the promise that the drought, as I saw it, in Nick's life would break. I felt his life was totally parched and dry where I was enjoying God's loving provision. The story about a cloud appearing on the horizon, even though only the size of a man's hand, was hopeful. I felt that the drought would end at God's appointed time. I was challenged that my focus needed to return to nurturing my relationship with Jesus. I needed to trust Nick and his choices to God so that I didn't miss the good things intended for me in this season. I worshipped alone regularly and lingered in God's presence, deliberately letting his nearness nurture my spirit. I hadn't got it all sorted in my head but I saw more and more clearly how painful it must be for God that he had given us free will. I began to see that he could influence circumstances in Nick's life and create opportunities but in the end, if Nick didn't choose to receive a fresh start, God would never force it upon him; not even for the sake of those whose lives had been shattered by his choices. I viewed Nick as a prodigal. If he chose not to return 'home' where would that leave me? I would need to be very strong.

Joy was a bit thin on the ground but Nehemiah 8:10 was a familiar exhortation.

Do not grieve, for the joy of the LORD is your strength.

The 'joy of the Lord'. . . Mmm. Well, I knew hundreds of reasons why I *should* feel joy. As a child of God I knew I was loved, chosen, forgiven, protected, promised a future, had a certain hope for life after death, could know peace in turmoil and many other amazing blessings. Hope and joy seemed intertwined in that; however tough the days, nothing could rob me of hope. I need never feel hopeless because the fact of the resurrection means that I can have a meaningful relationship with God right now. This 'hope' is certain because it has nothing at all to do with what happens in my day and does not waver according to what unfolds. It's all about my security in being a child of God. He loves and accepts me because of what is already a sealed deal. His love is this incredible constant in my life. I can't do a single thing to make God love me more and nothing I do will make him love me less. This is cause for joy indeed. As I practised reminding myself, or 'counting my blessings' as I used to sing in Sunday school, I had an experience of joy that helped push back the shroud of disappointment that hovered so often. I made an effort to cultivate joy: I needed strength.

It was nearly a decade later when it came but when it did, the revelation was life changing. I heard some teaching on 'the joy of the Lord is your strength'. There it was in the Bible; it wasn't my own joy at all, summonsed by act of will in order to create a better atmosphere in my day. It was *his* joy, the Lord's joy over *me* that generates strength. Outside, the atmosphere around my life was transformed forever. Inside? As I received truth, it set up camp in my heart. The centre pole was up and guy ropes were hammered in and pulled taut as I revelled in new understanding. God delights in me; I'm the apple of his eye. He thinks I'm gorgeous; he is totally *for* me because in his heart I am irreplaceable. How had I missed it all those years?

I'd had my suspicions standing in the freezing pew on endless gloomy Sundays whilst chanting in mournful monotone, 'And make thy chosen people joyful.' Heather and I (none too politely) had regularly challenged our parents' loyalty to the local vicar, purely on the basis that church was a joy-free zone and made us miserable. Now life would never be joyless again because that knowledge of God's delight in me, bred a profound sense of acceptance and liberty. Liberty that has brought wholeness in my spirit that nothing can touch. Every morning I get the divine thumbs up, a huge wink with a loving, 'Go Hazel!' How can that not give me the strength and impetus I need for my day? And that's the key for me: one day at a time, each resourced by heavenly affirmation as he joys over me.

Meanwhile, I was giving life my best shot and Nathan hit yet another grim patch where despondency engulfed him. I can't recall any particular trigger. He has a tremendous capacity for perseverance and I fear he had worked hard at appearing to be feeling better.

Looking back on that time it was as if a tropical storm were brewing. Each day a few more clouds gathered. It grew more humid as sadness pervaded everything. Electricity was building in the atmosphere. And then one morning, on yet another trip to the doctor, the storm broke.

'Now, Nathan,' the doctor was firm but gentle, 'I want to have a chat with you today, particularly about school. We can ask Mum to wait in the other room if you would be more comfortable?'

I held my breath and tried not to show the tension I felt as Nathan responded, 'It's fine for Mum to stay, thanks.'

The doctor continued, 'When you wake up in the morning, Nathan, do you ever feel . . .' he paused '. . . as if you don't want to go on living?'

Nathan was thirteen and looking intently at his knees as he said in a small, hoarse voice, 'Yes.'

It seems unbelievable that what was right under my nose was hidden. I had no inkling of the depth of utter despair in my own son. This section has taken me days to get on paper as I busily deferred the moment with chores, correspondence, laundry, cleaning. Anything to avoid revisiting this most painful moment of motherhood.

My faith felt wizened; I was praying with, for and over Sam and Nathan daily, so how had things got so bad?

16

Freedom Promise

I was too numb for tears. My heart was already broken but each shattered piece quivered under shock waves of pain. I struggled to digest what I had just heard. The crushing grip of the realisation that my gorgeous son had been ploughing through a mire of suicidal thoughts...alone...at only thirteen was so tight I had to work hard to keep breathing. My brain must have oxygen. This conversation was important. But the rush of icy water in my ears as the glacier of emotion engulfed me, rendered me as useful as Mr Tumnus after his encounter with the White Witch in *The Chronicles of Narnia*. I probably looked as smart, too. It was a truly awful moment.

Gradually the ice thawed and the blurring fog, which was the doctor's voice having an intelligent conversation with Nathan, thinned and became words again. Just in time, as he turned to me, 'Well, is looking at the possibility of changing schools an option?'

I tried to speak. It was difficult to see past the spilt bottle of tablets and the razor blades, dripping with blood that splattered my frozen thoughts.

'Umm . . .' I uttered intelligently and then again, 'Umm.'

The doctor cleared his throat and busied himself writing something down, presumably not my gormless contribution to the discussion. I looked at Nathan's white face then back at the doctor. With a rush of relief I remembered Dad's offer. The doctor spoke again, 'The thing is that if Nathan did want to consider a change, I could recommend a school in the area. It's...well, it's a different sort of school. They specialise really in helping young people fit in, you know, if like Nathan they seem to be a square peg having difficulty fitting into a round hole, that's where they excel. It's a boarding school but they take day pupils too. It is a fee-paying school but I would heartily recommend it for Nathan if it could be a possibility?'

We had long chats. The doctor encouraged Nathan that he could be making a positive choice for a better future for himself. He emphasised that this was in no way giving in to the less intelligent thugs at school whose ignorant bullying had contributed to his situation. This was very helpful for Nathan. I had heard of Bedales but knew nothing about it. General opinion as we talked with friends was mixed, ranging from some believing it to be a wonderfully creative environment offering a truly holistic education, to a spectrum opposite, where tales of lessons being optional and students being permitted to smoke in class abounded.

As we chatted and prayed Nathan and I agreed that since we had been praying about a way forward and each crying out to God for help, we would see this possibility as a doorway from him. We began to make gentle inquiries and I learned that the school did not require students to wear uniform, which would definitely appeal to Nathan who wasn't fond of restrictions. Also a viable 'Outdoor Work Department' was a great attraction; this offered experience in managing woodland, baking bread, laying paths, making chutney and generally presented educational opportunities that could be enjoyed in wellies under an open sky. Being outdoors, whatever the chore, was always Nathan's preference. Naturally independent, the concept of attending lessons and then having more personal responsibility for homework and further study also appealed to him. Everyone was on first-name terms from the school chef to the headteacher. Nathan decided the idea definitely warranted further inquiry and we learned there was an introductory open day planned in a few weeks' time. The school assured us we would be welcome to attend provided we understood that they had reached their capacity for pupil intake for the following September.

Another trip to Marsham Street came around. I continued to find it helpful to go and have my horizons expanded. It was encouraging to experience being a part of something much bigger than just what was happening in Hampshire. There were always exciting stories of God doing supernatural things around the world and the groundswell of expectation for our own nation, towns and churches grew each time we were all together. It seemed clear that God was positioning churches and individuals in readiness for a dynamic outpouring. And, personally, I was desperate to know that I hadn't just imagined or dreamed up the promise of family restoration. I was anxious not to waste emotion and longing on something that may turn out not to be God's intention. I felt I was staking my life on the promise and although God was also speaking other things and clearly unfolding my path, I didn't want to be hanging out for something that may not be him at all. I felt I'd rather God let me down gently now, or even abruptly, anything but find I'd lived my life on a whim.

I knew plenty of women who had married husbands who didn't share their faith and they appeared to crawl through life tearstained and desperate whilst wanting their husbands to change. They seemed to me like widows, longing for the dead body to rise up out of the ground and in most cases the dream happening seemed about as likely. I saw this as an undignified, draining way of living and I wanted no part of it. I'd had one encounter with an organisation in New Zealand for women whose husbands had turned away from walking with God, where they zealously 'named and claimed' on behalf of their backslidden men until blood vessels appeared at bursting point. It had left me stone cold and promising myself I would never indulge in such fraught measures. I didn't have a drop of emotional energy left in the tank but whatever God asked, if he just whispered that he was in it, I knew he would sustain me.

I went into the meeting and sat with John and Penny. Spotting some other friends I nipped across the aisle, slipped into the row behind where they were sitting and leant forward to greet them. The meeting began and I sat back to wait for a suitable moment to return across the hall to my own seat. I noticed a clean-shaven profile next to me and registered a crisp, pale-blue shirt just like one Nick had owned. I reined in my thoughts and focused on the voice coming from the front. Gerald Coates was leading the gathering. He showed a video and then told the story of a Baptist minister who had turned away from God, rebelled and lived in an adulterous relationship. He had my full attention. Gerald explained that when a friend invited this minister to come to a previous meeting at Marsham Street, God had wonderfully drawn him back to himself. Suddenly Gerald said, 'That man is here today, he can tell you himself.'

Absorbing the story and its possible implications I sat perfectly still. As the man next to me rose to his feet I experienced pins and needles all over my body. The crisp blue shirt made its way to the front and told his story in more detail. He concluded that he and his wife were talking about re-marrying. He returned to the seat beside me and at the next break I asked him to pray for me. God's redemptive power was clearly at work in his life, maybe something could be imparted. It surely wasn't chance that of the several hundred attending he was in the seat right beside me. He prayed reassurance for me and that I would be able to look Nick in the eye and speak truth with integrity. Nick had all sorts of ideas and accusations in his head at this time about my never having really loved him, my love changing, my love never having been really focused on him, but I knew if he stopped and actually asked me I could give a direct answer. He had made it harder and harder to respect him but it seemed that love wasn't automatically killed when respect dwindled and trust was shattered.

Later in the day we had a lunch break and there was an area under the building that had the feel of an old crypt about it. It was now a coffee-shop-cum-cafeteria area. I made my way to a table in the corner, a bit tucked away. Feeling there was so much to digest, I couldn't have eaten even if I hadn't decided to fast that day. My friends went off for a walk above ground and I went to the counter for a cup of tea. When I reached the till to pay it appeared I had ordered two cups. I just paid and took them to my table. Fairly quickly I became aware that an old lady had sat down opposite me. Sporting fingerless gloves she was very wrinkled beneath a wild mop of wiry, grey hair. She was dressed in a number of bulky layers, which were topped by a saggy, knitted cardigan in a variety of tired colours; hints of a faded rainbow. There were several scruffy carrier bags strewn around the legs of her chair. I vaguely wondered if she had left her shopping trolley out on the street and offered her my second cup of tea. Maybe it was meant for her all along? The day already felt very unusual. It suddenly registered that I hadn't seen her approach me and I briefly entertained the possibility of her being an angel. That was when she leaned across the table and her face lit up. 'I'm having a wonderful day,' she said. 'I've just come from Beulah: oh it's marvellous, so many are coming back.'

I hadn't the faintest clue what she was talking about. I presumed angels didn't suffer mental health problems and, not wanting to miss anything that might possibly be God, I drew my chair in, hoping I looked expectant.

She spoke again. 'Do you know it?'

I shook my head.

'Oh look,' she continued in an animated tone, 'if you know anybody who is divorced or in relationship difficulties . . .' (Mentally I allowed myself a rueful 'do I ever?') She hurried on, 'Truly, so many wonderful testimonies of husbands coming back, it's an amazing ministry.'

I couldn't speak. My head felt full of polystyrene and she had poked it, making a clean-cut hole. I feigned needing a tissue and leaned down into my handbag, rummaging desperately at floor level for an appropriate response. When I sat up she was gone. Completely disappeared. I just remained still for a while. Then I made my way back to my seat and tried to clear my head by writing down what had just happened.

In the car on the way home no one was familiar with 'Beulah' although somebody thought it may be from the Bible. Later I did a word search and found a reference in Isaiah 62:4. When I looked it up a deep stillness settled over me as I read,

> *No longer will they call you Deserted, or name your land Desolate. But you will be called Hephzibah and your land Beulah, for the LORD will take delight in you and your land will be married.*

The literal meaning of the name Beulah in Hebrew is 'married' and in John Bunyan's work he used the name Beulah for the Promised Land. I could relate completely with feeling deserted and desolate and it seemed clear to me that God was reaffirming his words from Amos. This specific scripture was surely saying we would be remarried. Very occasionally a tiny tremor of doubt would come towards the surface, but before it could rupture the membrane of faith around God's promise, I would pray and receive peace. By this time I was crying out to God that if I were mistaken he would release me from the belief of a future together.

Writing now about this time, I think perhaps a subtle shift was occurring. I wanted to move on in my faith journey; my love relationship with God had quite literally become my lifeline and it was steadily becoming more important to me than restoration with Nick. I wondered briefly if perhaps I could have read too much into the Amos verses. I began praying regularly that God's best would unfold and that He would be preparing me for it, especially if it was to involve relinquishing hope: but I knew I hadn't in any way manufactured the meeting with the little old lady.

Those close to me were slowly beginning to intimate that it was becoming difficult for them. Difficult to continue hoping for the restoration I dreamed of in the face of no evidence of change in Nick. It was brave of them to voice this as I continued to hope and think that the best outcome, especially for our sons, must surely be reconciliation. There was no evidence that Nick was making steps to regain a positive perspective on life. Nothing about the way he was living suggested that living with him would be a good thing for the boys or me. At times a despondent frustration would prowl around the precious promise and I would retreat to a place alone with the Promise Giver. I recorded all the things I sensed God saying and threw myself into the present. What was it going to take for Nick to turn his life around?

Increasingly, I accepted it was going to be totally up to God as it was obvious that nothing I said or did was making any difference. I had hope. Why would God cause such specific things to come across my path if he had no purpose for them? Abraham had believed God even when he couldn't see how God could possibly work out the promise. I believed God was speaking and I was so grateful to feel loved by him. I could trust him that the promise would be fulfilled this side of heaven.

In the few weeks that followed I experienced God being particularly close. One of the girls in the youth group had cataracts; we prayed and they cleared. I felt prompted to lick my fingertip and place it on her eyelids. I don't know what her parents thought but we were all very excited. At church it seemed we were being robbed of a bigger more powerful experience of God by people being focused on the nitty-gritty of sound systems, instruments, seating arrangements, etc. I felt pregnant with revival. I think a number of us did. That sounds rather dramatic but we were poised on the brink of a move of God that could change our nation, it would be spectacular.

The emphasis one Sunday morning seemed to be wholly on our environment and equipment. My journal entry at the time shows clearly the frustration I experienced.

I am pregnant with revival. My hormones are all changed so I get to church – I love the pastor and worship team – but after five minutes I feel the need to rush out and throw up!

I began to pray more specifically for Nick, declaring truth out loud. I strongly sensed the spiritual battle raging over his life. It did seem that he was able to lift his head over the edge of the trough of self-pity for a brief season as he expressed interest in things the boys were engaged in. I read some encouraging words in Titus 1:2, 'God, that cannot lie, promised.' I wrote in my journal,

> *Faith is not working up by will power a sort of certainty that something is coming to pass... God has said it so it is true. My part is to rest because God has said it will happen.*

It felt as if God was releasing a bit more of heaven. I had several dreams, which I wrote down in the night and then shared with the people concerned who were very encouraged. I felt a new compassion and offered to pray for people in the street if I felt God prompting me.

Nick suddenly announced he was going to talk things over with a pastor friend and I felt very hopeful. As I'd felt God speaking to me about a three-year commitment in Petersfield I had asked him to cause me to be a positive influence. I had felt prompted to commit and pray with certain people regularly, about ten in all. Some couples, some singles. Over the years we just carried on eating together each week and talking about what God was doing in our lives then praying together. I was encouraged and motivated when I read that someone had calculated that if each Christian discipled twelve others each year, over seven years that added up to 3,000,000 people.

The open day at Bedales was approaching. I felt I should visit a couple of other schools in the area just to rule them out, but inside I felt that God had used the doctor to speak into Nathan's situation and therefore it was likely that Bedales was the place. Tricky though: they were full for the next intake. I rang the secretary to confirm our attendance. The registrar contacted me to reiterate that there were no dayboy places available and to ask if we had considered the idea of Nathan boarding. I felt cold inside but quietly agreed we would attend the forthcoming open-day.

The following weekend we packed the caravan and went to our favourite spot on a sprawling farm not far from Goodwood. I couldn't relax. Nick brought his tent and we managed to be calm and peaceful for the boys. I found it very difficult to speak about Nathan's situation and trying only made me aware all over again of how self-absorbed Nick had become. He offered no support or understanding of the pain I felt at the prospect of Nathan going away to school. The school was only half-an-hour's walk from home but that wasn't the point. Life and my role in it would be changed all over again. I just didn't feel I had the resource to cope. I made myself go to church and was blessed in the worship when God showed me a picture about swimming out of my depth and Jesus being right there with me. The idea of either of the boys in effect 'leaving home' was just more than I could absorb but this picture gave me reassurance, not only that I was not in it alone but that being 'out of my depth' was okay too. Being out of my depth was possibly God's intention for me.

On the morning of the visit to Bedales Nathan and I prayed together. By the time the day came I was feeling pretty pent-up about it all. We asked God to give us clear indication if Bedales was his next step. During the preceding weeks there had been plenty of discussion with Nathan's head of year at The Petersfield School. He was genuinely concerned for Nathan's welfare and as he'd probed, plenty had come to light that was far from the best with bullying being a main feature. Nathan was making himself go to school.

Nick seemed to have lapsed back into letting life dictate the pace, which meant he took no initiative towards change. Although this was nothing new it palled as the possibility of Nathan moving into a world of considerable independence so soon, came into sharp focus. Life seemed all uphill. I still couldn't see any meaningful steps being taken towards us being able to be together again. I felt angry and resented the relentless consequences of Nick's sin yet again having an impact over which I had no influence. It was an ugly feeling and I tried hard not to let it surface. If Nathan had to go away to school I would feel punished. If he left home now then any chance of us being restored to enjoy family life, as we knew it, was gone. I'm not saying these were appropriate responses because it could be that Nathan would have changed schools wherever we lived. It is true that we would not have been living where we were if Nick had remained faithful but clearly these feelings demonstrate I still had some way to go in the forgiveness stakes. I did always find it hardest to forgive in situations where I felt powerless to relieve the boys' suffering.

There were over a hundred people in the room and we sat towards the back. After formal introductions and information about areas of the school that were on display the registrar stood to give a talk. He spoke about the ethos of the school and the particular educational experiences that Bedales had to offer apart from the academic. To my amazement, a few sentences into his talk he referred to the Bible and a passage that talks about the eagle dismantling her nest until the young egrets have no choice but to fly. He likened this to the Bedalian approach to education in that from an early stage preparations are being made for the young people to leave the 'nest' of school. The intention being that safe flight and a smooth transition to adult life would be the natural product of a style of education that seeks to give independence early on.

Nathan and I looked at each other. We both knew. This was it. The registrar could have used any one of a myriad of illustrations but he chose a familiar one, from the Bible. However, as we were leaving he spoke to us at the door, keen to reiterate that no dayboy places were available for September. I briefly outlined our circumstances and he immediately suggested that we fix an appointment for interview, stating Nathan could sit the entrance exam that week.

When the day of the appointment arrived the headmistress was charming. She seemed genuinely interested in Nathan and how he was feeling about the possibility of changing schools. She asked questions in such a gentle, clear way that he felt at ease and they had quite a discussion whist I sat silently praying. The head explained clearly to Nathan that the school provided options and had day pupils, weekly boarders and full boarders with variations available such as a day pupil living at school if parents were travelling. He had opportunity to ask questions and she explained that the general feeling was that because of the way the school was set up, pupils gained most from the experience if they boarded. But she emphasised that day pupils are in school for long days, integral to all activities and included in every function. Nathan went to do his test and I tried to read a book in the car.

Two days later the school rang to say the headmistress would like to see us for another chat. The registrar met us at the office entrance and Nathan was ushered into the head's office ahead of me. The registrar held me back. He quietly told me that though he was not at liberty to divulge details, Nathan's tests had revealed an exceptionally high IQ. The head was speaking as I moved to join them in her study.

'Well, Nathan, it's up to you. We are happy to offer you a place here and we would like you to come in whatever capacity you think would benefit you most, as a day pupil or boarder. You think about it and let me know.'

Over the next few days I held my breath. It looked as though God was 'making a way' but I could hardly pray. I couldn't bear to think of Nathan not living at home though I understood he was in a desperate place. I also seriously wondered what hope I had of nurturing an exceptionally high IQ in the way it surely deserved. We chatted together as Nathan mulled over his options. It wasn't easy for Steve and Heather either. What was God thinking? They had moved from the other side of the world to support our bruised little family unit. What was the point if Nathan now went away? Would Sam follow? I wrestled, knowing God instructs us not to worry about tomorrow. His calling, to live in the moment whilst sustaining a hope for better days, was demanding. In reality I could only manage one day at a time and I could only do that by continually 'taking my hands off' and leaving my future in his care. We all agreed it had to be Nathan's decision.

God gave me a big hint during the week I waited for Nathan to make his choice. As I worshipped at church my heart was heavy. I stood with my eyes closed and then I suddenly saw myself out walking in the countryside with Nathan. We approached a closed five-bar gate. Jesus stood on the other side with the most amazing expanse of beautiful rolling countryside stretching to the far horizon behind him. He opened the gate and extended his hand to Nathan.

I was not included in the invitation. Tears rolled down. I knew I was being asked to release Nathan but I saw God was showing me that if I could let go, Nathan would be led into a broad, spacious place of great freedom; and he would not be alone.

Nathan crept into my room early one morning a few days later and I made tea and brought it back to bed.

'Mum, I think if I'm going to Bedales that it probably would be best for me to board. I think I will get the most out of it that way.'

It required effort of superhuman proportions for me not to influence Nathan.

Mindful of the picture God had given I had tried hard not to show how I felt. In that moment I wished I hadn't done so well. I felt awed again by his maturity. Having been a daygirl myself in a boarding school I did know it wasn't the same experience as boarding but I desperately didn't want to have to let go so soon. And what about Sam? How would life be for him in an all-adult household? I hugged Nathan, assured him of course we could look after Branston and Nugget, and had another biscuit.

We called the school. They were pleased and Nathan began to experience a lightness of spirit, which was a relief beyond words but didn't dissolve the knot of dread I lived with all summer. I consistently reminded myself about the eagle picture. The school didn't promote any particular faith. What were the chances of the Bible actually being mentioned at the open day? I learned further down the track that the registrar was in fact a Christian and I found some comfort in that as Nathan faced the challenge of living in a dormitory and developed a life quite apart from family.

I reasoned it must surely still be best for the boys to experience us as a family continuing to reach out to their father. It was time for Stoneleigh again. Nick accepted the invitation to join us. But his heart wasn't really in it and the week didn't end well for me.

17

Silent Protest

There was only one more day of our week at Stoneleigh to go and I was thinking that things were going rather well. I had prayed much. We'd enjoyed easy meals together; Nick had been going to a few meetings, having time with our sons and generally seeming to fit in. Walking through the campsite together the last evening I was unsuspecting and ill equipped for a very painful conversation. It left me bruised and hurting all over again.

All the way through the disintegration of our marriage, and right up until the time I went to stay in New Zealand, Nick had actively encouraged me to maintain friendships that offered me strength. Andrew, the church leader and friend that had introduced us to life under the exciting influence of the Holy Spirit became Nick's mentor and had been brave enough to challenge Nick as he had begun to lose focus. Nick continued to be very angry about how this had changed the course of his life. However, he had consistently urged me to maintain the connection with Sue and Andrew and their three beautiful children. He would initiate my taking the boys round for coffee or meals if things were a bit tense at home. The boys and I gained strength from the ongoing love and consistent support that Sue and the family gave. When Nick suggested I went round to their house I thought perhaps there was an element of relief for him that others could give what he felt he could not. These friends longed for Nick to be happy and quietly honoured my particular belief that God intended restoration and healing. Our homes being a short walk apart made it easy for me and our friendship was a lifeline. I was thankful that, though Nick made it clear he didn't want contact, he hadn't lost sight of the significant role the friendship had for me as I struggled to maintain a rhythm of life for our children. The friendship had remained strong across the county border.

Much of the teaching that week was relevant and Nick went forward for prayer in response to a call for 'those who think they've heard it all before and been hurt by their involvement with church'. It was clear that God was creating opportunities for him to receive healing and hope. I wrote in my journal about a stirring to write and committed it again to God. On the last night the boys ran in front as we were walking together along the track through the showground, heading back to our plot. It was a mellow, pink dusk. We were talking about departure plans for the following day. People were snuggled around paraffin lamps enjoying hot chocolate with friends. Children scampered like carefree rabbits in pyjamas. Suddenly the atmosphere changed.

'What really gets me is how I'm always seen as the villain of the piece.'

In an instant Nick became vehement. I kept walking but slowed slightly. I recognised the accusing tone of voice but couldn't think what had precipitated it. Over time it had become obvious that in processing what had happened to him Nick had repeatedly recounted events and conversations. Now several years later it was as if there were little cassettes in his head and I knew that certain names, or referring to specific actions and conversations, had the ability to trigger a chain of thought. I was careful to avoid these trigger points, always apprehensive of what may burst to the surface. What he believed about things said and done were imprinted in his mind and he always said exactly the same. I had tried in vain to bring other perspectives or illustrate that people had good motives. I was optimistic that in the environment of the Bible week some softening or even healing could come. People, who loved God and had been singing rapturous praise all week, surrounded us.

As I nervously weighed possible responses Nick continued, 'Well, obviously I was the one accused but you're hardly above reproach yourself, are you?' That cutting tone again.

I stood stunned as a tirade of accusation hit me. Raising his voice Nick accused me of having been intimate with Andrew and disloyal in the very relationship he had encouraged me to foster. I was completely taken aback as his outburst reached its crescendo.

'Anyway…I'm not the only one who thinks it. Other people thought you had an affair with him!'

The enormity of this accusation rendered me speechless. My mind raced. I just couldn't take in what he was saying. The injustice of him thinking such things, especially some way into what I perceived as a reconciliation journey, paralysed me. What other people? Did others in the church really believe I had been immoral and never challenged me? Had Nick discussed this with other 'friends'? Had they all sat round commenting on my behaviour? I felt totally vulnerable. Hope exploded into tiny particles that scattered out into the night. I managed a quiet, 'I can't believe you would even think such a thing.'

The tentacles of pain sucked me in. I knew from bitter experience that this was not to be a reasoned discussion. As I turned to stumble between the guy ropes of celebrating campers, panic reached for me. I wondered dazedly about the boys. Surely nobody would have accused me in their hearing? Had 'the others' been in the church? Or the village? Surely not.

In recent months, as Nathan fostered the hope of the new school and in light of the Beulah promise, I had felt a deeper trust in God growing. It felt almost strange but I was able to pray more genuinely, 'thy will be done'. I was aware of God helping me with my feelings and it gave me confidence as I found there were an increasing number of days when my emotions were not dictating the atmosphere. I prayed that God would make the prophecy of being married again a reality in my life in his time frame, or release me from the promise that was deep in my soul. I experienced more peace and seemed to have at last clambered out of the emotional floodwater onto dry land; even tentatively daring to look ahead along the river bank. I was finding myself able to face each day and be thankful whilst still holding onto the hope that the Amos promise gave. Now, right there, unannounced, surrounded by Christians, worshipping families and faith-filled couples, the bank beneath my feet gave way. As I took a next step my foot went through the grass into a deep hollow and the sandy bank around caved in, sweeping me up in the landslide. I lost my footing and careened back into the swirling river of emotional turmoil below. Nick? He stepped over the gap where I had been and walked on. I thrashed around in the dark for a while. How could this be happening? Why had Nick waited till now to launch his accusation? The night offered no answers. I re-orientated myself and crept into my bed in the caravan still stinging from the slap of injustice.

When I awoke next morning I had lost my voice. Nothing so biblical as being struck dumb. A rasping, ugly, gravelly sound had taken up residence at the back of my throat, where my voice used to be. I felt as if a septic abscess had erupted all over me and I couldn't get clean, didn't know which antibiotic was needed.

As we went home, unpacked and then got back into normal routine, I experienced the suffocating weight of accusation and the pernicious resentment Nick had expressed. It was a tangible presence with me. My heart felt heavier than concrete in my chest. I was so disappointed and I felt confused. I must have been wrong when thinking that friendship was somehow being rebuilt. How could I have been so naive as to think we were making real steps towards a future together? The depth of the bitterness that had taken root in Nick's life and the fact that it exposed itself to be as strong as ever was traumatising. I felt the need to withdraw and followed the inclination to keep some distance between us.

The boys continued to see Nick, and Sam was beginning to initiate their arrangements thus providing me a measure of relief. A month later laryngitis still had a grip and I was bracing myself for the wrench of Nathan leaving home. I wrote in my journal,

> *I choose by FAITH to believe that you are at work but there is no evidence we are any nearer healing and release. I feel troubled knowing that on the money front things are slipping again for Nick (car insurance, etc.) but it is out of my control, even beyond any influence. Feeling so heavy-hearted BUT nothing said or done alters your word to me from Amos.*

I was troubled that the old signs were reappearing. I worried about the boys going in a vehicle that wasn't legal but so much of Nick's life seemed out of control and we had always viewed things like car tax and payment deadlines differently. As an act of will I chose to trust God each time the boys were with him. The alternative was to drive myself mad with anxiety.

In the weeks leading up to the new term at Bedales I was struggling with the whole idea of letting Nathan go, at only thirteen. He was entering a culture completely different to home and would be there for more weeks of the year than with family. Boarding school. I knew God had made the way and I didn't doubt he intended it for good in Nathan's life but that didn't immunise me against the wrench of loss. I frequently revisited the picture God had given me in worship and watched in my mind's eye as Nathan moved forward into a place of healing and wild freedom without a glance back in my direction. As we said goodbye in his dorm a couple of weeks later, I knew there was no going back and reminded myself again that Nathan was God's son before he was ever entrusted to me.

In spite of knowing God intended it all for good in Nathan's life I went home and abandoned myself to the lure of comfort eating. Waitrose trebled their sales of Boasters and I began to resemble a mound of chocolate chips. I was distressed about how Sam would fare being an 'only child' all week but couldn't seem to find a way of discussing it with him at any meaningful level. We both tend to process internally and find expressing our deepest emotions difficult. He liked to have any information about a situation made available and then to digest it over a few days before he ventured any comment. I explained that Grandpa had made it clear that his offer of funding was equally available for him. Sam was up to his neck in GCSE coursework at this time and couldn't conceive of initiating change that would separate him from his established friendship group. We knew his school didn't have a sixth form so a move was imminent but he had been thinking he would take the bus to college with his peers. He missed Nathan.

Six weeks after Nathan started at the school I bumped into the head as I collected Nathan one Saturday. She smiled warmly and said what a change they had noticed in my son.

'He is a different boy to the one who arrived here and has settled in very well.'

She spoke with obvious pleasure and Nathan was indeed happy. It seemed clear he'd made a right decision.

I could still only croak and by now was fighting the fear of something serious growing in my throat. Some rather unpleasant investigations involving plastic tubes and big swallows proved that my vocal chords, whilst having nothing 'growing on them', had become slack. I was informed they required complete rest in order to regain the elasticity needed for speech. I missed being able to sing and felt strangely isolated being with people who talked normally but not being able to join in and chat. I was mystified by how long it was lasting and, though I can't quantify it, I remain convinced that it was considerably more than a resistant sore throat bug that lingered. I felt as though something in my body had just ground to a halt on that summer night. The emotional turbulence appeared to have provoked a silent protest over which I had no control.

My parents suggested a few days away in the mountains and I gratefully accepted. The chalet, being on a mountainside in the Alps, had breathtaking views. I loved the sense of space and to be able to walk among the sheep and goats that wandered the pastures around the chalet. In the past I had found it to be a place of healing where I sensed God reaching into my heart and reminding me how much he loved me all over again. To sit in bed with tea, my Bible and journal with no time pressure was delicious.

Previously on a number of occasions when I had felt let down or hurt by Nick I had been tempted to 'draw stumps' and give up. Every time this had happened so far I had felt God speak to me from a verse in the book of Corinthians. This verse would 'happen' to be in my daily reading or be mentioned in church at a time when I was wondering if I could any longer believe the best. It comes in 2 Corinthians 2:6–7 just after Paul teaches about how the sin of one person affects everyone in the church family and he writes,

The punishment inflicted on him by the majority is sufficient for him. Now instead, you ought to

> *forgive and comfort him, so that he will not be overwhelmed by excessive sorrow.*

He goes on in verse 8,

> *I urge you, therefore, to reaffirm your love for him.*

This seemed crystal clear and I had taken all kinds of decisions and extended invitations to Nick on the basis of this instruction. I badly wanted to do the right thing and continued to care deeply about what was happening to him. There are several Bible passages where it talks about God testing what is in people's hearts. I didn't want to fail any test. Stories of Job's testing and a verse about the children of Israel when they fled from slavery in Egypt were familiar. It says God took them the long way around to test what was in their hearts, which had made a lasting impression upon me. I perceived there was a clear precedent for sticking with the programme and I was longing that God would use me for blessing despite everything. I didn't feel God was behind me with a big stick but I didn't understand then what I now cherish as his total acceptance of me, just as I am. Maybe subconsciously I felt that in some measure the desired outcome of restoration depended on my ability to hear God and do what he said.

The Sunday before I left for the chalet a lady had been sharing in church. She was bringing an encouraging word from Job 14 about a dead tree sprouting again. However, at the end of a week when I was crying to God to show me the next step in my reaching out to

Nick, it was the verse above that caught my attention. Verse 6 says, 'So look away from him and let him alone, till he has put in his time like a hired man.'

Several times I thought I had clear indication from God about time frame. I really believed that the year of the millennium was to have jubilee significance for us as a couple, particularly around the theme of liberation. In the Old Testament it talks about captives being set free and I believed God highlighted specific times and dates that would herald permanent change. Since they have all been and gone I won't list them here. I prayed, asking God to empower me to obey this word and I wrote,

How is it possible to still miss Nick and find the pain of longing for his happiness and freedom piercing each day? Each special trip and lovely experience seems somehow lacking... I yield again to your purpose, Lord, and pray you may accomplish all you intend in the pain.

The outworking of this obedience was the loss of what remained of 'joint parenting' as I stopped chasing and engineering Nick's involvement. I encouraged the boys to ring him and maintain whatever level of contact they wanted. Tensions arose as Nathan flourished in his new world and didn't want to spend every precious weekend with a depressed, increasingly distant parent. This put a terrible strain on Sam who continued to feel a level of responsibility for his unhappy hero. It was hard for him to be with Nick alone. He felt protective of Nick and cross with Nathan. It was excruciating for me as I felt powerless to resolve either issue and could not intercept the behaviours that were causing pain to both sons.

Towards the end of the week in the chalet I was encouraged by my daily reading from *Streams in the Desert* and copied it into my journal,

Difficulty is the very atmosphere of miracle... if it is to be a great miracle, the condition is not difficulty but impossibility.

She was commenting on a situation in the Bible where God brought much needed deliverance but only at the last minute, when it looked totally impossible. Returning home nothing on the surface was changed. I had to keep seeing Nick each week as he collected Sam. But in obedience to the 'let him alone' word, I deliberately withdrew. I avoided any conversation apart from polite greetings and I stopped looking for opportunities to include Nick. I didn't call him or write; no contact except the essential communication around him seeing Sam and Nathan.

I was encouraged as friends prayed for me. More than one shared the verse from Jeremiah 29:11(ESV) where God says,

I know the plans I have for you...plans for welfare and not for evil, to give you a future and a hope.

I continued to wrestle with how this misery could actually be his plan, this life that was unrecognisable from the happy family scenario that I had signed up for. But I was thankful for his whispers of love as I tried to continue reading and praying. My vocal chords had not recovered and a long-awaited hospital appointment with a specialist came up on the calendar.

The fateful conversation was now four months behind me. Not fond of hospitals and never comfortable in the role of patient, I found just the idea of the appointment stressful. I got myself to the right room on the correct day at the appropriate time but it became crystal clear to me that I hadn't read the small print. The female behind the desk rose, shook my hand, indicated a rather low, soft chair and then joined me on the wrong side of the desk. Alarm bells rang as her body language indicated she was attempting to put me at my ease. I registered the absence of tubes and torches and knew a fleeting longing for the familiar. I was jolted back into the present by the word 'divorce'. This uttered with a reverence that only a professional, preoccupied with the inner workings of a distressed mind and possibly nervous about the reception of their ideas, could muster. She appeared to me to have an unhealthy focus on the common need for counselling after divorce.

'Do you understand about the phases of grief?'

A gravelled intonation, accompanied by a leaning in of one shoulder and faint waftings of garlic.

'Talk to me about that time in July when you first lost your voice. How were things in your life?'

Exercising great self-control I swallowed the retort 'how long have you got?' that wriggled at the back of my throat. Instead I blessed her with my serene gaze; that would be the one intended to communicate an intelligent, impartial appraising of calm, rational inner thoughts. I thrashed around internally. Memories bumped into feelings. Words stung. Emotions swirled threatening to suck me back into the deep well of injustice. She waited.

We had been apart for over five years at this point and divorced for more than three of those. I was trusting God for healing, had a vision for my future and had known God whispering along the way. He'd given me dreams for other people and the courage to share them. I'd overcome my fear of snakes and thanks to my now dog-eared copy of *Suzie's Babies,* successfully navigated the treacherous landscape of puberty – twice. I did not need to talk about my feelings. She went on waiting until my determination not to open up caused so much internal pressure that I had an undignified coughing fit complete with runny nose and watery eyes. She spoke.

'The memory is making you cry? Have a tissue.'

I decided that by carefully choosing how much I said, I could abseil rather than freefall over the precipice of 'openness' yawning in front of me. I haltingly described the conversation that had triggered so much painful tension. In my heart I had wondered if it was possible I had been so deeply impacted emotionally by the words and atmosphere that night that it had had a physiological effect.

As the psychologist listened her eyebrows gently moved higher, encouraging me to continue. She didn't speak but now, leaning back, created a feeling of spaciousness between us, which the enormity of my feelings quickly filled. I felt thoroughly confused.

How in the world could deep-seated tension, relating to the divorce that was several years ago, be affecting my larynx now? 'Cope' was my middle name and I was baptised in a Brethren chapel. I had the ability to laugh at myself, could get a camp fire going single handed and the Holy Spirit had once given me a message for my Korean hairdresser, in her own language, so…Deep Inner Tension? I don't think so.

'You've probably had to be very strong for your boys?' she ventured.

No comment. Since I sat voiceless, apart from the rasping croak I could force out, unable to sing, all conversation a huge effort, I deemed none was needed. I couldn't even begin to talk about Nathan's struggle, Sam's pain and the end result of more loss as first one, then possibly the other, considered boarding school. I don't remember how the time concluded but I must have ticked some boxes as I had no further appointments. Strangely, a few days later my journal entry read,

> *I feel as though something I had stored up over years is seeping away, the plug is pulled – I can't face being with Nick and yet each week he must come. I feel isolated but if there were someone how would I talk about it all? Are you saying I need counselling? Please unfold the way, Lord. Should I see BS?*

I have no recollection of who BS was or is so presume I didn't feel the need to pursue that thought. However, just a week further on I wrote,

> *Life slowly moving on. I feel much better. Talked with A and he prayed – prayed along the lines of breaking any curse in the accusation spoken over me and slowly my voice is returning.*

In the last weeks before Christmas I let the boys set the pace for how and when they saw Nick. The young man who instructed Nathan's riding group at a local stud was made homeless and we had some good chats about God having a purpose for him. He had come with us to Stoneleigh the previous year so knew how we did life. He came to live with us whilst searching for a new place. Sam was processing my father's offer of funding for the sixth form if he would like to join Nathan at Bedales. One evening, when I had said goodnight and thought Sam had settled, he arrived beside my bed. Snuggling in he said, 'I don't feel really peaceful about deciding to go to Bedales, Mum, but can't feel peaceful about not taking the opportunity either.'

We chatted and it was clear to me that the subtext was about me, and his feelings having seen me struggle to release Nathan. I had tried very hard. All the books stress how important it is that children are not 'leaned on'. Particularly that they are not expected to fill the gap when dad leaves; the gap that is both mental and physical. I had made an effort to say outright to the boys that their father living elsewhere had nothing to do with them. I had emphasised that their behaviour had not influenced events in any way. I didn't want them to have any false sense of responsibility. I feel cross when adults who are moving on to pastures new as a result of marital breakdown, shrug and state authoritatively, 'Children are so adaptable and they are not really affected by us separating.' Extensive research demonstrates that second only to the death of a parent, divorce is hugely significant in the life of any child.

It became clear to me that Sam's underlying anxiety about abandoning me was holding him back from being able to make the decision to accept what would be a great opportunity for him. We chatted on and I gently encouraged him that if he felt there could be anything good in it for him he should jump. It would mean making new friends because his peers would go to the sixth form college a forty-minute bus ride away and that was big for Sam. Eventually he took a deep breath and looked at me, 'I think I'll do it, Mum; I think it's the right thing for me.'

We hugged.

'I don't think you'll regret it, darling, and you won't be very far away.'

I bit my lip as he pottered happily back across the landing.

18

Undignified Sacrifice

With my voice still far from normal another Christmas loomed. Festive seasons remain difficult, a shadow cast, to this day. Even walking through it all with God, receiving healing and faith for the journey, still public holidays and anniversaries are tinged. There is a sore place inside. I feel surrounded by happy families and loving couples who are blissfully celebrating with joy and abandon. I know this isn't 'truth' and I am well aware that many people have great struggles and sadness but it is no comfort. It probably should be and I know it doesn't sound terribly 'spirit filled' to admit it but I have to repel more than a niggle of failure when I reflect on my own happy childhood memories. All the amazing little rituals that made Christmas and Easter so special were woven into the fabric of my life, giving a profound measure of security. They make stark contrast with the barren landscape of my own thwarted efforts. How hideous for children to find joyous festivals such as Christmas and Easter become emotional hurdles that must somehow be managed. Divorce is so much more than just the death of a marriage. I decided to be brave. Brave as I had to handle the reaction of others, brave to go to a completely new environment and bravely I summoned the courage to enthuse the boys that this was indeed a great idea. The idea? Snow.

Rereading this first paragraph my need for bravery is conspicuous against the backdrop of the festive season. Decorations, bells, tree lights, carols and mulled wine each carried the sting of unfulfilled 'comfort and joy'. I recall the energy it took to plan anything remotely festive. The trip was vividly more about avoiding the pain of Christmas in familiar surroundings than an adventurous desire for fun. I was propelled by the determination to avoid painful memories – and Nick. Wanting to make it special for Sam and Nathan motivated me but bravery was necessary to disguise my own craving. I yearned to curl up under the duvet and not emerge until spring.

Christmas Eve found us settling into the Hotel Alpenblick surrounded by snow. Snow and other Christians. A Christian holiday company offered family ski trips with gatherings in the evening an option. I felt safe taking the boys by myself even though the skiing was challenging and their father, who was always larger than life on the slopes, absent. The atmosphere was friendly. I packed a little tree and a few decorations to try and make our room feel festive. I felt pretty hollow inside but could only give it my best. Sam had flu symptoms by day three and we spent a day in our room together. I felt a long way from home though strangely relieved to be away from the familiar rituals reminiscent of security, jolly celebration and happy family life. My parents must have thought it was an odd thing to do but they loved me through it and never criticised. At the time it never crossed my muddled mind that I could be diminishing their Christmas. All I knew was that I would not have to see Nick or navigate the waters of whose turn it was to have the boys on which day and I was grateful.

We arrived home in time to see in the New Year with Heather and Steve. I lit the remaining candle of the three I had lit in Russell Way and continued to feel that God intended a change at the end of our third year in Petersfield. Praying and mulling over the year ahead I realised how different life would look by next year. Sam would have completed his first term at Bedales; as a household we could be on the move and maybe Nick would be enjoying his relationship with God again? Looking back over the previous year and particularly through the word to 'let him alone', I could see that drawing back from emotional connection meant I was in a greater place of freedom.

I still had faith that God could and wanted to do a restoration miracle but as months passed I was able to acknowledge that it may be much further into the future. I was finding it possible to make plans and decisions without the filter of an imminent future with Nick. Sorting my room at the beginning of January, I found my birthday cards from the previous November. Nick had written lovingly in his:

Thinking of you now and always. Missing your friendship and love more than I can say. Loving you from far away xx

Surely we would share life again?

I also came across a page from a daily reading book that Sue had posted to me. The page was headed 'He led them on in safety' and one of the scriptures quoted was from Exodus 23:20 (NKJV):

Behold, I send an angel before you to keep you in the way and to bring you into the place which I have prepared.

I stuck this promise in the front of my new journal and took great comfort from it. I was not alone and God had something prepared for my future, something personal to me, something good. Faith believes in what we do not see. I continued to be obedient to the 'let him alone' word interpreting it in the context of emotional engagement with Nick. I made sure we spent no time alone together and left no opening for the painful, high-octane conversations about Nick's feelings and circumstances. My life was on a more even keel and I was thankful to God. I felt that to continue inviting Nick to join the family for the occasional Sunday lunch, birthdays and holidays could only create opportunities for him to experience love. Detachment is much easier in a group context. He had cut himself off from all Christian contact, and anger was always just beneath the surface. Nick appeared to be moved, softer and sometimes teary when collecting or dropping the boys but I was careful not to press in or inquire about his life, choosing to believe God was working in a hidden place.

On the church front in Petersfield there were leadership changes, which seemed positive. I often felt uncomfortable, sensing people were keeping me at arm's length. I felt like the odd one out but God reminded me that he was working through me as a catalyst. Being an agent for change doesn't mean lots of people want you as their best friend. I continued to pray about the possibility of a property being released back in Sussex. I dreamed of my rural cottage and had continued to call the estate office about twice a year because I felt so strongly that God had been in my conversation with the landowner. The countryside on the east side of the A24 is stunning. I was sure I could be happy there and, besides, if reconciliation were on the agenda how perfect it would be. The estate secretary was kindness itself but there was never any good news. I felt queasy before each phone call but I continued to trust God for the perfect timing. I knew that families had the option to remain after the death of an original tenant, so things would happen when they happened. I still believed that God could bring restoration to the church we had been committed to and heal relationships. How incredible it would be to see him fulfil long-ago promises, of impacting the region through a group of churches united in their vision to see God's life spilling out all over the county.

'The problem of getting things from God is being able to hold on for the last half hour.' So wrote Mrs Cowman. I was reading it nine years after the day we had renewed our marriage vows. That day when I had experienced hope that was quickly suffocated by disappointment. I've heard it said on several occasions that 'it is always darkest before dawn'. I consistently determined not to visit the list of times I had felt myself to be poised and ready for a full-on sunrise with surround-sound dawn chorus. Honestly, by now I could hardly count the deadlines that I thought I had sensed were from God. They had all been and gone swiftly on their way without delivering. There was a pull in my spirit to agree with the facts and accept there was no tangible indication that reconciliation was on the way. But then I would read about Joseph who had years waiting in prison before his dreams were realised, or Moses who was hidden away in the desert tending sheep as God prepared him to fulfil his vocation as deliverer of the slaves. It was clear God's purposes often involved prolonged periods of waiting. I was aware I needed every ounce of spiritual energy to keep my heart free; free from resentment and the sickness of deferred hope. I deliberately offered my feelings to God often praying familiar lines from the Lord's Prayer, 'Thy kingdom come, Thy will be done . . .' The longing for restoration didn't diminish but the depleting, painful sadness was easing. A genuine hope for each new day increasingly overshadowed the dragging disappointment of the past as I chose to look ahead deliberately trusting God to take care of Nick.

During this year I became more profoundly aware of the agony of God designing us with free will. It was clear to me that even if God answered my prayers and caused circumstances to bring Nick to a place of healing, where he could experience the reality of forgiveness and enjoy divine love in a more tangible way, God was never going to force the issue. God had put another picture of Nick in my mind when I was praying a couple of years previously. In the picture Nick had a suitcase attached to his ankle. The case was on a chain with a heavy cuff which had a lock. Now, God showed me the same picture but the cuff was unlocked. It seemed Nick was reluctant to bend down and just lift the cuff off because dragging the heavy case had become normal for him. I shared this picture by writing in a card and encouraged Nick to believe that there was reason to hope, that he had a future and it's in the Bible that God doesn't change his mind about people. I really struggled with the impression that Nick had no energy or inclination to make a change. By now he had been prayed for countless times at meetings to which I had invited him. He had asked several leaders in the area to pray for him but nothing seemed to bring what he was hoping for. I am not sure what that even was. I don't know if Nick did either. He still wore his wedding ring.

Feeling my very life depended on listening and being obedient to the voice of the Holy Spirit I was ruthless with myself. This led to some unusual things. Probably the weirdest was the time I felt, through my reading of Jesus washing the disciples' feet and the story of the woman who wept at Jesus' feet, that I should offer to wash Nick's feet. I thought it was probably just a wild idea triggered by the story but the impression grew stronger over weeks. In light of the decision to keep my distance I pondered how I could do it without connecting.

Eventually I decided I could obey the prompting if I was careful to just be gently clinical and not drawn into emotional communication. I decided to wait, pray and not rush anything. If it were a God idea he would unfold something. I know it sounds unlikely but if I'm writing my story it doesn't seem quite honest to leave out the parts that risk confirming any suspicion the reader may already have about there being a kangaroo loose in the top paddock!

It happened to be the weekend three years after that Sunday morning when I had first visited Petersfield. Nick unexpectedly asked me if I would like to go out for a drink. I had been praying and waiting, asking God about how keeping my distance tallied with foot hygiene. This specific invitation from Nick felt significant and, with the whole foot-washing thing on my mind, I accepted. I was trusting God was initiating this short time alone together for a purpose. I fasted and prayed the day before, asking God to keep me within his purpose for any conversation. Nick was completely unaware as I hopped into the car, that neatly in my bag lay a folded towel, a bottle of water and soap. Toads were milling about in my stomach as we set off. The prospect of physical contact, even if it was only his feet, was huge. It was a slightly chilly evening but when offered the choice of inside or the pub garden I opted for the latter and felt deeply relieved to find we were alone.

'Hazel, last year at Stoneleigh, did I offend you in some way?'

His question caught me completely off guard but when I quietly said I didn't feel able to talk about Stoneleigh, he didn't pursue it, moving on to other topics. The lurch in my stomach warned me it was far too soon to revisit a conversation that had been damaging.

If Nick hadn't come to the realisation that accusing me of being unfaithful had been deeply wounding I was not about to lift the scab risking a poke. He said he was considering moving into a flat, which sounded hopeful to me as it could be a fresh start for him and also give a base for him to have the boys. (I was very disappointed when later he didn't, renting instead a static caravan in the garden of a family who had used it whilst they renovated their home.) Next, the drum that Nick had been beating for years, 'The thing is I still love you, Hazel, I don't want to face life without you.'

But he never followed up with the question, 'Will you consider a relationship?' or 'Do you feel able to work on building a future together?' I had long since learned to listen and knew that this was not actually a conversation but just him making statements about his own feelings.

I tried to concentrate on conversation but the burning need to bring up the suggestion I had on my mind was paramount. I mentally communed with my Maker.

'It's okay, Lord, if you just let me know I can drop the whole idea, I will. But if you don't release me from the feeling I should offer, I'll go ahead. I'm happy, really happy to just give it a miss; maybe it was just a test? You know I want you to use me. Is this going to bless Nick?'

I continued to feel on the brink of a step of faith. I had that deep churning that starts in the pit of my stomach and travels slowly up to my voice box, causing various areas of my anatomy to become exceedingly clammy en route, where it swells until suddenly I speak or sing or read the thing that I sense the Holy Spirit prompting.

As Nick unsuspectingly sipped his drink, I took a deep breath.

'Nick?'

'Mmm?'

'I want to ask you something but it may sound a bit odd.' (Mistress of understatement eat your heart out!)

'Yes?' Nick was immediately yanked from his state of mental roaming into the present.

He was probably thinking something along the lines of, 'Uh-oh, now what? I should've known a quiet drink was too much to hope for.'

'It's just that I've been reading in John recently, you know, about where they get their feet washed?'

It all came out in a bit of a rush,

'Well, I want to say how sorry I am for where the process of divorce has hurt you. It was never my intention to cause you pain. I hope you can forgive me and . . .'

I was very thankful for the gathering dusk and hoping like mad that nobody was thinking of stepping out of the pub for a smoke. It was true. Whilst I didn't feel Nick's pain was my fault I at no stage wished to deliberately harm him through the divorce proceedings; once the ball was rolling I had just followed the steps shown me but I sometimes wondered if Nick had convinced himself I malevolently intended to wreck his future. I gulped for air and made myself slow down.

'May I wash your feet?'

With our combined impressions, mine of a dying goldfish and his stunned mullet, we must have looked as if we were on day release from somewhere. Then into the quiet Nick said, 'If you want to.'

I slithered off my chair onto the damp grass knowing the mounds of jelly that were once my legs definitely would not support me. Abandoning all attempts to appear anything akin to normal I unpacked the bowl (empty ice cream tub), laid the towel on the ground, poured some water and picked up the soap. Then realising there were shoes with laces to be navigated and then socks (help) I put the soap down and began to tackle the laces. I'm sure Nick will have said 'let me do that' or something similar but I felt that somehow this was part of a humbling process for me and I gently insisted.

I don't know exactly why or what, if anything, this act achieved. I know that the sense of dignity lost in obedience was liberating once I got over myself. Faith in this instance meant doing something just because I believed God was asking it. I didn't want to renege on my 'Yes' decision from when God drew me into the centre of the river of his spirit. Maybe it was to do with learning not to be inhibited by the thoughts and perceptions of onlookers.

I peeled off Nick's socks one by one. Mercifully I wasn't overtaken by a wave of attraction and didn't feel the urge to kiss or play with his feet but was able to quietly and deliberately soap, rinse and dry each one. I worked without speaking, silently praying that God would be present and trusting him that there was a purpose. Finishing the drying, I said once more that I was sorry for where my actions had hurt him. (This wasn't prompted by anything more than my earnest desire for peace between us and longing for Nick to understand that if there had been another option I would not have sued for divorce.) A wave of relief carried me back into my chair as I let Nick put his own socks and shoes back on. I exhaled silently feeling 'job done'. I can't remember what, if anything, we spoke of on the journey home and the evening's events have never been mentioned. If I hadn't recorded it in my journal at the time I would think it had been a dream. It only occurred to me recently to wonder what Nick was thinking, whether he contemplated refusing or thought he'd better go along with it, since crossing a person who was so clearly losing the plot had potential for a very unhappy ending, or what?

I've never felt prompted to wash another's feet in this manner before or since. I'd love to say this episode triggered amazing things, healing was released and incredible restoration occurred but the truth is I have no idea about any impact on earth. There is certainly a biblical precedent for loss of dignity, such as when David let it all hang out in dance before the Ark of the Lord. It could have been worse; I may have heard God ask me to perform foot-washing whilst lying on my side wearing only a loin cloth like one of the Old Testament prophets we read of. All I know is there is a process of humbling ourselves that frees us to care less about our reputation and more about obedience. I think it's about willingness to be seen as foolish. Years ago I felt God spoke to me clearly about attending a local country fair wearing a sandwich board with the text 'Jesus said, I am the way the truth and the life' emblazoned on it. I felt ill, daft and oh so conspicuous doing it but afterwards I sensed God's pleasure and approval. I know that I was obedient in humbling myself. Now, whilst not feeling responsible for it, I genuinely felt sorrow for the pain and wounding Nick had sustained. Anything that may've been accomplished on heaven's agenda has yet to be revealed.

I often sit on a train thinking, 'All these people who don't know you love them, Lord.' This is always followed by a heartfelt prayer of thanks that I don't feel prompted to stand and startle non-plussed commuters by proclaiming loudly that Jesus died to save them from their sins. However, the small lessons I am learning have meant that I do indeed care more about pleasing God than what the man next to me may possibly think.

Recently a businessman sat across the aisle from me on the 10.05 to Waterloo. (For anyone whose heart rate has gone up, since my name is not Agatha and this story is true, there are no dead bodies featured.) As I watched him, head bowed in his hands, I wondered if he was praying and immediately saw a picture of a large road junction, a Y with two clear choices of direction. It wasn't literally in a speech bubble above his bowed head but flashed across my other thoughts. I felt this man had an important decision to make and God wanted me to tell him that he, God, loved him. Then God wanted me to say that he was to be reassured and have confidence because he was facing a big decision and he was going to make the right choice.

How easy it is to be inhibited by the fear of what another may think of us. Even when we sense the Almighty himself at work. I think overcoming what is known as 'fear of man' is the essence of the whole losing dignity, being willing to look foolish thing, on God's agenda. By determinedly clutching the belief that how we appear to others is of any consequence in the scheme of the culture of heaven coming to earth, perhaps we risk missing a whole chunk of spiritual growth. I know I still have a way to go because I sat under the weight of these impressions toing and froing mentally.

The sudden damp, prickly sensation behind my knees intensified as I realised I had a choice. I could deliver the message immediately, whilst we travelled alone in our area of the carriage, or risk a cluster of passengers joining us at the next station and then have to deliver the message with an audience. I hastily leaned over.

'Errm, I'm a Christian.'

First major hurdle over. My shoulders drop two centimetres. He raises his head. Are his eyes watering? Is God already touching him?

'I think God may have a message for you. Would you like to hear it?'

This offer is hastily followed by a profuse reassurance that this means I would tell him something but that if it bore no relevance to him, his work or any part of his current life experience he should just ignore it and carry on with his day. He nods and I take this as an invitation.

'Firstly God wants you to know that he loves you and he understands you have a difficult choice ahead.'

I describe the picture of the fork in the road. He nods dumbly.

'God wants me to tell you to be encouraged and that you will make the right decision.'

Then, in a bit of a rush as we slow for the next station, 'And don't worry if this means nothing to you. Just forget about it. Thank you for listening.'

I slump thankfully back into my seat and make every appearance of calmly continuing to read my book until I register it is upside down and, with an awkward sideways glance across the aisle, furtively correct the angle under cover of reaching for my handbag. Just as my heart rate is beginning to settle and the glow of the Father's pleasure stealing into my limbs, the man rises. The two middle-aged ladies who are now ensconced opposite him are stunned into goggle-eyed silence as he leans over me clutching his brief case.

'Can we talk? Is it alright if I join you?'

Two pairs of arched eyebrows above pursed lips indicate our travelling companions are thoroughly unimpressed to be witnessing a blatant, casual 'pick up' but sensing genuine distress in the gentleman I resist the urge to frighten them by asking brightly if they have heard of Match.com. Such is their consternation they huffily gather their bags and coffees and move away from us.

As he slid into the opposite seat at my table the gentleman introduced himself. I'll call him Douglas. Before saying anything else Douglas began weeping, quite noisily. Out came the whole story of his terrible dilemma. A previous liaison ended long ago had come to haunt him through a work connection. Ongoing deception or coming clean with his much-loved wife of many years faced him. We talked. I listened mainly but the overriding thing was that God demonstrated how much he loved this man by causing me to be right there on the train to encourage and care. I prayed regularly for Douglas over the following months but have never seen him again.

As the weeks passed I kept thinking of Nick's question about the Stoneleigh conversation but knew it wouldn't help to have a discussion because, by asking, he demonstrated that he was totally ignorant of the impact of his accusations. From time to time, since we had been apart, I wrote letters when I felt I had expressed something badly or perhaps said things in the heat of emotion that warranted further explanation. Expressing myself on paper when I could order my thoughts and had my feelings in check meant that Nick could mull and digest what I wrote and was free to respond in his own time. Could this possibly be a time when he really wanted to understand? I felt too vulnerable to take the risk of a conversation bringing it all up again. Instead, on Sam's sixteenth birthday, I sent this letter.

Dear Nick,

I have been wondering whether to write since we went out that evening. You mentioned Stoneleigh last year. Perhaps you do want to understand. A particular conversation when you became very angry left me saddened beyond words. I don't want to relive any of it but perhaps these snippets from my journal over the ensuing weeks will make it clear.

"Tough time since Stoneleigh. Harsh words exchanged with Nick as he expressed his feelings and I realised I am unforgiven and don't quite know how that affects me – I feel somehow 'under' that. I don't feel guilty of what he accuses me but so heavy hearted, so disappointed…I thought that somehow friendship was being rebuilt: naive and wrong, obviously.

I feel the need to withdraw from Nick; quieted inside since his accusations…numbness towards him. I can see bitterness/unforgiveness has to rear its ugly head somewhere and I feel that's what happened but how can we play friendship anymore?

. . . so painful, Lord, I haven't been able to write for several weeks, so hard, will the letting go ever end?"

You made it so clear, Nick, that you believe yourself to have been utterly betrayed by me and you said you would never forgive me. I have come to terms with that and realise you could not possibly want a friendship based on distrust, bitterness and unforgiveness. Misguidedly I had thought something gentle but positive had been happening. I was wrong. I accept how you see me, and the initial emotional devastation has abated. You have chosen to live with your suitcase so I can only acknowledge that friendship – a relationship based on trust and mutual respect – is withheld from me.

I am glad for all kindly loving contact with our sons. I think I may always ache for what might have been; I remain, especially on this significant day, grateful you are the father of my children and I pray you may discover somehow, someday, the vision you long for,

Hazel

That week I wrote about the letter in my journal,

I think this brings closure emotionally on that agonising and shocking day when accusation destroyed what small hope remained. I can't imagine what he will think or feel. Mighty God, please help him find peace and wholeness... a purpose to life again. Seems it may be significant that Nick moves at this time but then... it has seemed so to me in my optimism on countless occasions.

Nick phoned when he received the letter, saying he was grateful I had written. He sounded appreciative, not cross or affronted. He said he thought I wouldn't want to discuss it over the phone but that he would be replying as he would like to 'respond to one or two of the points you've made'. He hadn't responded to any of my letters and I was sad that this time proved no exception. It may seem a small thing but coming in the wake of years of broken promises just one letter would have been indicative of a change of heart. Words trip so easily off the tongue.

By the middle of the year Sam was finishing his exams and I had taken the step of changing the car. I took heart from the lessons learned with buying the caravan and was more relaxed about the process. I loved the fact that Steve and Heather were more engaged with my church and for a season Steve led worship and made a considerable contribution, in both a prophetic and pastoral context, amongst the leaders. They were hopeful months and as a church it felt as if we were growing together more. I was asked to take on various responsibilities but each time I prayed and felt just to continue with the individuals I was praying with each week, encouraging them to grow in their faith.

Always at the back of my mind was the sense that God had brought me to the church for a three-year period and also that as the year 2000 arrived I was to lay down any ministry. In my thinking that was to do with needing to be available for the possibility of rebuilding a relationship and the belief that when God did move, to sit in the pew together would be far more constructive than me having a role in any overt sense. I still don't know if that was just me weaving a web in order to have hope to press forward. Or was it another missed opportunity, when God created a space and time for Nick to choose to step out of the horrendous consequences of wrong choices and into life.

19

The Cloud Moves

As the summer unfolded the prospect of Sam leaving home to board at Bedales, whilst I knew it was a great opportunity for him, clouded my days. Also I began seriously wondering if anybody anywhere on the planet had really 'got it' in so far as doing church was concerned. I journaled,

Church… good positive things happening yet I feel fundamentally disappointed – is the point that we learn all kinds of lessons trying to do/be church but realisation is meant only for the next life? Three years will soon be up and you have accomplished what you intended for us here… what next then, Lord? Let patience have her perfect work? Not many options. The build-up > Bedales is enough to cope with.

I still wonder if we will arrive in God's presence to find him standing, arms folded, tapping one foot and gently shaking his head. In my imagination I hear him say something along the lines of 'Oooh guys, what about church? You just never really got it, did you?'

Each time I go to a large Christian event, at some point in the proceedings I catch myself thinking about how there are so many thousands of Christians on the planet, well, millions and still the world seems fundamentally unchanged. How did twelve largely 'uneducated' men impact the course of history? What are we missing? It doesn't stop me feeling passionate about sharing life with God's people and longing for heaven to impact the relationships and communities I am part of. I know Jesus is returning one day for his church but what *exactly* is he hoping his bride will look like? At thirty years old I had most of the answers. Now, twenty-three years later, I have many more questions than answers. Is that normal?

In my own family I had attempted to be strong about the boys attending church till they were eighteen when they would be free to make their own choices about the way they wanted to do life. I felt a deep sense of failure and even shame as during this season they both decided that church was not where they wanted to be when they were home on a Sunday morning. I chose peaceful relationship over the routine I longed for and accepted their decisions. Sam was disappointed and angry as the youth group had been disbanded when leaders had moved away leaving his group in a vacuum. Nathan was finding the gap between school and home life meant church was less and less relevant. I had modelled my intentions on families that had strong loving fathers and felt an acute sense of lack as my good intentions came to naught.

I was very aware that Saturdays with Nick still had great potential for turbulence. Both boys resisted criticising Nick but it was clear that being with him left them struggling. I was anxious about the conflict between the example and attitudes we were cultivating in our home and the undercurrent of anger in Nick's life. Church was not giving the boys answers. It certainly wasn't bringing their parents back together.

In his book *The Art of Horsemanship* Xenophon writes,

> **For what a horse does under constraint...he does without understanding. Under such treatment horse and man alike will do much more that is ugly than graceful.**

He is referring to the riders at the Cadre Noir. This is the French National Horse Riding School where, working in perfect harmony, horse and rider demonstrate astonishing agility and balance. I think perhaps if only I could have held the reins loosely; trusted more.

Reflecting, my motives were driven by fear. I feared the boys sliding away from God and missing the happiness of fulfilling their potential. I feared others judging my influence as a mother and dreaded my sons becoming statistics. In a season when it was increasingly acknowledged that church needed to be more relevant for teenagers, I didn't want my sons to be among those who drifted away. The contrast between fear, with the negative, driven momentum it creates, and trusting in the 'perfect love' of God, which the Bible states categorically drives out fear, is much clearer to me now. Just like holding a pip between finger and thumb; if you squeeze too tightly the pip pings across the room. The revelation that in every situation I operate from fear or love came years later.

I tried to demonstrate respect for the boy's choices, knowing God was more able than me to meet their needs. Nathan had said he would like to be baptised in a service that was coming up. He was keen for Andrew, who continued to offer friendship and support and had in effect pastored Nathan since birth, to do the baptising but sadly the leadership at church didn't agree. The then leader was adamant that, even though he had no relationship with Nathan, he as 'the leader' should officiate. Confused, Nathan dropped the idea.

I had to manage my own emotions and struggled with feeling let down. It was another rejection and triggered emotions totally in conflict with those supposed to be a hallmark of God's family. I worked on keeping my attitude right but wonder what was so important to this man that he couldn't see past his own 'ministry' and endorse Nathan's decision. I looked into other possible options but the moment had passed.

What would have been a significant wedding anniversary came round and I received a tearful phone call from Nick saying he was aware of the date. I was also increasingly aware of the months passing and continued to sense things coming gently to an end for me in Petersfield. I knew a great sense of completion and peace as several friends were growing and being encouraged in their faith. John and Penny had been in the church since its conception and had held fast through all the storms. We continued to share meals and prayer times regularly and their faith, good humour and wonderfully inclusive spirit were a constant blessing.

I decided to share my thoughts about God's timing with Pen. I was apprehensive of her reaction if I spoke of moving away. We spent much time together. As it turned out I was blessed and encouraged by her gracious response, even expressing excitement about what God may have in store. She shared a great promise from Psalm 32:8:

> *I will instruct you and teach you in the way you should go; I will counsel you and watch over you.*

I was further encouraged on a Sunday morning when one of the leaders said he felt God was speaking to him about my life. 'A season is ending and a new season is beginning,' he said.

He also had a picture for me and it was of two trains. Each train had two carriages. In each train the front carriage was named 'Future' and the rear carriage 'Past' but he said he could see clearly that the couplings were different.

In the first train the Past carriage was pushing the Future carriage along but in the second train the 'Future' carriage was definitely pulling the 'Past'. This spoke to me of being in a greater place of healing and strength so that the failure and pain of the past was having less influence and I was free to move into the future. I felt in the context of my relationship with Nick it was significant that in both pictures the coupling remained intact and possibly affirmed my reluctance to sever all contact. I was glad that God seemed to be indicating that my past, in appropriate perspective, was not wholly negative and could therefore have a part to play in my future.

Stoneleigh that third summer had a recurring theme about exiles returning and we were challenged to look to the 'rock from which you were cut and the quarry from which you were hewn' that are talked about in Isaiah 51. I would make notes and then reread them in the evening mulling and praying. Was my 'rock' West Sussex? Was God indicating that my time of 'exile' over the border was coming to an end? Was he going to release a cottage for us to live in? But how could I move back into a place that had held so much pain?

The next talk was looking at the apparent barrenness of Abraham's wife Sarah and the verse, 'Is anything too hard for the Lord?' Then at one point in the story of Abraham it speaks about him pitching his tent in the hills east of Bethel. The home that had to be sold when our marriage ended had been called 'Bethel' and the rural estate I had prayed about moving to (where I had my name down for a vacant cottage) was just on the Downs about a mile and a half to the east. It felt to me that God was indicating a move back in the direction we had come from. I wondered if God could restore our original vision and whether he was really going to impact the county through the group of churches with whom we had been partnered. Many of the people who had shared the original vision remained in their homes and churches. This only emphasised the sense of 'exile' I felt in my own life. As the week went on God was saying more and more through the story of Abraham and Sarah as he encouraged them, 'Come out and I will show you.'

I was praying much about when to give notice on the house in Love Lane. By the time the week at Stoneleigh was over Heather and Steve felt confident the next move for them would involve going to a New Frontiers church but I had no such clarity. They began to speak about a season living with my parents in Fittleworth whilst they visited churches, prayed and decided where to move. I, on the other hand, had heard in another session at the Bible week, 'leave your father's house' and was convinced that being based with my parents was not the right step for me.

We were mutually dependent for the rent so it was imperative we all felt peaceful about the timing of the approaching move. I was beginning to think that the application for me of the teaching I had heard around the command 'come out and I will show you' could mean we should give notice and then I would trust God to make clear the next step.

The time between Stoneleigh and the beginning of the new academic year in September was uncomfortably full for me. We had a stream of overseas visitors and lots of activity at a time when I felt I had a mountain of information and emotion to process and pray through. I needed to plan. I was also desperate for the clock to stop as the days leading up to Sam going to board at school galloped past. September and the new term arrived far too quickly for me but we had had long chats all together when away in the caravan, and the boys expressed excitement about a house move.

Leaving them both in their respective dorms I would have felt utterly bereft if God had not been so faithful in causing us all to feel a sense of anticipation. I was praying that wherever the next step took us we would be less than an hour's drive away. It was a sunny day, which helped, and I felt excited for Sam that he had had the courage to take this opportunity.

My mother has loved God all her life and faithfully supported whichever local church we worshipped in. She is not given to claims of 'revelation' or 'words' so the occasions when she does step out usually have significance in my life. That week she gave me a card with a scripture from Isaiah in it explaining almost sheepishly she felt it was 'from the Lord'. She had written,

> *Forget the former things; do not dwell on the past.*
> *See, I am doing a new thing!*
> *Now it springs up; do you not perceive it?*
> *I am making a way in the desert*
> *and streams in the wasteland.*

I was still unsure how I would really feel about returning (from exile) to live in a place that had so many memories. The day after leaving the boys at school I travelled back to the area we had left.

As I drove through the familiar villages on the way, I was surprised and pleased to find that the by now familiar tight knot in the pit of my stomach had completely gone – even driving past the house of the friend who had taught the aerobics classes. She had so horribly betrayed me. It stung for years. But that day I felt only peace. I had gone forward for prayer on several occasions during Stoneleigh. It was clear to me that God had done some more healing because since learning of the adultery ten years previously, I had never been able to pass the house (which gallingly lay on the main route between many friends' and my parents' home) without having to suppress a wave of nausea. I drove through the village and then turned right up Chantry Lane and onto the Downs.

I sat overlooking the area, savouring my freedom and thanking God for the lightness in my spirit and so much to look forward to. But I was still not completely sure and I asked him to show me clearly how I should follow what I perceived as his signposts. I decided to visit the estate office and talk to the secretary I had been telephoning regularly, in hope of a property coming vacant. She was as charming as ever and encouraged me to write again to the landowner explaining my current situation. No cottage yet.

Driving home through the stunning countryside I felt lighter and more hopeful than I had in a long, long time but pondered what exactly was 'my current situation' and how could I best explain it? I hadn't been using my copy of *Through the Bible in a Year* in my daily readings for some time but on impulse picked it up that week. The reading for the day was from Nehemiah 1:9 (NLT),

> *But if you return to me and obey my commands,*
> *then even if you are exiled to the ends of the earth,*
> *I will bring you back to the place I have chosen for*
> *my name to be honoured.*

There was that word 'exiled' again. Maybe God was going to do a miracle and all the things Nick and the team had dreamed of could still come to pass.

Over the next couple of weeks we received notice of a rent

increase; I began to wonder if half-term could be time for a move but I am often in a hurry to implement what I think God may be saying when he is much more concerned with preparing me on the inside. Steve and Heather had been building links with New Frontiers people and there was a new church being planted in Sussex. They were now sure that back in the Worthing area was the next step for them. Steve had written to Terry Virgo to inquire about training the organisation may have to offer. He was keen to gain as much understanding and experience within the New Frontiers context as possible before returning to share it in Auckland. They decided they would definitely base themselves in Fittleworth with my parents. Steve could travel to work easily from there and Heather would get what shifts she could in the community.

I felt clearly that I was not to join them and I began to wonder about another season in the caravan. I wasn't ready to be too far from the boys and was not clear about my next step. I was praying about the possibility of work and adjusting to the reality that life would be very different from here on. With both sons at school all week a whole new vista was opening up. I felt daunted and increasingly aware of the jubilee element of the coming millennium celebrations. I remained convinced that it was to be a significant time for my relationship with Nick. I felt a twinge of anticipation each time I read or thought about the historical implications of jubilee, the celebration of emancipation and restoration. Maybe we could actually be involved together in church life again back in the area we had received so many promises. I reminded myself often that nothing is impossible with God. After chatting with Heather and Steve and letting all the scriptures and impressions I felt were from God settle into my spirit, I was convinced. I began speaking to friends back in the area we had moved from. I let it be known I was looking for a home to rent in the region whilst I continued to hope and pray for a cottage on the Wiston Estate to be released.

So the question was, 'What is your timing, Lord? Do we pay the rent increase and wait here for your direction or hand in our notice and move out?' A friend called to say she was praying for us. She felt God had highlighted a verse in the Bible where God spoke to some people telling them to remain where they were and be at peace.

It seemed another period of waiting beckoned as Steve heard that there would be no reply to his inquiries for some weeks because Terry was overseas.

During this time it dawned on me that actually I hardly needed to pray about if and when to move because we were interdependent. My housing benefit and their earnings were all part of one calculation so for me there was no issue: if Heather and Steve moved I would have to. Far from being anxious I felt an element of relief, and focused my prayers and listening to God on the question of where next for me. Heather, Steve and I talked together about how God led the people of Israel via the scenic route (rather than through terrain inhabited by wild beasts and enemies) and recognised that God always has a purpose in what may appear to us to be delays.

One Sunday some friends that the boys had attended church and school with before we moved into Hampshire, were being baptised in the pool belonging to a lady in our old church. We were invited and I felt strong enough to go back. It was a special time of seeing old friends. Sharing memories of when the children were small felt restorative. It was a chance for me to let more people know I was looking at the possibility of returning to the area and share stories of God's sustaining love.

With the realisation that Steve would wait till the next step was clear for them, and sensing he had decided to line up a connection within New Frontiers before moving, I tried to relax. I could do nothing to make Steve hear more quickly from Terry and any plans on my part could not be made until the others had a time frame. It was a delicious autumn with an abundant crop of blackberries. I had discovered the joy of making sloe gin and we had long walks, searching out the purple berries, followed by cosy evenings chatting endlessly about trusting God and the incredible possibilities in front of us all.

I was adapting to the boys being away and very thankful that they were settling into a rhythm of coming and going. I had been aware that as a solo mum it could be easy to slip into the trap of making the boys my life. This knowledge didn't save me from missing them terribly. I would stand in their empty rooms wondering what they were doing and how they were with a cramping feeling in my stomach.

The days were not long and empty: I had regular slots in the week when I prayed with others, the three of us entertained often and I set to sorting and tidying cupboards. There was always someone in the neighbourhood ill or in need of support. A friend with a horse was injured at this time and asked if I could help out. I spent many hours in the saddle, soaking up the wide-open spaces and exploring field and forest. It was good to have time to absorb and process the enormous change that no children at home brought to my routine.

Wednesdays were a half day at school when the boys could come home and there were only a couple of weekends a term when staying in school was compulsory, so in one sense I was broken in gently but it was a huge adjustment and I wondered what God was going to unfold. Who exactly was I? Obviously my identity up to that time had been integral to my role as a mother and I wrestled to come to terms with the fact that in the context of restoration with Nick, the boys were now young men and the experience of 'family life' I had longed to re-capture was gone forever. Lost.

The grieving process took some time and I was very grateful not to be living alone. The peace of God was a sustaining canopy over each day. It kept the rain of hopelessness at bay as I held still inside, knowing I had been promised a future even though it remained hidden. I wrote in my journal,

I continue to enjoy the knowledge and experience 'He himself is our peace' and am trusting God that he is unfolding the next step behind the scenes. Terry is back in England next week – please, Lord, reveal your timing very plainly for giving notice on this house.

I wrote, as I had been advised, to the landowner in Wiston and the strong sense I'd had that we would one day live in the sprawling area of countryside beside the old school route never waned. If it were God's purpose it would happen. I was thankful to have such peace in my heart and, knowing it could be several months before the next step was fully clear, I ordered a load of logs for the fire and settled my mind to a final winter in Petersfield.

20

New Beginnings

Through connections he was making in the Worthing area Steve was invited to speak at our old church, where many who had been part of my story still attended. I was surprised at how vulnerable it made me feel. I knew most people had an opinion about my situation and how I came to be living in the next county, and I still felt troubled and disquieted about how the church had rejected Andrew and Sue. I wasn't worried about what Heather and Steve may hear or say. I felt totally supported and safe in our relationship but the water of community looked murky. Feelings had been vehemently expressed and I was unsure about what they would encounter. I wondered if Heather and Steve were going to have a role in bringing healing and restoration and how it would all play out. All that eventuated was several Sunday invitations and some helpful conversations with people who were still damaged by the way things had unfolded.

Meanwhile the church in Petersfield was having a 'fresh commitment' time and I felt I was watching things unfold from a distance. Yet another encouragement to recommit seemed rather hollow to me. But relationships with those where friendship rather than church was the focus, blossomed. I just enjoyed the love and growth that was happening as people came and went from our home and was grateful to be feeling free from any previously felt responsibility.

Even though the boys often struggled after time with Nick, they experienced profound disappointment when at short notice he said he was busy and couldn't see them. I wrestled with helping them to manage their emotions whilst feeling frustrated that even years into the process these last-minute changes of plan had such an impact on us all. The emotions of the moment were powerful and I was tempted to doubt; doubt that anything really good could ever come out of such turmoil. Mrs Cowman wrote that week, 'Is anything too hard for the Lord?' from Genesis 18:4 and 'That thing if it is in line with what we know to be his expressed will (as a son to Abraham) he, God, intends to do for us.'

I wrote in my journal,

His expressed will... the verse in Amos? Could I have misinterpreted? Could God have been meaning his personal contract with Nick? Obviously more letting go to do.

I wrote this question but continued to believe implicitly that reconciliation was on God's agenda. It just felt clear that I had monumentally misread the timing. The belief remained strong that without relinquishing the conviction that our family would be restored there was still a place of greater personal liberty available to me. I believed that with God it must be possible to know a sense of peaceful fulfilment even in the waiting.

Claire was a dear friend who had been divorced some years earlier. She had a Catholic background and we chatted often about faith. She had four sons and we encouraged each other as we faced the challenges that having an absent father presented. I can't remember now whose idea it was but it must have seemed a good one to us both at the time. In the gloom of a November Friday evening we found ourselves arriving at a retreat centre somewhere near Godalming. This was to be our 'Beginning Experience' (B.E.).

B.E. is a programme run as a ministry of the Catholic Church over a weekend. It is a weekend designed to bring a measure of closure to those in the aftermath of divorce or loss of a spouse, by creating the opportunity to process emotions with hope of receiving healing. The idea is to be away from all distractions. The weight of my suitcase indicated that I was not up for the loss of *all* distractions, well not the bottle-shaped ones anyway. Besides, I knew from the brochure that periods of time were to be spent in silent contemplation in the solitude of our rooms, and these places were often chilly so, a glass of something red and hearty was verging on the medicinal. Having been educated by nuns Claire was nervous of discovery but I suffered no such inhibition. On the contrary, if a thing was banned, in a religious context, I was finding increasingly that I wanted to do it, bring it, try it. The programme is run under the Catholic banner and has some spiritual content but it is clearly non-denominational and all are welcome.

Looking at the process and stages of grief the B.E. gives the opportunity to evaluate how far along you are and how thoroughly one is dealing with death. Divorce is viewed as death of a marriage and the weight of loss experienced is soberly addressed. Opportunity is given for personal evaluation. We were encouraged to look back at our marriages as through a door with a glass panel in it and deliberately call to mind happy and positive memories.

Through the structure of the programme the facilitators, all of whom are peers who have been through the programme themselves, do not give advice. Instead, through sharing their own journeys and the posing of questions, they stimulate participants to review where they are in their own process of grieving. Sessions were created when we had to spend time writing in a notebook provided in the quiet of our rooms. By the answering of questions we were expected to confront issues and organise our thoughts. There is opportunity to share these thoughts, feelings and discoveries in small groups. I had rather disturbing experiences of group therapy in the psychiatry module of my nursing training, when we were encouraged to indulge in serious conversation with patients who believed they were someone else and often had a parallel existence.

Small group work and soul bearing are not my forte. You wouldn't believe how many people out there believe themselves to be the mother of Jesus or who enjoy conversation with amicable aliens on a regular basis. I found it all thoroughly unnerving. Did I mention my phobia? That would be the one that surfaces in the 'sexless socks and sandals' arena. Our particular course had plenty of potential and I worked hard at keeping my line of sight well above the knee as we sat in our small group circle.

A more conscientious mother would probably have been on the lookout for hints on facilitating deeper healing and healthy grieving in her teenage sons. I was poised; convinced I was about to be prompted to put my dream to death. Other than the general recognition that the more whole I was the more I would have to offer the boys and the better mother I would be, I was preoccupied with my own need to hear direction from God. Sam and Nathan seemed settled and comfortable in their own rhythms of home and school life by now. Perhaps I needed them to be. I didn't have answers...even for myself.

Contribution to the discussion was optional with those who took the plunge clearly finding it helpful. I had approached the weekend with several things on my agenda. Clearly it is far too risky to arrive at such events with no agenda; anything could then happen and I would only have myself to blame! I harboured hope of arriving at a place where I could achieve a measure of closure and healing whilst still retaining the hope of things to come; preferably with Nick.

My life was by now studded with people who were keen for me to 'move on' and I felt sure that the Holy Spirit could accomplish something in me that would keep them happy without me having to deny the promise.

In spite of all that, I was praying earnestly that if I had misunderstood God or embellished his word to me that he would take this opportunity to root out of me all the longings and dreams that involved restoration of my marital relationship with Nick. My journal entry the day before we went away reads,

Had long chat with Steve and I ended by saying so much is milling around inside – like a huge ball/muddle of wool and I need, am asking God to show me this w/e which is the one thread that will begin the unravelling... Am fasting and praying today... Lord, please do something amazing in Claire's life.

Topics such as grief, guilt, trust and forgiveness were among those covered with the chance to accept responsibility where appropriate, assign blame or relinquish it where relevant, and arrive at some healing with a sense of completion. Some of the unveiling of the grief process illuminated various parts of the process Sam and Nathan were experiencing but it is clear that individuals express the recognised stages of the journey in their own unique way. At one point a punch bag seemed a helpful thing for Sam. Nathan wanted to read a good deal. Nothing is promised but everyone on the course is offered gentle respect and understanding as they come to appreciate where they are in their own process. I had some good times with my pen and wine glass, wrapped in a blanket at the little writing table in my room, and appreciated the chance for reflection and review. I hadn't heard God say anything clearly but felt peaceful.

The culmination of the weekend was a moving closing service. In the morning my reading in Mrs C. had been reassuring.

We shall find it impossible to commit our way unto the Lord unless it be a way that he approves.

*However extraordinary and unexpected may seem
to be his guidance, however near the precipice he
may take you, you are not to snatch the reins out
of his hands.*

The talk in the final service was a very moving exposition on the story of the prodigal son. I was challenged by the wholehearted absence of judgement in the welcome given to the prodigal by his father who, let's face it, had every right to be wounded, offended and furious. His unfettered joy and acceptance of the wayward son spoke to me. Was I willing to reach out again? Was God letting me know this was the next step? I wondered if this was an indication that I should invite Nick to spend Christmas Day with us all and prayed asking God to make it clear to me if this was his idea.

Nothing in my readings of the next few weeks caused me to feel restrained and references to God helping and strengthening were many. I wasn't in a rush but I began asking God about the 'How?' of my reaching out. Could it be that I had been so faithful to the 'let him alone' instruction that Nick had no idea that I longed for and dreamed of a glorious reunion? I believed I had put myself deliberately in a place where God could have just removed the dream but he hadn't. Instead I felt he had reinforced it.

I tentatively shared my feelings with my Dad. I told him I didn't want to be carried away with hopeful intentions but was still feeling I wanted to work towards reconciliation. I shared about the prodigal son talk and explained how I was feeling challenged about my attitude in wanting Nick to 'sort himself out' before risking extending myself again. What did he think? Dad was supportive and talked about believing a joined future could be possible if Nick were prepared to allow me to oversee the finance and administrative side of things. He was positive, even offering to chat to Nick if it would help.

In real life there were signs that Nick was slipping into debt again and I dreaded him telling my father. I knew in the long term, provided Nick were willing to let me take care of things like renewing insurance and car tax and paying the bills, managing the finance needn't be an issue. I could see that much drama could have been avoided if we had been enlightened years previously but it hadn't occurred to either of us. It was clear that in my naivety I had presumed that Nick would carry all that weight just as my father did. Nick contributed many practical skills that my father, who never even learned to change a plug, did not but I lacked insight back then. When some friends made it known that in their marriage it was the wife who managed the finances and admin side of things, I remember thinking it odd and somehow out of balance. The concept of the wife taking a lead and shouldering responsibility for those areas was so alien to me that it even seemed less spiritual. Unwittingly I was entrenched in what I viewed as the appropriate model of doing things in relationship so that this deviation from my perceived norm felt threatening.

At that time my emotions were taut. Our relationship was floundering and the daunting possibility of my needing to apply myself to any version of mathematics could only have resulted in a terrifying equation: maths + me = camel-straw-broken-back. The peak of my mathematical achievement at school was being demoted to 'D division'. Having struggled to master the mystifying theorem of someone with the unlikely name of Pythagoras in C division, I was grouped with a number of others and we were instructed in the art of opening a bank account. That exorbitant school fees were clearly not wasted is happily illustrated by my mastery in the realm of cheque writing. This remained with me to great effect. Subsequently learning to move money using only a keyboard has provided hours of fun.

It was only weeks before another Christmas but two major events were about to unfold, on opposite ends of life's spectrum. My youngest brother David had by now been living and working as a chartered accountant in Hong Kong for several years. Encouraged by old friends who had settled there he had migrated in the wake of a painful divorce compounded by a redundancy and was thoroughly settled. This was a great relief to my parents as David has an innocence about him that lends a certain air of vulnerability.

I previously mentioned that my siblings are all three blue-eyed blondes. Heather is most definitely blonde, in every understood meaning of the word; everyone loves her and we just explain that we are 'laughing with you, not at you' on a regular basis. David has, from time to time, exhibited behaviour that demonstrates he, too, has the 'blonde gene'. The signs were there quite early on. He was about six when we were all in church one Sunday morning for the family service. In our local Anglican church attempts to be culturally relevant were in full swing; a crossword appeared on the overhead projector screen with coloured felt-tip pens available for audience participation.

Vicar: 'Now, children, this is your opportunity to show us what you have learned today. We have heard the story of Noah and his ark. Noah, all the animals and his family were shut in the ark in all that rain. They were tossing about on the floodwater day after day locked inside, but God was looking after them. Our first clue is a four-lettered word. We have the first letter, which is S. The wind was blowing furiously and the water kept swirling and rising. The first clue is, "How did the people in the ark feel?" They were all inside and God was looking after them as the ark rose and fell on the huge waves. Hands up if you think you know. Anyone?'

David raised his arm and was beckoned forward. He faced the screen, pen in hand. S_ _ _ then solemnly turned and wrote on the acetate S I C K. My brother returned to his seat emanating an innocent air of quiet achievement. His parents unsuccessfully attempted to hide their mirth but no handkerchief would have been large enough as eyes watered and throats struggled to contain real belly chuckles. Andrew is the next eldest and grinned broadly as his younger brother returned to the pew. My sister and I giggled and enjoyed the spectre of a pink-faced vicar hastily explaining that sometimes a clue may have two correct answers and, 'Oh look, on this occasion S A F E also fits. We'll go with that for today, shall we children?'

There was also the time when Dad took him to a cricket match and David, then about ten years old, needed the toilet. My father indicated the public conveniences and returned to the fixture list. A few minutes later he entered the Gents but found no sign of David. Returning to the spot where they had parted he scanned the crowd for a curly blonde head. Anxious minutes passed then Dad gaped, open-mouthed, as a nonchalant David emerged from the Ladies.

When challenged, my brother calmly explained he just followed the sign for the 'Lad…ies.' An easy mistake but one that he didn't make again – as far as I know.

After a decade as a single man again David had met somebody new and my parents invited me to go for a short holiday with them, to meet Maria and experience David's new culture. Maria is Pilipino, dark, gentle and very attractive. She had just completed an Alpha course and was clearly excited about her faith and the new relationship. It was wonderful to see David so happy and to have a whistle-stop tour of his new life. His little flat was on the 37th floor of a building overlooking Aberdeen Harbour. It was designed to sway rather unnervingly in the wind to minimise damage in the typhoon season.

The city of Hong Kong is wall-to-wall people all in a hurry. Living space is at a premium with Chinese families often living twelve or thirteen to the space David had. His bedroom only accommodated a small double bed because he sawed off one corner and slept on the diagonal. So many people lived in the block and the consumerist mindset of always having new possessions, combined with frequent moves, meant David completely furnished his place with things left in the skip in the basement of the building.

Dave has always loved boats and was saving to purchase a launch of his own. I was dubious about his dream of setting off on the high seas. Although time had passed, this is David who, graduating from Newcastle University some years before, had wanted to get his thesis bound before submitting it. He emerged from the 'Bookmakers' at his local shops genuinely bemused as to why the sign intimated that they actually made books on sight! I consoled myself with the thought that nobody would let him loose in a nautical arena without thorough training in chart reading, wind speeds and hopefully much more.

We had prayed for ten years that a new love would come into Dave's life and it was special to see God bringing him a partner. Maria was no stranger to great sadness. The father of her children in the Philippines had been violent, abusive and unfaithful. As happens for many in her culture the only option for survival meant leaving her three sons to be raised by their grandparents and going overseas in order to earn money to send home. Poverty is endemic in the Philippines and unless you are born into the very wealthy minority, life is tough. Bribery and corruption are rife and work is scarce. Maria had also experienced unscrupulous employers in Hong Kong but had never lost hope of a better future and dreamed of being reunited with her sons. She has an infectious giggle and was warmly affectionate, immediately having a connection with my mother which blossomed into strong friendship. Dave and Maria have now been happily married for some years and Maria's sons are an important part of their life.

The other incident that life had in store in those short weeks before Christmas was truly terrible. Death. In the boys' boarding house at school there was a bit of a tummy bug going round so when Nathan's friend Sandro began feeling unwell and started vomiting he was put to bed in one of the sick rooms. Nathan went in to chat briefly and say goodnight to his friend. The next morning we learned that Sandro had developed a high fever late that night and been moved to the cottage that was the school sanatorium, staffed by trained nurses. In the early hours he had rapidly deteriorated and died. It was meningitis. It was shocking and the community reeled with grief as it struggled to understand how this could possibly have happened. Term ended early and Sam came home. Nathan and his friends lingered needing the support of being together.

I was appalled that Nathan, on top of everything he had had to manage, was now called upon to process this enormous event, something many adults never encounter. I felt inadequate and powerless as his main source of support was clearly the friends with whom he shared life but I had not had opportunity to get to know yet. I had met but did not 'know' Sandro. As the shock subsided I battled fear and the horror of what might have been. Nathan was among a number who had to take heavy-duty antibiotics. I kept thinking about Sandro's mother and her terrible journey from London to the school the morning of what must surely have been the most terrible phone call of her life.

Nathan remained calm and coherent during the whole ghastly week. I saw him each day and then when he was ready to leave his friends he came home. We had a few days skiing booked and I thought Nathan may want to remain in England in order to attend Sandro's funeral but he solemnly explained it would not make any difference to Sandro if he attended or not and he would like to come away. On the day of the funeral we sat up late by a roaring fire in the chalet, sipping port, while I prayed fervently I would say something helpful.

Prior to going to the chalet I had tentatively spoken of my idea to 'reach out' to Nick by inviting him to share Christmas Day with us. As a family we were in agreement, although some misgivings were aired as the time drew nearer. These were mainly around the topic of potential disruption as Steve sensed my expectation building once again. Heather and Steve were protective. They knew Nick's mood and demeanour would influence not only the festive celebrations. It could undermine the stability they saw growing in Sam and Nathan who were always desperate for their father to enjoy himself.

Maybe I was blind to how much the boys carried that weight. I think perhaps things were happier for them when I didn't try so hard to combine the life and strains they had when alone with Nick with the more relaxed, affirming atmosphere we lived in. Years later it was much clearer to me that whatever we were or did had little ability to improve how Nick saw his life. I think it was also clear to those living with me that I did feel increasingly positive. I knew we would be moving in the coming year and I felt optimistic that significant things were going to happen in my relationship with Nick so there was much to look forward to. Steve remained reluctant for us to risk our hard-earned stability.

Not long before the festive season dawned it transpired that Nick had broken his wrist and it felt good to be able to extend the Christmas invite. It was a special time with my parents joining us. They were really amazing in the way they consistently included Nick and never made it more difficult for me than it already was. My mother must have been desperate to tell me to shake off the dream and throw myself into a new life, not holding out for a miracle and keeping my life on hold. But then she loved him too, and as Christians we can't afford for our hearts to harden, can we? It felt very good to be able to give Nick a hug. I savoured this basic physical contact and I felt relaxed; it must surely be indicative of good things ahead?

Forgetting how well Nick can 'play a part' and emboldened by how peaceful being together on Christmas Day had felt I was hopeful that seeds of a new, genuine friendship could be sown. I suggested meeting for a walk on one of the days during the Christmas break. We walked and talked more than we had for some time. I think the entry in my journal the following day says it all,

Met Nick... Had a walk and talk – so much unresolved, he expressed so much unhappiness and disappointment – I almost felt perhaps I am out of my depth; I restrained myself from reaching out and kissing his face all over... I thanked him for risking friendship again and was left feeling completely inadequate. But, Lord, you never said it would be easy and he is crying out for relationship with you and me. I picked up Every Day With Jesus at Mum's afterwards. 'Loved into Loving' was the heading and I remember the tree picture... I know you are God of the impossible and I'm trusting that my love for you influencing and initiating my love for Nick will cause a softening of heart which will enable him to find restoration, peace, full forgiveness.
Mrs C. today 'Arise... enter to possess... God hath given...' Judges 18:9,10.

When New Year's Eve arrived I had previously already burned the three candles that represented my understanding of God having a commitment for me to fulfil in Petersfield. I prayed, thanking God for the enjoyment of the completion of three years. I wondered how his timing was going to unfold. I was unexpectedly alone. Heather and Steve had at the last minute decided they would love to be in London to see the millennium celebrations.

As I came face to face with my own emotions I realised I was close to repeating my previous mistake. 'Mistake' because God was teaching me he was to be my first port of call whatever the need and I wanted my default position to be relying on him first. Looking to those around me, leaning on them for support and succour could seem like less effort but it was no good slipping back into my old way. Heather and Steve were married and it was wholly appropriate they should feel free to catch the historic moment in London if they wished. I was thrilled for them but a bit sorry for myself. I knew I was God's woman of faith and power appointed to love Nick back to wholeness but I felt quite alone in my appointment.

Nick was at a New Year's party having declined my invitation to spend the evening together, stating that it just felt 'too hard' to spend the evening with me…whatever that meant. I'm not sure it occurred to me to question his statement but I knew growing a new relationship would take time and he had never hidden his desire for fun. I wanted him to be speaking the truth and he was always convincing when describing his own emotions. He had accused me of 'taking life too seriously' in the past and I wrestled old emotions as I tried not to think about him leaving the party. I was still dogged by something he had said to me in days gone by. He had been confessing to an occasion when he had taken a woman he'd met in a shop where he was working, to a party. He'd explained (in a tone that implied the only possible reason for my apparent ignorance of social etiquette must be that I had just emerged from the Ark) that it was quite simply the 'expected thing'. If you took a woman out for the evening, it followed that on dropping her home she expected sex. I had been astounded by his sincere tone and shocked at his ability to deceive himself.

The boys slept and I watched a service on television. The bishop of somewhere-or-other prayed a blessing over me as I attempted to leave all that rubbish in the past where it belonged and sought to embrace the hope and anticipation that the New Year offered, a new century at that!

21

Not The End Of The Story

Several months have passed since I completed the previous chapter. During this time I have consumed quantities of chocolate that even Willie Wonka hasn't dreamed of; amounts completely disproportionate to any possible appetite. This appetite induced by restless movement, from chair to desk to pacing to music collection to laptop to pen and paper and back to desk, in a state of semi-neurotic abstraction, for days at a time. I feel as if I am in a particularly gruelling episode of *Call the Midwife*. The baby has got stuck. The front wheel has fallen off the midwife's bicycle. She simply isn't coming. In my mind's eye is a vision. My final full stop miraculously gives birth to a paperback sporting an alluring cover. It is bulging with words of life and hope.

I do understand that in real life the 'ending' will in fact only push me slithering, vulnerable and mewling into a process with yet more strain and panting; a whole different journey called 'the possibility of publication'. I guess if you are reading this (and you're not my mother) somebody somewhere took the risk. Rather than any kind of 'ending' I think this could be the start of a new season for me when I commit to honing and practising my writing (some even refer to it as a 'gift') in case in some far-flung corner of the earth, by some means, my Editor in Heaven may use it to bring hope. My current dilemma? How do I write a final chapter? How can I finish a story that has not ended?

As the year 2000 unfolded, Heather and Steve remained supportive as I hesitated. I was open with them about feeling I needed to be sure of the next step for me, and wanting to remain near the boys. I talked with Sam and Nathan and explained Claire had offered me a spot on her land, just outside Petersfield, where I could live in the caravan. This would mean they could continue to come out of school whenever they were free, and that I would be nearby whilst praying about our next home. I thought I might be there till the end of the summer term by which time I anticipated having a clear sense of direction. We talked together about the likelihood of going to rejoin Heather and Steve once they had found a place to rent in Worthing. The boys were happy with the plan. Sam was busy choosing degree courses and lining up for his A-levels; Nathan continued to grieve over Sandro but was able to talk about it more; and Steve had applied for a transfer to the Worthing office with his job.

When I went to talk to the leaders of the church about the impending move they were excited on my behalf and completely affirming. John said God had shown him a picture for me. It was of a plant that was pot-bound. He could see new soil in a flowerbed being prepared for this plant. A space where the roots could spread and prolific, healthy growth could occur. I felt that this helped explain the sense of discomfort I was experiencing as I was being extricated from the 'pot'. The pot is often knocked to loosen the plant before it is shaken free. 'Pot-bound' inevitably means the plant will not slip out easily. I had a sense I would be laid to one side, perhaps in the caravan at Claire's, for a while as final touches to the fresh soil in the new flowerbed were being made. I mused that may possibly last for the length of the summer term.

I experienced moments of unease knowing that nothing new can be built till the old has been cleared away. So much of the past lingered. Was it really possible for a healthy new relationship with Nick to emerge? Then I read in the Old Testament about the rebuilding of the temple in Jerusalem. It says that 'they proceeded to lay the foundation of the new temple amid the massive ruins'. I felt reassured that God has a track record of weaving old into the new for his purpose.

In the Easter holiday I took Sam and Nathan away for a few quiet days on our own to a cottage in Dorset. It was good to snuggle in together and have a space in which to talk about all the changes. I chatted with them about my taking some time to be sure, rather than presuming we would just move to Worthing to be with the others, and they were happy.

I was a bit concerned about feeling cut off whilst in the caravan and also acutely aware that for the first time I would be living alone. I wondered if I would be lonely. When I had moved to Petersfield God had spoken to me through Elisha's story. I was reading in the book of Kings again that week away, where Elisha tells a widow to shut herself in with her two sons and then they experience miraculous provision. As we travelled home I prayed again that God would give me wisdom and stop me pursuing relationship with Nick if it was going to result in further damage to ourselves or our sons.

Nathan hit a dark patch and was able to attend school as a dayboy for a while. He and his friends were trying to process the enormity of death grabbing one of their number and many of them experienced depression. I had moments where so many emotionally challenging situations being unresolved threatened to make me feel overwhelmed. Nathan's grief and Sam making life decisions, both with a father too absorbed in his own issues to engage at any meaningful level.

Heather and Steve were understandably champing to get into the next phase of their lives. But God consistently reminded me of his faithfulness and the week we decided to hand in notice on the house I read, 'He who called you is faithful and he will do it' and 'Blessed is she who believes that all the Lord has spoken to her shall be accomplished.'

And then visiting Heather and Steve's new church with them this exhortation was read out, 'So do not throw away your confidence; it will be richly rewarded.'

On the planned moving day Claire rang to say it was too wet and the ground too boggy to move the caravan, so I hastily collected a few things and scooted to my parents house for the night feeling let down and bone weary. There was a brief moment when a friend got in touch to say she had a cousin who had property in the area and I thought maybe God was going to save me from the caravan chapter but it came to naught. I was missing the boys terribly, felt all at sea and was fleetingly tempted to feel sorry for myself, but by early May I was thoroughly settled in the caravan and loving the freedom. I relished being in the paddock with sheep and horses as my nearest neighbours.

Heather and Steve moved to be part of the church in Worthing and after a stint living with my parents they rented a bungalow. Claire generously allowed me to have the dogs with me. Together we enjoyed a glorious spring surrounded by lambs and all not far from Sam and Nathan at school. Mid-week and some weekends they joined me. Time together lingering over barbecues and late-night chats was precious. I felt something was being brought to birth in the realm of potential restoration. It was uncomfortable and time seemed to drag but I read in Ephesians about God building things and the value of foundations. This helped me accept the possibility that God was putting in foundations for the new thing, and for it to be done well would take time.

Nick began to be more relaxed and open. He began dropping in to see me in the caravan when the boys were at school and I felt we were really learning to communicate honestly. I was always aware that he was fundamentally disappointed whereas I was enjoying God's presence and knowing him speaking love and direction for my life. I tried to be sensitive and respect what I discerned as Nick's rather fragile feelings. I was hopeful and encouraged as we shared suppers, chatted and listened to music. Was this to be the turning point? I looked forward to his visits but continued to feel I needed to be careful. I wasn't certain Nick's actions meant he was moving towards restoration but the signs were all good. A journal entry during this time reads,

> *Wonderful to be at peace with Nick, I still feel so attracted to him – please keep me very wise in all I say and do. I am seeking to be a faithful friend but of course feelings are being unlocked so then enjoyment levels are lowered if he is not there. Don't really want that to happen but it isn't possible to just 'act' caring – I do care and inevitably his sadness and the reality of how he is living start to get to me. Nick states he doesn't believe talking to anyone can help.*

I met and prayed with Sue regularly during this time. She was nervous for me as I prepared to embark on what I perceived as a new relationship with Nick and she gently expressed loving concern without in any way judging. Her loyal support of my dream of restoration meant I felt safe to share my dreams honestly. She must have been busting to warn me from risking my heart again but her willingness to empathise with me on the faith journey, and to be open to God's leading, strengthened me. Sue managed to be honest about her hesitations whilst remaining fully supportive of me, a quality of friendship to be highly valued. I was fully convinced I was to keep pressing in for full reconciliation and God spoke reassurance whenever I wavered.

As intimated in the first paragraph of this chapter, in recent weeks I have felt completely desperate to finish the book. I have been assaulted by doubt. The enemy of God mutters:

'Whatever possessed you to think you could write *anything* worth reading, much less a book?'

'You? A writer? Pah, I don't think so!'

'Has anyone *actually* said they would be interested to publish your work?'

'It was all in your mind; how likely is it really that God asked *you* to write your story?'

And so the barrage goes on. But still I am not able to settle, to put the manuscript in a drawer and move on, so here I am at the page . . .

The boys completed the academic year and we all moved to join Heather and Steve in the bungalow in Worthing. Whilst waiting in the caravan God had spoken to me about continuing to share a home base and preparing for a return to work. Nursing homes were prolific in the local area with several in easy walking distance. Summer term ended and Sam signed on with an agency for holiday work. Nick was regularly around our table. He also came to church with us. I was very excited, as things seemed to be moving positively towards restoration.

Some months on I felt it was time to put my cards on the table. Nick had always made his perspective clear; that I had ended the marriage. I had instigated the divorce so I reasoned that perhaps he needed me to take initiative.

We decided to have a go at being away as a family, just the four of us. It was my suggestion. Seeing Nick as a 'wounded soldier' motivated me to keep reaching out. Friends in Yorkshire were on holiday and generously said we could use their home. While we were away I took the plunge; after all, the prodigal's father had 'run to meet him'. I shared with Nick how serious I was about building a life together and I said I would like to wear a ring as a token of that commitment. He was quiet; very quiet. Then he said I had given him a lot to think about. He didn't pursue the subject until we had returned to Sussex. He explained then that he needed time. Ouch.

I was profoundly disappointed but not crushed. We had reached the middle of the year 2000, the year of jubilee, the one I had felt could finally be our year of 'cancelled debt' and a new beginning, I wrote in my journal,

I have been feeling anxious about Nick's inability to commit, to see anything long term but I do see that is unreasonable. He is right; he does have a journey to travel – I trust you and must be patient. You have spoken, Lord, and you will take responsibility.

Thank you: in days when I am tempted to think I got something wrong you realign my focus. My reading in Daily Light yesterday, 'Keep yourselves in the love of God, abide in me…without me you can do nothing.' Of course, Lord, it is all about YOU and the timing is in your hand. I will settle into your commandment 'that ye love one another'. So, Lord, I realign my desire with your timing (I felt you spoke about this year but it is only half-way through) remembering Jacob's encounter with you at Peniel which broke his natural strength so you could clothe him with spiritual power – YES PLEASE!

I truly felt God was doing a deep work in my life that would culminate in a new marriage.

I focused on getting back into the workplace and accepted a number of regular shifts. One day I had a thought, like a snowball landing on a warm stone it dawned on me, as I pondered what increasingly felt like reluctance on his part, that at no time had Nick sought to reassure me that he was not seeing anyone else. I had heard of men who managed to live a completely double life. Briefly disconcerted by the thought I told myself that kind of idea could not co-habit with faith and pressed on. A small damp patch lingered on the stone and quickly evaporated.

Looking back I can see that during the next two years we had some milestone conversations. One such exchange occurred as we sat in the car on the seafront after a lovely meal. I had prayed about it and felt it was time to broach the subject of commitment again. I explained to Nick that I loved him, that I would like to share life with him and wanted to be his wife. I told him that so long as his heart was towards God and he wanted to grow in his faith that it wouldn't be an issue for me if he didn't feel able to go to church. I was ready; he had consistently said he wanted to 'grow old together', why waste any more years? I emphasised it was him, as a person, that I loved. I wasn't concerned about him having any overt church role or ministry.

Nick listened. Then firmly and quietly explained that he had financial and other 'issues' that he wanted to resolve before he felt he could live with me again. I struggled for breath under the weight of blatant rejection. A paradigm shifted at my core but it was subtle, no cracked evidence appeared on the surface. Another significant exchange happened many months later when I visited Nick one afternoon and finally the crater split wide open as truth erupted.

Meanwhile, Heather and Steve moved into a bigger rental home. Sam went off to university. Nathan was in the sixth form. After several part-time nursing roles I was delighted to gain a job at Bedales. It was a residential term-time post and Nathan could, if he chose, live in my flat. I felt God restoring to me the years I had missed through him boarding so early. I loved being part of the school culture, getting to know Nathan's friends and thoroughly enjoyed working in a boarding house full of teenage boys.

Nick blew hot and cold after that seafront conversation. By that I mean that if I initiated it, we would meet or he would attend a parents' meeting or come to church. But things came into sharper focus as I developed in my new role and viewed our situation from a distance.

Sam was living away and both he and Nathan were managing their own relationships with Nick. God didn't give me a word or any indication that he had changed his mind about restoration but I felt urged to create room for my own life to develop.

Faith at that time looked to me like two things. Firstly, allowing a large space in which Nick could make his own decisions so that he could reconnect with God and accept healing and forgiveness in his own time. Secondly, demonstrating the awesome, liberating love and power of God in my own life by living it to the hilt. It was clear that whatever was going on in his head Nick remained, in his own mind, the victim. He was not taking any actions to facilitate us being together. I was still convinced that he would make this journey and I pondered again the picture God had shown me of the hidden pathway near the caravan. So many years had passed. My dream of being a family again before the boys left home was six feet under.

It was late summer. I was curled up in the corner of the static van Nick rented.

'The thing is, Nick,' I heard myself say as it took both hands to steady the mug of tea I was holding, 'I think perhaps you are in love with the *idea* of being with me, of us being a couple, but I don't think you actually love *me* anymore.'

Nick did not deny it.

I drove away feeling at one level numb realisation. This was a huge conversation. Then release seeped into my body like heat in a sauna: this was it. Nick's future was his concern. It would be wonderful for his sons if he could cease to live as a victim but change must be absolutely God's responsibility. Trusting God to fulfil his purpose did not mean keeping my own life on hold. God is God and he completes what he begins. God sighed gently over me and his breath infused me with acceptance. Time to accept it could be many years . . .

Time then to embrace a life alone with God and demonstrate belief that he would work in Nick's life in his own unique time, in a place not visible to me. A God of love had given opportunities for Nick to step back into wholeness. He loves too much to overrule the free will he has given and Nick exercised his freedom to choose. Sam, Nathan and I live with the consequences of that choice. Bill Johnson writes in his book *Face to Face with God*,

> **Yes, God can use tragedy for his glory. But God's ability to rule over bad circumstances was never**

meant to be the evidence that those circumstances were his will.

Jesus paid the ultimate price for our freedom; God could pull strings but who wants a puppeteer for a God?

A beautiful cottage did become vacant and I settled into a rural lifestyle at the foot of the Downs I love so much. It was so old the boys couldn't stand fully upright in parts but their friends loved to come and stay. It had a rambling garden, an Aga in the kitchen and a long-held dream of mine...a stable door off the kitchen. I was living in a miracle. I occasionally saw Nick when he collected Sam or Nathan but no longer initiated any contact. I was content that God would fulfil his promise in his time frame.

It was a shock when it came to light that Nick had a girlfriend. Learning the relationship had been ongoing for some years (and, yes, overlapped with times when Nick was speaking of a future for us) was painful. But the worst was that he had made our teenage sons promise not to tell me. This meant them having to lie, over time, about where they had been and who they were with thus constructing a burden of deceit in their relationship with me. I struggled to forgive Nick for that but it forced me to face the truth. Without fundamental change I could no longer like the man he had become.

After a few carefree months in the cottage my Dad became ill and I moved in to help Mum nurse him at home. I was shattered when just over a year later I could only watch helplessly as cancer sucked the life out of the mast that had held the family sails aloft all my life.

Incredibly, within a few months of his death I received a job offer in Australia and God made it clear the adventure was his purpose. I went and experienced a whole new way of life working in a busy Accident and Emergency Department. Sam and Nathan remained in England happily living and working independently. We see each other regularly.

At the beginning of my story I wrote about being cast adrift on the hostile, churning breakers of divorce. I yearned for shore and cast about in search of a safe cove with a firm sandy beach. What has changed? Everything. God's faithfulness in sustaining and leading, protecting and strengthening has drawn me way, way out to sea. I crave the wide rolling ocean of God's love. It's a mystery. The substance of the very environment that threatened my life has morphed into the one place I hope never to leave. My tears have become not just pools, as in Psalm 84, but literal wells of unspeakable joy. The source of his love has lured me into a place of wild abandon, where his delight in me injects every day with hope.

Nick is now an absent father in the fullest sense of the term. I long for him to enjoy God and encounter unconditional love and for that to turn his heart towards two sons who need him. The loving priority of heaven doesn't change and I remain convinced that restoration of relationship with the Father, with his sons, with those he perceives as guilty, is fully available to Nick, to any prodigal willing to return home. Peace with God transforms any life but the Holy Spirit loves to be invited. God's nature is to restore, he loves to perform the impossible but step one is always to welcome his son or daughter home.

My experience is that he has become my home, the place I inhabit. God perfectly fathers me, is my wild adventure, rampant lover, faithful husband, and closest friend. He is, quite simply, enough. ENOUGH? Did I just write that? That is the whole point, the 'glory' of what God has done. I cannot get enough. My marital status, my career pathway, the décor in my home, my body image, others' opinions, nothing matters anymore by comparison. And it's no longer about any promise of a dream fulfilled. I don't know how God has done it but quite genuinely in a way I never imagined or asked for (that ring a bell?) all I want is him. His presence. Gifts are great, health is wonderful, friends are valued, family is precious, work is an adventure, church is good BUT it all pales besides being actually *with* him, physically impacted by his presence and knowing a love that infuses every cell in my body. I want his love to spill out of me so powerfully that those around me taste heaven.

This yearning has precipitated a new adventure. I have heard Jesus is pouring himself out on the poor and destitute in a corner of Africa and he has made a way for me to go. I am off to visit Pemba in Mozambique. God has told me he has keys to give me if I will go. He has shown me I am to learn from the children and serve the poor. I have no idea what that looks like but I heard Heidi Baker speak and read her books and I believe even my normal Christian life can be transformed. It has to be so because without power how is the message of the New Testament 'good news'? I am pursuing God with all my heart because I am convinced my mundane can become his miraculous.

My mother keeps slipping into a trance-like state and can be found, eyes glazed, her stare fixed on some invisible horizon muttering,

'Africa?…Hazel?…It must be GOD.'

Bibliography

Bird by Bird, Anne Lamott (Anchor Books, 1995).

I Am With You, John Woolley (O Books, reissued edition 2004).

Face to Face with God, Bill Johnson (Charisma House, 2007).

Love Must Be Tough, Dr James Dobson (Kingsway Publications, 2006).

Streams in the Desert L.B. Cowman (Zondervan, revised edition 1997).

Surprised by the Voice of God, Jack Deere (Kingsway Publications, 2006).

The Art of Horsemanship, Xenophon, edited and translated by Morris H. Morgan (Dover Publications Inc., 2006).

One Year Bible: The Living Bible, (Tyndale House Publications, 1985).

Walking with God, John Eldridge (Thomas Nelson, 2008).

The following excerpt is taken from

H A Chilver's new book

'Pemba Pennings' coming soon.

Introduction

Perhaps, like me, you have wondered what the key is, whether there is a heavenly formula that unlocks God moving in power in your life? A spiritual pathway that if walked could release the kingdom, which in the gospels Jesus consistently claims is 'here'. One might be forgiven for thinking that if it were possible to be more like someone whose life already overflows with evidence of this kingdom there could be hope... Mmm. Since this story, this chapter of my journey was greatly accelerated when a kind friend called Kathy 'innocently' leant me a book about Heidi Baker. I'll take her as an example of the futility comparison breeds.

Heidi was born and grew up in a millionaire's paradise in America called Laguna Beach. I was raised with three siblings in a three-bedroom semi-detached red brick home in suburban England. By the age of sixteen Heidi was preaching, I was fervently renewing my commitment to Jesus as Lord at regular intervals and optimistically going along to youth group anticipating romance. Heidi was exploring all things 'Pentecostal' whilst I was obliged to sit on a hard pew each Sunday declaring in doleful tones that he 'makes His chosen people joyful.' The complete absence of fun, laughter or anything remotely suggesting hilarity led me to the only possible conclusion. Our church had not been 'chosen'. Heidi was learning to take risks and already adventuring in the power of the Holy Spirit whilst I was being warned. Warned that there were Christians who may 'need an extra baptism' but the general qualifications were deemed to be mental instability or possibly being an American TV evangelist, because any overt emotion was definitely not appropriate for a committed Bible-reading British Christian.

You can probably see where this is going but I will just finish. As a young woman Heidi experienced great passion and concern for other nations; I was busy avoiding any gathering where a missionary on furlough was showing their slides in case I got 'called'! Africa was a specific non-starter after a brief visit with Grandparents living in Zimbabwe (then Rhodesia) introduced me to corruption, armed guards, poverty, intimidation and human need on a scale beyond my ability to process. Heidi studied, gained degrees (yes, plural!) and later a PhD. I didn't even go to university. Heidi was working on the streets in London seeing homeless people's lives radically turned around as she introduced them to Jesus and I was preparing to walk up the aisle and on into middle-class motherhood.

I don't want to be another Heidi, but any of us who feel ordinary or normal in comparison can be hungry to be in a relationship with our heavenly Dad that overflows with power and love to the world around us. Wanting to be just like another person, striving to emulate someone else God is using will not fully release God moving in power and is likely to be a distraction or even a trap. 'Fix your eyes on Jesus' is in the Bible because nobody else will do.

The one thing we can share and do need to have in common

has nothing to do with our upbringing or standing in life; it is a heart posture. A posture of hunger, desire, longing for God. It is the description of this hunger that so powerfully challenged me as I read the book.

By the time I visited Kathy I had been exploring living in the fullness of the Holy Spirit for twenty years. I was passionate about seeing Jesus loved and celebrated but miracles, signs and wonders were painfully conspicuous by their absence. I read Heidi's story because I had heard things and I was desperate for more of God in my own life. That day, when I got to the part where Heidi's hunger for more resulted in God coming so powerfully on her that she was, in effect, glued to the floor for a week, I spontaneously slipped out of my chair and found myself continuing to read on the floor. There was nothing at all 'British' about the experience she described. She was embarrassed, uncomfortable, emotional and helpless to the point of absolutely no control over her situation.

My reading ground to a halt as I tried to imagine. It didn't compute. What about the bathroom? What about food and drink? No. It was totally extreme, surely that couldn't be part of God's purpose in 'the normal Christian life?' Aagh . . . could that be the point?

I had had 'normal' for years. What if . . . ? I sensed an invitation. It was unexpected and it came unannounced on an ordinary autumn afternoon in England as I waited for Kathy to return from work. The thing is, I didn't have to accept. I let choice hang in the atmosphere as I took a deep breath and decided to read on.

By the end of the book Heidi was seeing God do many miracles. I had heard stories of blind seeing and deaf hearing in Mozambique through Kathy who had visited Maputo. I had also noticed in recent months that her prayers were different, more direct with a new authority. She had prayed for me over the phone and my chest infection had cleared. So it was clear to me that the encounter that Heidi wrote about was a catalyst in her life with God, as though the awfulness of feeling humiliated and embarrassed, and particularly being unable to control anything that happened, in some way catapulted her into a new release of God moving in power.

I pondered: what if in order to see signs and wonders in my own life, this, or a similar experience is required? I don't know if the Holy Spirit holds his breath but in that moment I stepped back from the detail. Basically I was looking at a person moving from being glued to the floor in public to seeing God bring dead babies back to life with countless other miracles in between. How could I hold back when those were the possibilities? As I lay on the carpet and said yes to whatever it was Love was drawing me into I felt heaven sigh with pleasure.

December 2014: Piercing, electric blue eyes combed the upturned faces as she pondered response. Most glistened with humid sweat, many streaked with red dust; all were focused on hearing the answer to the question. The air was pregnant with expectation as hungry hearts from many nations ached for resolution. It was hot, flies were busy and everyone was sitting on the cement floor in the meeting hut in Pemba, Mozambique.

Harvest School 21 would soon be over and we had a final question and answer session with Heidi. Ann had voiced the heart cry of 249 other students:

Introduction

'Heidi, we have been here for nine weeks. Many of us have connected with children; we have been involved in all the activities and loved serving where we can. But we are all going home tomorrow. Just . . . leaving. Some of us sponsor children but what more can we do? We will all be back in our own nations but is there anything we can do? How can we help and continue to make a meaningful difference here?'

Smiling, Heidi spoke; slowly turning her head as she did to ensure every student was included. 'Some people give up a month each year and come to help us. That's fantastic and we really appreciate it. How can you help? The thing each of you can do, the thing that really is the most help, is to tell people, leave here and tell your story.'

I heard Heidi's voice but it was God who spoke to me. Excited hope stirred. Just over a year before I had begun writing about Pemba but had got bogged down and convinced myself that it was unlikely anybody would ever want to read my ramblings. The project lay incomplete in the labyrinth of documents and folders on my laptop.

Now, many months and writing hours later, this is my story.

The Off

D earest Ma,
Here I am on the 12:26 from Exeter St Davids to Waterloo. It was good to chat briefly on the phone. Sorry the Auckland summer is less than you hoped but at least if the roof is fixed you can relax. With no phone or internet contact where I am going, I thought I'd just get you up to speed with a couple of letters as I set off, and then I will be out of contact for a while whilst I tackle this project. Will obviously let you know as soon as I am safely on my way back to London.

Rather a lot to catch up on as things have gained momentum so I'll try and start at the very beginning. To be honest chatting to you about the adventure as it begins makes it feel less lonely. I really appreciate your support, even though I know a part of you probably wanted to dissuade me, and although I admit to feeling completely blown away that God would orchestrate such an unexpected turn of events, in my spirit I hear Him clearly saying, 'Come on, Haze, further up and further in,' and I am magnetically drawn by love to respond.

The weird thing is the train looks just the same as it does every day, just like all the other times I have caught it. My suitcase, with fluro-pink strap clicked firmly around its bulging midriff waits patiently in the corner rack. I like to wedge it outside the other bags, poised for a smooth pick-up as I exit en route for the tube. I'm sitting in my preferred spot; an aisle seat at a table facing the way the train is travelling to defy nausea. (Even going the wrong way on the train makes me feel queasy since I had that paroxysmal vertigo thing in my ear last year.) My preference is the first table that offers a view right down the length of the carriage. I like light and space even when I'm travelling. I can't bear the bulkhead seat in a plane, like being tied up and dumped in a dead end.

So, on the surface this journey looks for all the world like just another routine trip home to Australia. Only there is actually nothing routine about this journey. From the foreign objects of mosquito net and water filter through empty jewellery pouch in my case, to borrowed 'Fitness First' rucksack replacing stylish leather hand bag, to crisp new visa on page 11 of my passport. Golly, Ma, nothing is 'normal'.

Sometimes when I travel friends give me a card to wish me well. This morning (remember I have been renting space in the large shared home in Exeter) it was 'house prayer'. At 7 a.m. I was striding the canal bank and deep breathing, gulping in the last Devon air for a few weeks. Others gathered in the lounge to pray and later I received an envelope bulging with encouraging notes, pictures and Bible verses God had prompted them to share with me. True to the creative nature of the household, as I opened the envelope just now a golden shower of glitter erupted. Bursting with relief at being released, it enthusiastically coated as much as possible within its reach. The unsuspecting gentleman opposite tried not to respond (how very British!) as his *Daily Mail* took on a lustrous shimmer. I thought of Joanna chuckling as she stuffed the envelope. Hopefully it will prove to be a prophetic sign of God's presence visiting me in power. I do know of meetings where 'gold dust' appears on worshipers but I only experienced it that one time when the Toronto blessing was influencing things in our church in Petersfield. I'll keep you posted.

I didn't have time to go into the detail on the phone, Ma, but honestly, this journey only really began in earnest four weeks ago which is why I am feeling pretty breathless about it all. You remember I went to that conference in Cardiff? It was actually a training school intended to equip and teach us to pray for people to receive healing from God. At lunch break on day two I met a young couple called Fred and Chloe. As we chatted I shared my frustration and longing for God to break out and transform the lives of the desperate homeless people I have been getting to know in Exeter. As she breastfed her tiny daughter, this young mum calmly levelled her gaze on me and said,

'Hazel, I think you should go to Mozambique.'

In the next session I went forward for prayer and received a prophetic word: 'A new chapter is beginning. It will be bold. It is a long chapter'

The following day I connected with Fred and Chloe again. They prayed for me and Fred said, 'I see you on a stage with a spotlight on you. It's God shining the light. His attention is specifically on you. This is a time of preparation. It will be short so savour the process. I feel God also reminding you that he saves the choicest wine till last.'

With mellow thoughts around Pop and his passion for Chateau

Neuf with beef, I went happily into the next session.

Randy Clark shared that he had been in a meeting where Mrs Mahesh Chavda, Bonnie, described seeing a number of angels, all about six-foot tall, moving among the people and strengthening the saints. She then saw three huge angels, all over nine feet tall. These angels went to just a few and handed them commissioning scrolls before stamping a number on them. Randy said God had told him there were a number of people who were at the conference to be commissioned and that there would be opportunity, specifically for those who knew it was for them, to respond later in the week. Something leapt to attention inside me. I resolved I would be among those responding. At the time it didn't feel like an issue that I had no clue what a 'commissioning' may look like. I just knew God drawing an unconditional response from my heart and felt a deep excitement about being in the right place at the appropriate moment.

When it was time for those of us who identified with this sense of being drawn into a specific new chapter to respond and to receive a commissioning, I went forward with a huge 'Yes' in my spirit. When Randy spoke about the likely cost and gave people the opportunity to return to their seats many did but in my heart I had already stepped off the cliff. As Randy prayed for me God's presence was like a soft, heavy cloak covering my whole body. It was heavy and I fell to the floor. As I lay on the ground I had thoughts about Heidi and heard the words, 'Spend time in Heidi's shadow and write about it.' Much later, as I came to as if from a deep, peaceful sleep, that phrase was going round and round in my head but I had no idea what it could mean. How could I begin to support or connect with an international miracle worker? Was God planning for me to work for Heidi or 'carry her bags' for a season? That would obviously be a season when she was going to be in Europe then.

You know, from time to time in life somebody will say something and it has a 'ring' to it, a sense of purpose all its own, a prophetic edge? Chloe's comment was one of those and her dart landed a bull's eye. However much I wriggled I couldn't dislodge it. I had been back in Exeter for a week and the thought of emailing Heidi Baker surfaced every time I began to pray. Googling her I actually found a contact address. It was in Mozambique. I had no intention of actually going there but God's spotlight was on the next stepping stone and I knew from experience only obedience would move the light to the next step. Obviously he would show me the turn that would enable me to fulfil what he was asking but just in that moment the process required me to email Africa.

Finally, I sent a tentative email of inquiry to Pemba (where, it turned out, this young couple had done a training course when Chloe was still pregnant). Obviously God was just testing me; had to be. He knows my heart, I want to follow him 100 per cent but he also knows I don't really do Developing World.

With missionaries in the family I have strong feelings; you remember me returning from visits to Nigeria and Zimbabwe as a teenager and announcing I need never return to Africa and I was definitely *never* going to be 'called'? And to make jolly sure, I have successfully boycotted any gathering or feedback evening that could possibly have even the vaguest risk of said 'call'. The word 'furlough' has sent shivers up my back since I was seventeen.

My initial tentative inquiry about offering 'support' was greeted with a reply email that positively gushed joy and led to a request for 'basic information'. Reasoning no harm could come from my sharing simple details I quietly responded, all the while thinking how well God must think I was doing. Communicating with *Africa* of all places! Each time I pressed 'send' I smugly thought I'd hear nothing for a couple of weeks at least . . . nothing happens quickly in that part of the world, does it? God had other ideas.

Friends began spontaneously sharing dreams and words that could indicate a particular step of faith was imminent for me. Meantime the community in Africa (who surely would have all vacancies for short term volunteers booked up well in advance), gleefully emailed saying, 'Welcome to Pemba. Please send your arrival details as soon as possible and we would love to meet you at the airport.' In obedience to a prompting I had made a polite inquiry about the volunteer programme at Pemba. Convinced it was simply the next 'stepping stone' (in my mind there was no risk of my actually *going* there), I had placed my confidence in a friend's comment that only one in three applications to visit the base were accepted, therefore I was quite safe.

I know you will be thinking about the boys, Ma, and possibly feeling that responsible parenting rarely looks like placing sons under the strain of needing to ponder Mum's mental stability. I have been astounded... in a wholly good way! Firstly, when I got back from the conference and sat with Sam (who is now 30 remember), explaining all I sensed God might be saying he was not in any way disparaging. He listened, asked a few thought-out questions and then endorsed my sense that this seems to be a God idea. Although admitting it was unexpected, to the level of 'flying pigs delivering milk' (we were actually able to laugh together about that), Sam agreed that I needed to pursue the idea and trust that the door would close if I were on the wrong track.

And Nathan? Having a son in an active war zone has been one of the hardest things I have had to walk through as a mum. I explained to God that the timing was all wrong because Nathan was due home from Afghanistan. I desperately wanted time with him. And then... God brought him back two weeks earlier than anticipated. I wanted to discuss the detail of the timing with him and give him the opportunity to say he would prefer Mum not to be dashing off to 'the jungle'; probably he would gently say he would really like me to be around for his birthday. But God.

To say Nathan was excited is an understatement. He leapt up and immediately ordered me a top-notch mozzie net and a water filter flask such as the army issue, then whisked me off to purchase antimalarials. I could not have felt more supported. I was stunned and blessed but I couldn't afford to just buy a plane ticket and my air miles are all with Qantas, who surely don't fly into Africa? Next, the travel agent found a Qantas ticket was available and unbelievably, as I sat at her desk (registering exactly where Mozambique was on the house-sized map on the wall), an instrumental version of that worship song, 'As the deer pants for the water so my soul longs after you' began playing. I presume everyone in the office could hear it? I managed to wade through all the forms . . . and then sent my visa application with no payment; but the visa was granted anyway and I paid later online. I began to feel 'snookered'.

Ma, I hope you are sitting down . . . I am on my way to Mozambique.

Printed in August 2021
by Rotomail Italia S.p.A., Vignate (MI) - Italy